CW01083160

GUNFIRE TARGET
Six Years with the Royal Artillery

GUNFIRE TARGET

Six Years with the Royal Artillery

Edward A. Oates

The Book Guild Ltd.

Sussex, England

The Book Guild Ltd.
25 High Street,
Lewes, Sussex

First published 1996
© Edward A. Oates
Set in Times
Typesetting by Poole Typesetting (Wessex) Ltd.
Bournemouth, Dorset.
Printed in Great Britain by
Bookcraft (Bath) Ltd, Avon

A catalogue record for this book is
available from the British Library

ISBN 1 85776 066 2

CONTENTS

Acknowledgements		vii
Preface		xiii
1	Final Years of Empire	1
2	Iraq 1941–42 and the Forced March to the Western Desert	15
3	The Battle of Ruweisat Ridge	26
4	The Second Battle of Alamein	41
5	Alamein and Aftermath	56
6	Alamein to Tripoli	74
7	The Tunisian Campaign	89
8	Return to the Delta	106
9	Welcome to Italy	116
10	Monte Cassino (1)	126
11	Monte Cassino (2)	141
12	Break-Out on the Adriatic	156
13	Central Italy and the Battle of the Gothic Line	172
14	The Greek Campaign	189
15	Finale: Northern Greece	209
Epilogue		220
Bibliography		225
Index		226

ACKNOWLEDGEMENTS

My father, Edward A Oates, passed away on 1st June 1995, unable to see his book through its final stages to publication. With the information left available to me, I have made every effort to discover and cite his sources. Although at times it has been impossible to determine a source – either from my father's notes or from my own research efforts – I have acknowledged every source to the best of my ability and can only apologize for any omissions.

On behalf of my father I wish to gratefully acknowledge the contribution of Lt. Col. G R Stevens OBE and his history, *Fourth Indian Division* (McLaren & Son Ltd., Toronto, 1948); *The Tiger Triumphs* (the Director of Public Relations, New Delhi, 1946); and *The Gulag Archipelago* 1918–1958: An Experiment in Literary Investigation 1–11 by A I Solzhenitsyn. Copyright © 1973 by Aleksandr I. Solzhenitsyn. English language translation copyright © 1973, 1974 by Harper & Row Publishers, Inc.

I also acknowledge information from various regimental and battery War Diaries from the Public Records Office, London. The quotations of Rudyard Kipling were taken from The Definitive Edition Rudyard Kipling's Verse (published by Hodder and Stoughton, London).

The battle maps 'EI Alamein' and 'Theatre of War' are reproduced from *War in the Desert* by James Lucas by permission of Arms and Armour Press. The map of 'Monte Cassino' is from *Fourth Indian Reflections* (D C Blomfield-Smith, Cambridge, 1987).

Many thanks to Noeline Bridge for compiling the index, and to Cyril Mount for permission to reproduce some of his paintings, both in the book and on the dust jacket.

Elizabeth Turner (née Oates)

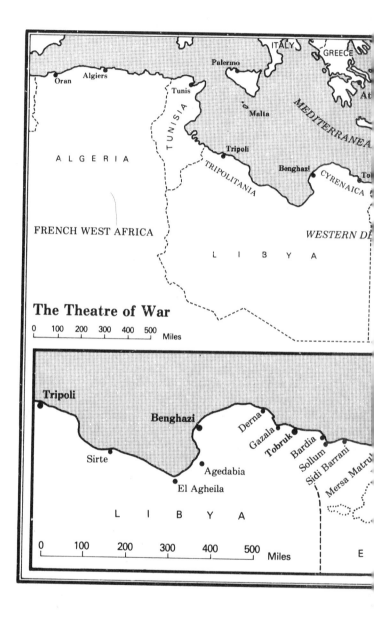

The Theatre of War

0   100   200   300   400   500 Miles

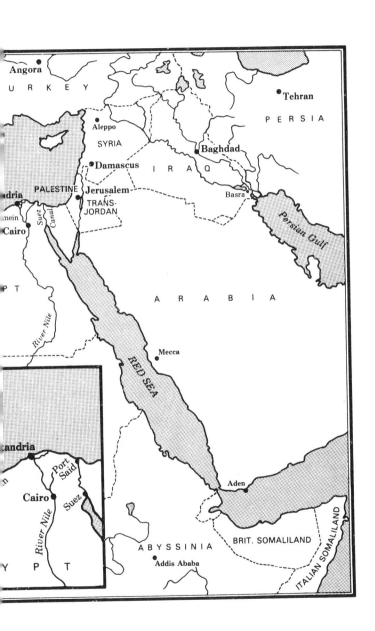

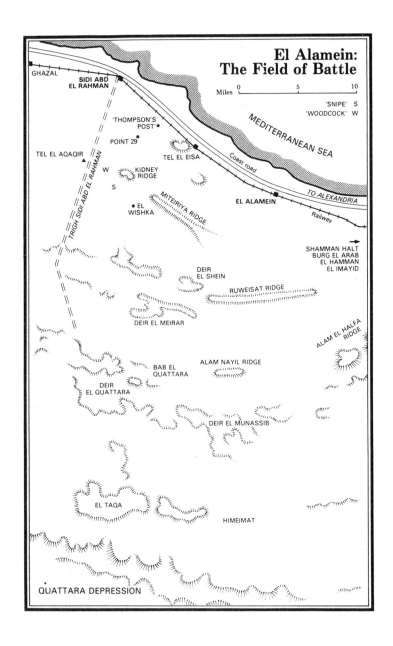

El Alamein:
The Field of Battle

Miles 0   5   10

'SNIPE' S
'WOODCOCK' W

MEDITERRANEAN SEA

GHAZAL

SIDI ABD
EL RAHMAN

'THOMPSON'S
POST'•

POINT 29

TEL EL AQAQIR

KIDNEY
RIDGE

TEL EL EISA

Coast road

W

S

EL ALAMEIN

TO ALEXANDRIA

• EL
  WISHKA

MITEIRIYA RIDGE

Railway

TRIGH SIDI ABD EL RAHMAN

SHAMMAN HALT
BURG EL ARAB
EL HAMMAN
EL IMAYID

DEIR
EL SHEIN

RUWEISAT RIDGE

DEIR EL MEIRAR

ALAM EL HALFA
RIDGE

BAB EL
QUATTARA

ALAM NAYIL RIDGE

DEIR
EL QUATTARA

DEIR EL MUNASSIB

EL TAQA

HIMEIMAT

QUATTARA DEPRESSION

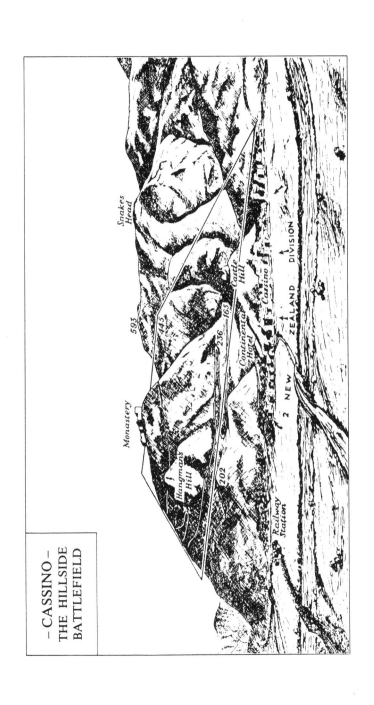

– CASSINO –
THE HILLSIDE
BATTLEFIELD

Snakes
Head

Monastery

Hangman's
Hill

593

445

236

165

102

Castle
Hill

Continental
Hotel

Cassino

Railway
Station

2 NEW ZEALAND DIVISION

PREFACE

The role of the Field Branch of the Royal Regiment of Artillery has been and continues to be the close support of the infantry. From the colonial wars of the nineteenth century through the First and Second World Wars the field gunners, with pinpoint accuracy, have supported the poor bloody infantrymen: they have placed a curtain of fire in the form of a barrage to protect his advance after destroying or at least neutralizing enemy strongpoints and gun positions; they have rallied him when under attack, breaking up enemy counterattacks and have employed smoke screens to conceal his movements.

How many infantrymen on the Western Front in the First World War, huddled in their trenches or clinging to parapets under intense enemy shellfire as the British shells burst over and in enemy trenches and gun positions, have exclaimed, 'The guns! Thank God, the guns'?

However, in the Second World War in Egypt on 2nd and 3rd July 1942, at the First Battle of El Alamein, on a rocky outcrop called the Ruweisat Ridge, the field gunners were thrown into a very different role.

Field Marshal Erwin Rommel's Afrika Korps, after breaking through the British Eighth Army's lines in Libya, had shattered and nearly destroyed the British armour and had chased the British and Commonwealth forces back into Egypt. General Sir Claude Auchinleck, the British Commander, had decided to make a last stand on a 40-mile front at El Alamein. The 1st South African Division held the north of this line and the 2nd New Zealand Division defended the south. The centre was held by exhausted remnants of broken British and Indian formations. The way appeared open for Rommel to break through in the centre with his two panzer divisions, roll up the South

Africans and head for Cairo and Alexandria, only 60 miles to the east. The Ruweisat Ridge, a rocky elevation running east and west, jutted out from the centre of this line and was the key to the battlefield. If the enemy captured the Ridge El Alamein was lost.

In the early morning hours of 2nd July 1942, 11th Field Regiment, Royal Artillery after a 2000-mile 10-day forced march from Baghdad in Iraq and forming the nucleus of a desert battle group named ROBCOL, was ordered to advance west along the Ruweisat Ridge and engage and destroy any German armour attempting to penetrate the Alamein line at that point.

For two days, under a blazing African summer sun and intense enemy artillery and mortar fire, supported only by a company of infantry, the gunners of the 11th Field Regiment with their 25-pounders fought the 15th Panzer Division over open sights down to ranges as close as 300 yards. At one point the regiment was down to only one gun while fitters and artificers worked desperately under fire to restore additional guns to action. On the evening of 3rd July Rommel withdrew his depleted panzers and commenced to consolidate his positions.

Although the First Battle of El Alamein continued for another 15 days the battlefield had been secured for Montgomery's final victory in October, the turning point, with Stalingrad, of the Second World War.

Although this is the story of only one regiment it is also the story of all the regiments of the Field Branch of the Royal Artillery in the Second World War of which there were over 150 at the height of mobilization.

Because of the close relationship between field gunners and infantry it is also a tribute to the extraordinary fighting qualities of our Indian infantrymen of the 4th Indian Division.

It is dedicated to the memory of all gunners who lost their lives while serving the field guns in any capacity.

1 FINAL YEARS OF EMPIRE

> You may talk o' gin and beer
> When you're quartered safe out 'ere,
> An' you're sent to penny-fights an' Aldershot it;
> But when it comes to slaughter
> You will do your work on water,
> An' you'll lick the bloomin' boots of 'im that's got it.
> *Rudyard Kipling*

We crowded the carriage windows as the troop train huffed and puffed its way slowly into the station, its ancient locomotive releasing clouds of steam along the low platform. Craning my neck I read the station sign mounted on a sturdy steel frame – British style. I read 'Meerut U.P.'

Posted along the platform like penitentiary guards ready to take a new batch of convicts into custody were a number of NCOs dressed in immaculate khaki drill shorts and turned-up shirt sleeves pressed to a knife-like crease with topis evenly adjusted to correct military angle.

Carriage doors crashed open and, like wild animals suddenly released after prolonged captivity, we hurled ourselves onto the platform. The three-day journey from Bombay was finally at an end. As NCOs rapidly formed us into the conventional and now familiar three ranks our creased and rumpled khaki serge stood out in startling contrast to their spotless tropical uniforms. As we stood at ease, enduring the almost ritualistic waiting period, I reflected on the events of the past month.

It was 29th November 1939. Four weeks previously, recruits all, we had assembled at the Ascot Race Course near London, England after 10 days' draft leave. We were all numbered amongst the initial rush to join the colours after the British Government's declaration of war on Germany on 3rd September. The Ascot Race Course had been appropriated by the War Department under the War Measures Act as a temporary assembly and holding military area. We were all partially trained recruits, a mixed group of infantryman, artillerymen with small numbers from the service regiments included.

On 2nd November we had entrained for Southampton and, crossing the English Channel to Cherbourg, we had spent the next three days enjoying the wartime hospitality of the French railway system. Arriving at Marseille we embarked on the troop ship. After a brief stop at Malta to drop off some naval ratings we arrived at Port Said in Egypt. The journey down the Suez Canal and the Red Sea was hot and humid but uneventful. Making another brief stop at Aden to release some RAF types, the troopship continued across the Indian Ocean to Bombay. Then followed the long and boring railroad journey to Meerut in a solid seat troop train. Along the way I was reminded of a verse from the barrack-room ballad *Gunga Din* by Rudyard Kipling:

> When the sweatin' troop-train lay
> In a sidin' through the day,
> Where the 'eat would make your bloomin' eyebrows crawl,
> We shouted 'Harry By!'
> Till our throats were bricky-dry,
> Then we wopped 'im cause 'e couldn't serve us all.

All in all the journey was the classic overseas military trip courtesy of HM Government. It was a tour which was to continue for many years and for some would end on a foreign battlefield.

My train of thought was brought suddenly to a halt by a sergeant making a roll call. We had by now been separated into our respective arms of the service. Infantrymen and gunners formed the two largest groups. We were marched off the platform to where a number of ancient Bedfords were parked. They all looked as though they had been salvaged from a First World War battlefield.

2

We climbed aboard with our kit bags. An hour later, after a bumpy and dusty ride, we arrived at the end of our journey – the Regimental Headquarters of the 11th Field Regiment, Royal Artillery. We were greeted by that august personage, the regimental sergeant-major. The passage of so many years has erased his name from my memory but not his face. I can seem him now, tall, square-shouldered, an outthrust jaw with sharp blue eyes capable of seeing through any guilty offence. His medal ribbons stamped him a First World War veteran. He gave us a kindly welcome but completed his address with a thunderous exhortation: 'You are members of the Royal Regiment of Artillery. The Right of the Line, the Pride of the Army and the Terror of the Enemy and you now belong to the 11th Field Regiment, one of its finest units. You may give your soul to God but you give your Loyalty and everything else to The Regiment, including your life if called upon to do so.'

At this relatively early stage of the Second World War Britain's Indian Command was still operating on a peacetime footing. It was two years before Pearl Harbour so the Japanese threat had not become an issue in British military planning. Europe was a long way off and the ghost of Queen Victoria still hovered over the capital of India, New Delhi. In the armed services commissioned ranks enjoyed a life that was dominated by social factors rather than military considerations. Other ranks were more concerned about the forthcoming regimental sports than by the war in Europe.

For over 100 years Britain had governed India, supported by a number of factors. The first of these was an efficient, fair, and rigidly moral civil service. The second was Britain's uncanny ability to recruit native soldiers and, trained by British NCOs and commanded by British officers, indoctrinate them with loyalty to the Crown. This loyalty was tested over many instances in two world wars and was rarely found wanting. Finally there was a small but well-trained British regular army garrisoned at key locations throughout this vast and populous country.

One of those garrisons was maintained at Meerut in the United Provinces about 50 miles north east of Delhi. In addition to the 11th Field Regiment of the Royal Artillery there was a battalion of infantry from the Royal Warwickshire regiment.

3

Placed as it is in the centre of the Indian plain Meerut registered summer highs of over 100°F. Winters, however, were quite pleasant.

Meerut's major claim to historical fame was related to the Indian Mutiny in the nineteenth century. The Indian Mutiny commenced in Meerut on 10th May 1857 when Indian troops, or *sepoys* as they were called, rebelled against their officers. Waiting until a major part of the British garrison were at church parade at the Anglican Church, and therefore unarmed, they broke into the church and in a frenzy of blood they slaughtered officers, other ranks and many women. The following day the mutiny spread to Delhi. It wasn't ended until 20th June 1858 when British troops recaptured Gwalior. From that date until British troops were finally withdrawn from India after the Second World War all church parades to the Anglican Church at Meerut were accompanied by an armed party of 12 men and an NCO. Notches were cut into the prayer rails to hold the Lee-Enfield rifles. It may have been the only instance of the Church officially sanctioning the admission of an armed party.

Our first major shock was to learn that the 11th Field Regiment was still a horsed or mounted artillery regiment. It was equipped with 18-pounder field guns still in use after service in the First World War. We watched our battery, the 83/85th, return from training exercises the day after we arrived. I was forcibly reminded of that well-known First World War painting entitled *The Retreat from Mons*. It depicts an artillery field battery galloping west from the town of Mons, drivers fighting to control their six-horse teams, 18-pounder guns jumping crazily on the shell-torn road, gunners hanging on grimly to the plunging limbers and an outrider, struck by shrapnel, writhing on the ground beneath his fallen horse.

Our introduction to the equestrian aspect of life in the 11th Field Regiment was not without its lighter moments. A daily ritual, except Sundays, in a mounted unit, was rough exercise. Gunners, as well as drivers, took part. This involved each man riding one horse, bridled, but unsaddled, and leading a second.

In single file (two horses abreast) we would proceed out of the cantonments and into the country, under the eagle eye of a sergeant. It was with some trepidation that I mounted, assisted by a friendly heave by another gunner, on my first 'rough ex'. After a couple of miles at 'the walk', I began to gain confidence and settled down to enjoy the cool morning air and varied scenery. We had reached the Royal Warwicks cantonments and were now passing their parade square.

The Warwicks were on parade at battalion strength, rehearsing for a forthcoming ceremonial event. As we watched in mild curiosity, the Warwicks Band struck up with a roll of drums. My two horses, knowing by now that they were controlled by a novice, went into a trot and then a canter and broke ranks. I threw away the reins of my second horse, needing all my concentration to stay on the back of my mount, which cantered off up the road. My comrades cheered me on with gusto, shouting confused advice. My mount, deciding he was in control of the situation, kept going on and on and out onto the *maidan* or plain and through sundry patches of bush. Eventually exhausted, he came to a walk and there I was, lost on the *maidan*. I need not have worried. The horse knew his way around and brought me safely back to the cantonments where I arrived in time to miss breakfast.

As a prelude to our commencing gun drill, the last joined draft was taken out on horseback under a sergeant instructor to watch the regiment, comprising two batteries with 16 guns, coming into action. It was an inspiring sight, one of the final pages in the story of the romantic era of the Royal Regiment of Artillery. The first arrival on the gun position was the gun position officer or GPO, accompanied by his assistant or GPO ack, a lance-bombardier. They quickly scouted the selected gun positions and placed markers. They were followed by the battery sergeant majors who remained mounted. Then came the guns, enveloped in a cloud of dust. They came at the canter. The gallop was never used in training. The NCO in charge of each gun travelled as an outrider and came onto the gun position to direct his gun to the correct marker. The six-horse gun teams controlled by three drivers, lead-driver, centre driver and wheel driver brought their guns to their respective position and pointing towards 'the enemy'. Gunners jumped down from the ammunition limbers and unhitched the horses. Limbers were unhitched behind the guns. The horses moved back to the wagon lines under the direction of a BSM. The GPO, who had set up his command post, now began to bring the guns onto the selected line of fire with all guns parallel. From the moment of the arrival of the GPO on the gun position, until the last report of 'Ready!' from the detachment commanders, not more than 10 minutes had elapsed. It was impressive and memorable.

As the last joined draft we were the new boys on the block and, as such, were the butt of many jokes and tall stories by the old sweats. One of these was how to obtain relief from the mosquitoes by fooling them into thinking you had gone to the 'hill country'. This was achieved by placing your kit in the big box at the end of your bed and being careful to remove your best boots and spurs, with great-coat, from the shelf above your bed! Another was that, during the monsoon season, the bullfrogs grew so big that many an unwary gunner with a hangover had tried to saddle a bullfrog instead of his horse! Gradually we learnt to take information and advice from the old soldiers in India with a large pinch of salt. Eventually another draft of recruits arrived from Blighty. We immediately graduated to premature old soldiers.

Training by way of gun drill, foot drill, musketry practice and small arms instruction continued through the winter of 1939–40. In March of 1940 we went to firing camp at Tughlakabad. This was our first experience firing live ammunition. We had, as a draft, now reached the end of basic training and graduated without ceremony.

The Tughlakabad area, in addition to the location of the artillery firing ranges, boasted a number of historical places of interest and antiquity. One of these was King Tuk's Fort which was in a remarkable state of preservation and had survived intact from about the twelfth century. It possessed a fascinating labyrinth of passages and mysterious rooms, the purpose of which has been lost in the mists of history. However, the outstanding feature was and still is, I am sure, the Qutb Minar. The Qutb is a tower rising perpendicularly from a flat plain and about 400 feet high. The columns of stone that comprise its construction alternate between squared and round. They form a perfect circle, being wide at the base and tapering as it rises into the air. It is divided into five sections, each section having a balcony or viewing platform at its top. The architectural style varied from section to section, indicating different architects and/or time of construction. With its different colours of stone it would represent a dream study for a modern architect. According to local legend, construction was commenced in the eleventh century by orders of the local rajah who planned to build it as a personal monument. He died before construction was completed. His successor continued construction but also passed on before his plans were completed. Another successor fell heir to the limitations imposed by man's mortality. The Qutb Minar

6

was finally completed in the thirteenth century by another ruler of the same dynasty. His objective varied from the Qutb's originator. He had apparently taken to wife a remarkable lady reputed to be the most beautiful in the world. She had demanded, as part of the price of her hand, that her lord and master arrange for her to be the first person to see the sun rise in the morning. This request was, of course, based on the belief that the earth was flat. Accordingly, the first morning after completion, the lady climbed to the top, by way of the winding staircase, then committed suicide by throwing herself from the balcony to the ground 400 feet below. Just legend, but then like most legends there are likely some truths.

Soon after our return from Tughlakabad, I was involved in a macabre experience.

It was the custom in India at that time to bury deceased persons very quickly after death. Embalming was not practised. A gunner had died in hospital early on this particular day. His funeral was arranged for the following morning. The body had been transported to the regimental morgue, located near the boundary of the regimental cantonments where a guard was placed. This was again the custom because of the danger of body-snatching, not uncommon in India. The morgue was a dark grey stone building without windows and with a single heavy door, secured by an enormous padlock. With its thick walls and surrounded by huge trees, it remained relatively cool, even in hot summer weather.

The guard was mounted at 17.30 hours and we were immediately marched to the morgue guardroom, located about 100 yards from the morgue. I drew the second relief, 20.00 to 22.00 hours. Guard duty itself was simple and straightforward. The relief on duty was posted outside the door and there he stayed, alone and vigilant for two hours until relieved. In addition to the standard Lee-Enfield and 10 rounds of .303 ammunition, he was equipped with a whistle, which hung on a lanyard from around his neck. After a boring and uneventful shift I was relieved at 22.00 hours. It seemed that I had hardly dozed off before I was awakened by the shrill sound of the regulation whistle. I could see our NCO jumping from his seat behind the battered desk and grabbing the hurricane lamp that hung from the ceiling. Deprived of light and minus the reassuring presence of our NCO, both myself and first relief felt the first twinge of unspoken fear. Acting in unison, we took off after the bombardier, mutually deciding that authority could take second place to the issue of the moment. We reached the morgue almost on the heels of the NCO. We found an obviously frightened young gunner pouring out a torrent of words that made little sense.

Speaking in a tone of authority the NCO said, 'Shut up and start again, slowly this time.'

The relief calmed down and replied, 'There's a noise, Bombardier ... inside the morgue ... sort of a moan-like ... I've heard it a few times, it starts and stops, then starts again!'

The bombardier looked at him intently. Then, raising the lamp, he inserted a key in the big padlock, and removing it, pushed open the heavy door. Crowding close behind the NCO, we peered into the dark room, barely illuminated by the flickering flame of the oil lamp. We perceived the faint shapes of the three raised slabs. On the extreme right slab lay the white shrouded figure of the deceased. The steamy silence was oppressive, only broken by the incessant bellowing of the bullfrogs. The NCO had lowered the lamp and was about to close the door when we heard the sound, an anguished moan. It was a moan that seemed to rise from the bowels of the earth, half-human. As the lamp was quickly raised, we stared in shocked wonder, spiced with horror, as the form on the slab raised itself to a semi-sitting position, the sub-human moan still spilling from beneath the white shroud. For the space of about five seconds, we were frozen into immobility. Then the NCO galvanized into action. He locked the door and, ordering the three of us to stay outside, he took off for the guardroom and telephone. He quickly returned and sent us all back to the guardroom. No more than 20 minutes elapsed before the medical officer arrived, followed shortly by an ambulance. We were dismissed and given no further information.

I learnt later that the incident, as described, could happen in India in relation to a certain disease and under certain conditions. The soldier involved was taken back to the hospital sedated. He was returned to England by air without any further contact with personnel of the unit. It is doubtful if this incident was entered into the regimental history.

The old British class system, very much in evidence in England up to the Second World War, was even more pronounced in British India.

However, the military funeral was the great class leveller. Whether a senior officer or a humble gunner from the last draft, the deceased was given equal treatment. The funeral cortege was just a grand sight. The coffin was transported to the cemetery on a gun-carriage covered with the Union Jack and hauled by six black horses, adorned with black plumes, followed by drums muffled in black velvet and finally the firing party. It was a fitting finale to any soldier's military career. Kipling wrote a poem about that too.

At that time we felt we were suffering great hardships whilst doing our part in holding the Empire together. In retrospect, we enjoyed an easy life. We had most of the benefits and advantages of peacetime military life with little personal risk. Possibly the greatest threat to life and health was malaria, followed closely by dysentery. There was, of course, always that universal scourge of military life – venereal disease. However VD was personally controllable, preferably by total abstinence.

As the pleasant winter days gave way to the increasing heat of spring, the local rumour mill went into overtime. The most bizarre had us going to Egypt as a horsed artillery unit because the tractors couldn't pull the guns in the deep sand of the Western Desert! This one was nailed to the wall in late April with the first arrival of 15 cwt. and three-ton trucks or lorries as they were termed. The 11th Field Regiment RA had finally arrived in the age of mechanization.

Driving instruction and MT maintenance commenced soon after and it was fortunate for local inhabitants that the Indian plains afforded ample room for error and sometimes just plain crazy driving.

Conversion from the 18-pounder horsedrawn guns to tractor equipped 25-pounders proceeded at a rapid pace. This gun, replacing both the 18-pounder and the 4.5in. howitzer, was the standard field gun of British and Commonwealth forces in the Second World War. It may be truly said that the 25-pounder became a legend in its own time. Apart from the obvious fact that it fired a heavier shell, the 25-pounder combined both the merits of the 18-pounder with its 'flat' trajectory and the 4.5in. howitzer with its steep or high trajectory, necessary for deployment in mountainous terrain. This was accomplished by employing different charges. It could also be brought into action as fast as its two predecessors, less than one minute. It was equipped with a platform or base for the gun wheels, which was carried and secured under the trail when travelling but would drop almost under wheels by pulling a lever. When brought into actions, it would prevent the gun from 'digging in' during action in soft ground. It also facilitated the 'laying' of the gun. One man could swing the gun through 180 degrees in a matter of seconds. The 25-pounder gun howitzer weighted only 1.75 tons, had a range of 13,400 yards and had the advantage that a worn-out barrel could be replaced in action relatively quickly. It fired both high explosive or solid shot so could be used in an anti-tank role. In the hands of a well-trained gun crew, the 25-pounder developed such a high rate of fire that the Germans initially believed that it was belt-fed with ammunition.

The 25-pounder had a muzzle velocity of 1200 feet per second in Charge III which could be increased to 1400 feet per second by super charging. At this MV the 25-pounder could pierce the heaviest German armour at 500 yards.

The 25-pounder required a crew of six men to bring its fighting potential to the optimum: one man laying, one man opening and closing the breech, one man loading, one man feeding the loader with ammunition, one man preparing ammunition and an NCO commanding the gun.

The summer of 1940 passed rapidly in training, mechanizing and, in particular gun drill. We came in and out of action so many times that we were doing it in our sleep. Our horses were gradually 'taken off the strength' and, with the shipment of the last animals, the horsed era of the 11th Field Regiment came to a close. There were, I suspect, some sad hearts and damp eyes amongst many of our drivers as they said goodbye for the last time to their horses, or 'hairy-assed wheelers' as they were affectionately called.

In late June of that year I was selected to take an artillery survey course. Field survey as a trade was, and still is, peculiar to the artillery. The system of indirect shooting or firing on targets unseen from gun positions, required accurate mapping or fixing of both gun positions and targets in order to establish an accurate bearing and range. The primary role of field artillery in the Second World War had not changed substantially from the First, which was close infantry support. The set piece infantry advance was to move behind an artillery curtain of fire or barrage. The infantry would maintain a line of advance as close as 100 yards or even less to the exploding shellfire.

All this called for a high degree of accuracy from the gunners. Prior to any infantry advance, selected enemy targets, such as strongpoints, machine-gun emplacements and defending infantry, would have to be destroyed if possible or neutralized by gunfire. All of those factors called for reliable survey preparation.

Eight of us were enrolled in this survey course. Some of our number had not been educated beyond grade 8 so some of the work became heavy going. However, one of our group, named Topper Brown, an Oxford University undergraduate, obviously knew more about trigonometry than our instructor, Sergeant Turberfield. When the sergeant first unveiled the basic formula of all artillery survey, the right-angled triangle formula, we all listened with keen interest. I can see him now, placing that formula on the blackboard:

$$\text{Base} = \frac{\text{perpendicular}}{\text{tangent}}$$

He turned to the class and asked evenly, 'Are there any questions?' in a tone which indicated that he did not expect any.

Brown raised his hand and in a dead-pan voice asked, 'Why does the base equal the perpendicular over the tangent, Sergeant?'

We thought, 'This is it, he can't answer,' and waited. Sergeant Turberfield slowly approached the table in front of him. He placed his hands on it, palms down, and he barked rather than spoke, 'The base equals the perpendicular over the tangent because I bloody well said so!' To this day my answer to the same question would not vary.

This statement effectively terminated any further questions in this vein.

The annual vacation period was cancelled in 1940. The Indian Command maintained a number of summer holiday camps in the hill country, located in the foothills of the Himalayas. These summer camps provided a welcome break from training, the monotonous routine of life in the cantonments and the heat of the plains.

In late summer we moved again to Khanpur Camp near Tughlakabad for another firing camp. All ranks were impressed with the performance of our 25-pounders, although our efficiency was something less than optimal. Obviously, we would need further training to bring us up to war readiness. The survey party, in addition to

11

assignments related to the firing camp, also completed a four-day field trip into the lower levels of the hill country, surveying and mapping as we travelled. Shortly after our return to Meerut we took our survey trade tests. Topper Brown, who had passed his third class test a month previously, took and passed his second class. The rest of us successfully completed our third class test. It was with some pride and a lot of satisfaction that we placed our brass 'S' badges on our uniforms.

The intensity of training was gathering momentum, and it was obvious that our life of relative comfort and safety was building toward a finale. However, regimental HQ maintained its customary, stony silence. Even the adjutant's batman, normally a reliable source of information, was as dry as a parched sponge.

In early December I was shopping in the Meerut bazaar with two colleagues, Watkins and Les Garfield. Stopping at the local photography shop to buy some film, I got into a conversation with the proprietor, a Rajput.

'You are looking forward to going to the Middle East, sahib?' he asked, rather than stated, as he totalled my purchases.

I was immediately on my guard and replied, 'Not really, but what do you know about that?'

'I know, sahib,' he replied. Then, lowering his voice to a conspiratorial tone, he added, 'You will be going to Basra next summer.'

I tried not to show my surprise and decided to terminate the conversation. Paying for my purchase, I left the shop. The incident served to reinforce what we had often heard, namely that the local bazaar could supply more information about British military movements than regimental HQ.

I had discovered that one of the best ways to explore the Indian countryside was by use of the humble push bike. One of my weekend day trips was to the beautiful Roman Catholic chapel in Sardhana, about 15 miles from Meerut. It had been built under the direction of an Irish priest in the late nineteenth century who had inspired its construction.

The current priest-in-charge supplied me with a lot of local history and legend. His most interesting story concerned a certain Colonel G.W. Dyce. It seemed that Colonel Dyce was a British officer stationed in Meerut before the First World War. He met, fell in love with, and married a local beauty in this Roman Catholic church. In the eyes of the British military authorities and his fellow officers, Colonel

Dyce had committed an unpardonable crime. One might go to bed with a native woman, but never, no never, did a British soldier marry one and certainly not an officer. Colonel Dyce was forced to resign his commission, and being possessed of independent means, he settled in India where he died, never returning to England. His native wife died in childbirth at a young age. I located her tomb in the churchyard. It was a highly ornamental white marble tombstone inscribed in a Hindustani dialect, with a clock indicating the time of day she expired. Inscribed in gold leaf and set in a black marble plaque in the wall of the crypt, were the following lines:

Alas, in this neglected spot is laid
A heart, once filled with celestial fire
Hands that Rod of Empire might have swayed
Or wake'd to Ecstasy the living lyre

Yes, Colonel Dyce loved his lady very much.

By 1st May 1941, we had reached war readiness and both batteries were now up to full strength in both personnel and equipment and were both equipped with 25-pounder gun howitzers. The tractors or quads were all four-wheel drive and fitted with winching gear. The regimental survey party was supplied with two North American-built Ford V8 three-four ton pickups with a canopy over the cargo area. They were left-hand drive, which initially caused us some problems. Our third vehicle was an English built four-cyl. Austin convertible. This was apt terminology for a vehicle that was converted from civilian to military use. More about this vehicle later.

In May Topper Brown was promoted to a full bombardier, Watkins and myself getting our first stripe. The operational complement of the regimental survey party was also established as follows:

NCO in charge:	Bdr. Basil Holgate
Second-in-command:	Bdr. Topper Brown
Surveyor:	L/Bdr. Watkins
Surveyor:	L/Bdr. E. Oates
Surveyor:	Gunner Les Garfield
Surveyor:	Gunner Jock Adams
Surveyor:	Gunner M. Colley

Bombardier Holgate was a pre-war regular soldier with over six years' service in India. A decent man and a reliable comrade.

Bombardier Topper Brown was an Oxford graduate and volunteered for service in the first year of the war. A whiz kid with figures, we could always rely on Topper to solve those knotty problems.

Lance Bombardier Watkins or Watto, as we usually called him, had joined the Royal Artillery as a boy at the age of fourteen, and had served as a bugler. He was quiet, serious, conscientious and dependable.

Gunner Les Garfield was a Sussex man given to few words. Solid and stubborn, one could always rely on Les.

Gunner Jock Adams was a Scotsman, as his name implies. He was the wit of the party. Possessed of a dry sense of humour, he was the classical grumbler in the best British Army tradition.

Gunner Colley had specific responsibilities for the care and safe keeping of our survey equipment. Conscientious, but a difficult man to get to know. Normally the survey party was the responsibility of a junior officer, but as at May 1941, no one had been appointed.

Finally, in early June, initial orders went up on the bulletin board. The 11th Field Regiment RA was assigned to the support of the 8th Indian Infantry Division. Further information indicated we were bound for the Middle East in the near future.

In late July 1941, the 11th Field Regiment finally left Meerut, UP and entrained for Bombay. We travelled during the hottest part of the Indian summer, following the end of the monsoon season. Detraining at Bombay, we embarked with only a modest delay on a tramp steamer converted to a troop ship.

Thirty six hours later we took leave of the sights, smells and sound of India and, escorted by a lone British destroyer, we watched the lights of Bombay disappear below the horizon as we sailed west to the Persian Gulf.

2 IRAQ 1941–42 AND THE FORCED MARCH TO THE WESTERN DESERT

UBIQUE
(Royal Artillery)
Ubique means that warnin' grunt the perished linesman knows,
When o'er 'is strung an' sufferin' front the shrapnel sprays 'is foes;
'An as their firin' dies away the 'usky whisper runs
From lips that 'aven't drunk all day: 'The Guns! Thank Gawd, the Guns!'
Rudyard Kipling

After enduring the heat and humidity of the Persian Gulf we landed at Basra in early August. The regiment went under canvas at Shaiba Camp about 10 miles out of the city. Although all ranks were well acclimatized to tropical soldiering the daytime temperature at Basra overwhelmed the majority rising as high as 135°F. All one could do was lie in the shade of the tent with both ends open, hoping to induce some slight air movement. Because of their immense height it was truly said that the palm trees of Basra had their roots in hell and their heads in heaven.

Training and maintenance was restricted to the morning hours but Shaiba Camp left no pleasant memories with the gunners of 11th Field Regiment.

In late August Movement Orders went up on the regimental notice board without information in respect of destination. The night before

15

we broke camp one of those interesting personal wartime incidents occurred.

A member of the regimental survey party who shall be nameless had developed an attachment for a young lady who plied her profession in the red light district of Basra. Resisting our advice he decided to make a final trip to visit the lady. As the evening passed we became gradually concerned that our colleague was going to make a break and desert. The disgrace and consequences of such a move were too awful for us to contemplate. Late in the evening Jock Adams and Les Garfield agreed to go to Basra and, if necessary, bring the lovesick soldier back to camp by force. Jock conceded that he knew the red light district on River Street very well. In the wee hours of the morning Les and Jock returned with a dishevelled and angry surveyor. Apparently, after running their quarry to earth, or rather to bed, they were obliged to fight their way through a buxom bevy of bordello beauties to reach safety. It was only by threatening to call the military police that they were able to escape at all.

We had looked after our own and the honour of the regiment had been preserved.

The regiment pulled out of Shaiba Camp early the following morning and, passing the refineries of Abadan to our south, we headed east towards Persia, or Iran as it is known today. The following day we reached Ahwas, a small town inside the Persian border, where we halted. After several hours cooking in the hot sun we swung northwest heading back into Iraq. There was no explanation for this odd incident. Crossing the border again we cut into the Basro-Baghdad highway and turned north towards Baghdad. The term 'highway' was rather a grand name to give this road that was a combination of hard-top, gravel and basic earth.

The political situation in Iraq at this time was uncertain. This placed a heavy responsibility on British military commanders who were obliged to be firm but diplomatic.

Although Iraq was bound by treaty to allow British bases on its territory a number of problems had arisen since the fall of France in 1940. The French authorities in Syria had come out firmly in support of the Vichy Government under Marshal Pétain. In addition they were co-operating with and supporting the Iraqi rebel leader Rashid Ali. Rashid Ali was fighting to overthrow the Iraqi Government and eliminate British power and influence in Iraq. Their efforts were aided and encouraged by the Nazi government in Germany. Hitler's Directive No. 30, dated 23rd May 1941 read: 'The Arab freedom movement in the Middle East is our natural ally against Britain.'

The same month Winston Churchill, losing patience with the intransigence of the French in Syria, authorized General Sir Archibald Wavell, British Commander in Chief, Middle East, to take action. After expending his considerable diplomatic skills trying to convert the Vichy French to the Free French movement without success Wavell took military action. On 8th June two divisions, including the 7th Australian Division, crossed the border from Palestine. The Vichy French were defeated and Syria and Lebanon were brought under British control.

At this time the German spring offensive in Russia was showing rapid territorial gains. British Intelligence had good cause to believe that Hitler, after defeating the Soviets, would direct his panzers south through the Caucasus, bypassing Turkey and invest the oil fields around Mosul and Kirkuk in Northern Iraq. This would constitute the Eastern jaw of a gigantic pincer movement which would close when Rommel and the Afrika Korps defeated the English Army in Egypt. They would then seize the Canal Zone and move east and north east through Palestine and Jordan to meet near Baghdad. It was a bold and ambitious plan.

The 8th Indian Infantry Division had been ordered to move to northern Iraq and prepare a defensive line north and east of the Mosul-Kirkuk oil fields.

In early September the regiment entered and passed through Baghdad. Continuing north we passed through Mosul and then turned north east viewing the oil field in the distance as we closed towards the Persian border. A regimental advance party, under the 2nd I/C Major P.R. Waterfield had gone ahead and as a cool evening breeze dissipated the heat of the day we arrived at a camping area that was to be our home for the next eight months.

In the distance the purple snow-capped outline of the Zagreb Mountains stood out in sharp relief against the eastern sky. We were located not far from the small Kurdish village of Altun Kopru.

In the next few days we completed the chores of setting up camp in an area which sustained up to 30 inches of snow most winters. The huge task of preparing defensive positions against a German panzer army then commenced. The divisional defence line faced the only pass through the Zagreb Mountain that could be negotiated by a mechanized army. Gun positions with alternatives were prepared. OPs were placed, artillery and infantry anti-tank position were laid out with infantry strongpoints and fields of fire. Finally thousands of local labourers were hired to construct a massive anti-tank ditch under the direction of Indian engineers.

The first snows arrived on Christmas Eve and when it ended we were under 12 inches of the white stuff. It was a hard miserable winter but the spring of 1942 came early to northern Iraq and as we spread out our blankets in the warm March sunshine the early emerging wild spring flowers painted splashes of colours in the surrounding valleys.

March, April and May passed rapidly, assisted by a rigorous training programme initiated by our CO, Lieutenant Colonel A.O. McCarthy. Absolute and comparative calibration of the guns was completed in early June.

On 9th June an ominous omen for the future disturbed the normal tranquillity of military life when both batteries were ordered into the field for practice in anti-tank gunnery. To field gunners drilled and trained in the concept of close infantry support at ranges that fell comfortably between 4–12,000 yards this was not merely an enormous waste of technical expertise, it was downright heretical.

The regimental notice board was daily scanned for additional news of the impending move.

On 10th June the regiment was paid a courtesy visit by Major-General C.O. Harvey, commanding the 8th Indian Division and Brigadier R.V. Garry, commanding Royal Artillery. On the same day Topper Brown, who maintained close contact with the adjutant, obtained the official news that the 18th Indian Infantry Brigade, including the 11th Field Regiment in support, had been ordered to join the Eighth Army in Egypt.

On 11th June 1942 the regiment moved out from Altun Kopru area on the first leg of its long journey to Egypt and the Western Desert. It was with some degree of sentimental sadness that many gunners said goodbye to an area that had been their home for over eight months. In spite of the rigours and hardships of that miserable winter, buried at times under heavy snow, the spring had provided ample

18

compensation. With a last look at the towering, snow-capped Zagreb Mountains gunners faced south on the way ahead to Baghdad.

Arriving at Lancer Camp the regiment collected stores and vehicles. Sergeant Hall of 83/85 Battery was astonished at the ease with which he was able to replace a gun tractor. Sergeant Hatfield, Battery Clerk 83/85 Battery, commented drily that the army appeared to be doing its best to satisfy the last requests of the condemned!

The regiment pulled out of Lancer Camp soon after dawn on 15th June. Crossing the Euphrates for the last time the column headed west along the same road that centuries earlier had been travelled by the Medes, the Persians, the Assyrians and the Roman legions. Also, no doubt, it had been traversed by the tribes of Israel in one of their many migrations. On 17th June the column passed through the Iraqi town of Ar Rutba. Crowds of small children ran excitedly alongside the guns while anxious mothers watched impassively from behind partially shuttered windows.

The regiment arrived in Al Mafraq, Jordan on 19th June. Soon after noon the next day the artillery column crossed into Palestine, descending from the mountains to the fertile plains below. By nightfall the regiment reached Hadera on the Mediterranean coast. One thousand miles had been logged since leaving Altun Kopru.

Lieutenant Colonel McCarthy ordered a travel break of one day in order to complete necessary maintenance and repairs. Every effort was to be made to avoid time-consuming breakdowns on the final leg of the journey into the Canal Zone.

There was now an opportunity to catch up on news from the Western Desert. The Afrika Korps was on the Egyptian border; Auchinleck desperately needed tanks and anti-tank guns that could stop the enemy advance; the 9th Australian Division had been ordered to move up to the desert front from Syria and the 18th Indian Brigade, which included the 11th Field Regiment, had been ordered to accelerate its move.

The Mediterranean at Hadera rolls into a long sandy beach ideal for swimming. It rises gradually to a series of sandy hillocks covered with scrub grass. Later in the afternoon following the regiment's arrival, after vehicle maintenance had been completed, the beach at Hadera was invaded by gunners of the 11th Field Regiment. Local inhabitants retreated in amazement as hundreds of stark nude bodies plunged into the clear warm water in ecstasy and reckless abandon.

By 08.00 hours the following morning the regiment was on the road following the coastal route south through Netanya, bypassing Tel Aviv with its modern white high-rise apartment buildings reflecting the morning sunshine. Passing through the ancient biblical towns of Ashdod and Askelon the column negotiated the towns of Gaza and Ratah, then swung west into Egypt and across the Sinai Peninsula. On 23rd June the 11th Field Regiment entered the Canal Zone and into a prepared camp at Ismailiya.

There was a general expectation by all ranks that there would be a rest for a few days at the next stop, Cowley Camp, outside Cairo.

The journey from Ismailiya to Cowley Camp was short but agonizingly slow; it almost seemed that the Egyptian government, encouraged by German intelligence was making every effort to delay the movement of Eighth Army reinforcements to the Western Desert. Pedestrian traffic wandered aimlessly across and along the roadway; camel and donkey traffic would stop in front of gun tractors. Efforts to order or persuade individuals to move out of the way were often met by sullen looks and outright obstinate refusal.

It was a sad fact that in late June and early July of 1942 the arrival of General Rommel and the Axis forces in Alexandria and Cairo was expected daily. Subtle and not so subtle insults were directed at British and Commonwealth personnel of all ranks.

To be fair, much of this attitude could be directly placed against the conduct of base and HQ staff. A general mood of defeatism swept through various army bases. Loose talks in bars and cafes, picked up by waiters, then distorted and magnified, conveyed the impression that the Eighth Army was defeated and all that remained was for Rommel and the Afrika Korps to drive unopposed to the Nile Delta and into the welcoming arms of King Farouk!

Any hopes that the regiment might have a lay over at Cowley Camp were soon dispelled. One day only was allowed to complete all necessary exchanges and draw supplies. Cowley Camp was a major vehicle park, so this included bringing vehicle strength up to par, exchanging vehicles as necessary, loading ammunitions, correcting signals and communication equipment and stocking food and fuel. One new issue at Cowley Camp was the sun-compass, a navigational instrument used in the desert. RHQ and battery specialists were given a one-hour lesson in its use. Working without rest all that day regimental and battery quarter masters supervised all necessary replenishment. By nightfall the regiment was ready for departure.

At 05.00 hours on 26th June, as the first faint shades of dawn lightened the eastern skies, as Eighth Army and Middle East Command Headquarters personnel in Cairo destroyed files and sensitive documents, as the navy transferred British servicewomen to ships in Alexandria Harbour and as dignitaries of the Egyptian government prepared to roll out the welcome mat for General Rommel, the 11th Field Regiment moved out of Cowley Camp. As the spires and minarets of the Cairo mosques receded in the background we moved ever deeper into the vast expanse of the Western Desert. We were just one formation against pitifully few reinforcements moving up to the battle front. On that day also Sir Claude Auchinleck, Commander in Chief, Middle East Command, relieved General Sir Neil Ritchie of his duties and assumed personal command of the Eighth Army. Around mid-afternoon the guns rolled through El Alamein. Only the sign, with a row of sand-filled barrels marking the limits of the road, informed the traveller that there was or had been a town of some sorts. It was completely deserted. A small rail station looked as if it had been lifted straight out of a Wild West movie.

The sun had moved well into the western sky when the regiment reached El Daba after covering nearly 250 miles since leaving Cairo early that morning.

A general swell of increased excitement and heightened expectation permeated all ranks that evening. Afrika Korps armour had already reached Mersa Matruh. Information gleaned from garbled radio traffic indicated that heavy fighting was taking place in the desert south of Mersa Matruh. The situation could be described as mercurial, not just fluid; 18th Indian Infantry Brigade now came under the command of the 5th Indian Division.

The following morning, following orders from Divisional HQRA, the regiment moved out of El Daba at 06.00 hours, continuing west on the coast road towards Mersa Matruh. At 08.00 hours we were brought to a halt at a place called Sidi Haneish and instructed to await further orders. There was almost no wind that day and as the sun moved towards its zenith it was hot, unusually hot. To their north, less than 1000 yards away, gunners gazed longingly at the blue, placid waters of the Mediterranean with hardly a shimmer disturbing the surface.

By midday west bound traffic had ceased. In the opposite direction it had dwindled to an odd lorry loaded with walking wounded, bandaged heads and bloodstained faces etched with exhaustion. Occasionally an overloaded ambulance would come through, the driver trying to avoid the larger potholes in the broken road surface.

It was mid-afternoon when orders for action came to Lieutenant Colonel McCarthy. The regiment was to form part of a battle group with infantry and a small number of armoured cars. There would be no armour in the form of tanks. The column would proceed due south from Sidi Haneish, intercept, engage and destroy any enemy forces encountered.

Shortly afterwards the remnants of two companies of infantry arrived at Sidi Haneish. The first company was the Green Howards and the second the East Yorks.

It was decided that both regimental and battery 'B' Echelons would remain at Sidi Haneish under the command of Captain Evans-Lawrence.

The light was rapidly failing as company and battery warrant officers assembled the column. Bren carriers, which were lightly armoured tracked infantry vehicles, headed the battle group, followed by lorried infantry with the guns bringing up the rear. The few armoured cars operated ahead and on the flanks, reminiscent of the outriders in the days of mounted warfare. At 19.30 hours the battle group rolled out, due south into the desert. The terrain was good, generally hard stony ground. Towards midnight the column was forced to make a wide detour in order to avoid a belt of treacherous soft sand.

It was close to 02.00 hours when the crew of an armoured car reported enemy vehicles approaching on a bearing of 280 degrees. The battle group came to a halt on the reverse slope of a gentle ridge. Bren carriers and two armoured cars moved forward. The guns were deployed for tank action. Maintaining complete silence and no lights, the unsuspecting enemy column was allowed to close to under 500 yards. Illuminated only by desert starlight the guns went into action. Three vehicles were immediately lit, one bursting into flames. Raking the column with Bren gunfire the carriers moved forward. It was all over inside 10 minutes. Seven prisoners were taken. A number of enemy vehicles withdrew at high speed towards Mersa Matruh. It was decided not to give chase.

Towards midnight 'E' Troop of 83/85 Battery, bringing up the rear of the gun column, became separated from the main battle group and either fell behind or veered off in a wrong direction. Eventually the troop reached the belt of soft sand and became hopelessly bogged down. Guns and limbers were unhooked. Resorting to a combination of winching power and manpower the troop finally extricated itself from the sand trap. At this point there was only one commissioned officer with 'E' Troop, Lieutenant O'Day. O'Day was actually on the strength of the 97th Field Regiment also supporting an Indian Division. He had been on leave when 11th Field Regiment came under movement orders and was attached to the regiment at Lancer Camp on 13th June. He was a young and inexperienced officer faced with making a major decision. After conferring with Battery Sergeant Major Harvey it was decided to return to the 'B' Echelon group at Sidi Haneish.

The main battle group maintained its position for the remainder of that night. No further enemy movement was detected.

The column continued south at dawn. At 07.00 hours a cloud of dust ahead, rising high on the still morning air, brought the group to an abrupt halt. After cautious investigation by the armoured cars they were relieved to find they had run across elements of the 2nd New Zealand Division. This division was commanded by General Freyberg V.C.

According to information supplied by the Kiwis, the division, rushed forward from the Canal Zone, was thrown into the melee south of Mersa Matruh. It sustained initial heavy casualties and was cut off. Hurling themselves against the Axis forces in a narrow wedge the Kiwis had broken through their encirclement, salvaging their guns and equipment. The division was now withdrawing south east to take up defensive positions between the Ruweisat Ridge and the Qattara Depression under orders from General Auchinleck.

As the final cloud of dust settled behind the departing Kiwis the battle group turned east. The wind increased through the morning and by midday the column was in the grip of the desert dust storm known as a *khamseen*. Experience in the desert had taught the Eighth Army troops that if caught in a *khamseen* of this ferocity the safest course was to halt and wait it out.

Late afternoon the wind decreased and the group continued their journey eastward. At 18.00 hours the column halted and were ordered into a leaguer, a circular defensive position with armour and guns on the outside. They were now about nine miles south of El Daba. There was little sleep that night as Signals Section radio operators maintained a listening watch. What battle-hardened infantry officers feared most was encirclement by the Afrika Korp's fast-moving panzers.

Early the next morning the battle group continued northwards. After careful investigation by two armoured cars the groups occupied the El Daba aerodrome and again formed a leaguer. The aerodrome had obviously been vacated fairly recently by the Desert Air Force. It showed all the signs of a hasty evacuation. The wreckage of two Hurricane fighter planes and a transport plane were silent testimony to the fortunes of war. One of the Hurricanes had crashed on landing; the other, presumably unable to take off, had been blown up.

It was past noon before orders came through to the battle group. They were short and to the point: retreat to Alamein immediately; Mersa Matruh had been captured and El Daba was outflanked. If surrounded the battle group was to fight its way out. No help could be expected.

Two of the armoured cars returned after a sweep in the desert south of El Daba. Their crews reported German armour supported by anti-tank guns and lorried infantry moving east on a bearing of 135 degrees. There was no time to lose. Quickly refuelling petrol tanks from the ample supplies still at El Daba the 11th Field Regiment took the road to Alamein. With lorried infantry at front and Bren carriers bringing up the rear the gun tractors were stretched to the limit of their speed. Guns and limbers plunged and reared wildly on the broken road surface and sandy dust billowed out from the column and clung, like a permanent pall, to the vehicles. The armoured cars maintained a flimsy screen three to 500 yards inland, driving parallel with the column. Enemy forces were sighted but were too far away to cause problems.

As the head of the column passed the Tel El Eisa feature mobile patrols of the 1st South African Division were sighted. The Springboks were holding the northern sector of the hastily assembled Alamein defenses. Cheering wildly the gunners and infantry men of

24

the battle group passed through the South African defenses on the coast road and into temporary safety.

The 11th Field Regiment had arrived at Alamein.

3   THE BATTLE OF RUWEISAT RIDGE

The red sun sank beyond the Deir El Shein,
Soft darkness covered you: the tumult died;
The soaring lights marked out your stubborn line,
Beneath the shadow of Ruweisat Ridge.

What was the worth of your stout hearts that day?
Who tells the sum of all your sacrifice?
But for your staunchness who can say
The autumn victories have never been.

Is that the answer to your sweat and pain?
Your requiem in the desert's dusty breeze?
When the bells peal for Alamein,
Remember these.
– Brigadier Rob Waller, late RA.

Early the following morning the regiment moved forward in response
to an urgent call by the South Africans for additional artillery support.
Deploying south of the road the guns were laid out on a bearing of
270 degrees. Throughout the day harassing fire was brought down on
German armour moving south on the Rahman Track. It was calculated
that Rommel had driven and exhorted the bulk of the Afrika Korps to
advance over 50 miles in the preceding 18 hours. He had 'bumped'
the Alamein defences. Axis formations identified included the 15th

26

and 21st Panzer Division, the 90th Light Division and the Italian Brescia Division. Another dust storm developed towards noon. By mid-afternoon, artillery observations became impossible and the guns ceased firing.

As the sun dipped near the horizon on the last day of June the regiment came out of action, limbered up and withdrew to a position between El Alamein and El Imayid. We went into leaguer which, considering we were nearly 10 miles behind the 'front', didn't auger well for the following day. The 18th Indian Infantry Brigade, which had been detached from the 8th Indian Division, had arrived by rail from Iraq. They were currently constructing a defensive 'box' at Deir El Shein, a large depression between the coast road and Ruweisat Ridge. Although we were, at this point, without orders for the next day, it was expected that the regiment would deploy in support of the 18th Brigade.

The loss of the Regimental 'B' Echelon was confirmed that night. Together with the 83/85 Battery 'B' Echelon they had been cut off at Sidi Haneish west of El Daba by Rommel's lightning advance on the evening of 27th June. Surrounded by the enemy they had attempted to fight their way out to freedom but were unsuccessful. Sergeant S. Hatfield of the 83/85 Battery, with two gunners, escaped the trap by going to ground in a deep *nullah* when the battle was at its height. They later walked east into the desert and were picked up by a 10th Corps Signals vehicle. Sergeant Hatfield later provided a detailed report of the destruction and capture of both 'B' Echelon and 'E' Troop which had rejoined the group in the early hours of 28th June.

Hatfield reported that the first warning they had of their danger came less than two hours after our battle group moved south into the desert from Sidi Haneish on the evening of 27th June. The petrol lorry was filling up at the petrol dump when it came under machine gun fire. The enemy had cut the coast road east of their position, effectively preventing any withdrawal. Captain Evans-Lawrence ordered both 'B' Echelons into a regimental leaguer while Captain Breakell went to the headquarters of the 5th Indian Division, located further west, for information. Vehicles and personnel had moved into an area of scrub grass and sand dunes about 500 yards north of the coast road. The machine gun fire was coming from an enemy mobile column in the desert.

In the early morning hours of 28th June Lieutenant O'Day and BSM Harvey reached the coast road with three guns of 'E' Troop. They had blundered into a small detachment of German mobile infantry about a mile short of the coast road. Challenged by a German sentry, Lieutenant O'Day ordered his driver to hit the accelerator. Increasing speed, the small column thundered through the enemy leaguer. Although they came under small arms fire they reached the coast without any casualties. It was reported that Sergeant Penny was seen standing up in his gun tractor giving the horse artillery signal to break into a gallop! The column turned east on the coast road. They encountered an infantry patrol of the 5th Indian Division which directed them to the 11th Field Regiment lines.

Soon after dawn, Captain Evans-Lawrence made a careful recce of the position and ordered slit trenches to be dug and vehicles dispersed. At about 07.30 hours the enemy commenced shelling the position with high explosives. The soft sand neutralized the effect of the shelling to a major extent.

Lieutenant O'Day and BSM Harvey deployed 'E' Troop and the three 25-pounders went into action, hurling HE into the enemy positions. Later that morning a depleted company of the Durham Light Infantry arrived from Divisional HQ. They deployed around the guns and began to prepare weapon pits. Bren guns were set up in anticipation of the inevitable enemy attack.

Sporadic artillery and machine gun fire continued throughout the morning. At about 14.00 hours heavy concentrated counter-battery fire came down in the gun positions with the obvious intention of neutralizing the British artillery. The gunners were ordered into slit trenches. A tractor and two ammunition limbers took direct hits, one of the latter exploding in a tremendous orange flash. As the intensity of the shelling diminished enemy tanks were observed approaching the regimental position at a range of about 2000 yards. Gunners were ordered to 'Take Post!' and 'laid on' the approaching armour over open sights.

At 800 yards, with guns loaded with High Explosive Charge III, cap on, the order to fire was given. One tank was hit and exploded, one tank was hit and stopped. The panzers went into reverse and withdrew. The panzer commanders evidently decided not to close with the 25-pounders. Casualties were now mounting and it was obvious that the unequal battle could not indefinitely be prolonged. Only the guns prevented the German armour from overrunning the outnumbered regimental 'B' Echelons.

It had been noted that as a general rule the Axis forces avoided attacking in darkness. Under the present situation it was believed they would overcome this dislike and attack either during the hours of darkness or just before dawn.

As the heat of the day diminished with the first cool breeze of the Sahara night and the shadows cast by the setting sun rapidly lengthened the brigade commander issued orders for a breakout at 21.00 hours. Petrol and rations were issued to all vehicles and any correspondence that could be of any use to the enemy was ordered destroyed. Seriously wounded men were assembled at a clearly marked 'First Aid' post. They would have to be left behind. A medical orderly volunteered to stay with them.

As the vehicles commenced to form up behind the Durham Light Infantry who were to lead the breakout Jerry opened up with another artillery concentration. Two three-ton lorries loaded with 'walking wounded' Indian Other Ranks (IORs) were hit. One vehicle caught fire and the cries of trapped and wounded men penetrated the HE explosions and chilled the hearts of nearby gunners who were helpless to effect any rescue.

Captain Breakell went forward to bring 'E' Troop out of action. BSM Harvey was still behind his guns, directing fire and encouraging gunners. The remaining guns were to bring up the rear of the column. One gun had lost its tractor and was 'spiked' by its two surviving gunners.

At 20.45 hours the order was given to break out. As the Durhams walked bravely forward into the enemy positions, their Bren guns chattering and bayonets fixed, enemy guns opened up on the column behind. Enemy infantry of the 90th Light closed up on the road behind the fire of their field guns.

Sergeant Hatfield was in a 15 cwt truck near the end of the column and behind the cookhouse lorry when it took a direct hit. Hatfield picked up Driver Barty and Gunner Woodward who were unhurt. Two hundred yards further on his vehicle lurched to a stop with a shot through the engine. They scrambled aboard the three-ton MT lorry and almost immediately it was hit and caught fire. Sergeant Hatfield and five gunners jumped clear. By this time the road was a shambles of blazing and exploding transport. Finding a relatively deep *nullah* crossing the road, Hatfield jumped in, calling on the gunners to follow. They followed the *nullah* north from the road, bending low to avoid enemy small arms fire. Here the small group remained most of the night.

At 04.00 hours the next morning Hatfield led his party out, walking east into the darkness. They were eventually picked up by a 10th Army Corps signals vehicle. It was Hatfield's opinion that all the personnel of RHQ and 83/83 Battery 'B' Echelons, including the survivors of 'E' Troop, were captured.

Ten words in the Regimental Diary of 1st July 1942 sounded an epitaph for those men who lost their lives at Sidi Haneish and a sad farewell to those who marched into captivity, some of whom never returned: 'B Echelon lost by enemy action, 201 men believed captured.'

Captain Evans-Lawrence escaped captivity a few days later, rejoined the regiment, but died of wounds received on Ruweisat Ridge in late July.

During the night the enemy moved artillery forward west of El Alamein. Shortly after sunrise they commenced ranging on the coast road west of El Imayid which culminated in accurate gunfire on our positions. Sergeant Hall, one of our popular and respected NCOs, was killed. Slit trenches were hastily dug and we went to ground.

On that first day of July, as Auchinleck desperately organized the Alamein defences, as the Eighth Army scavenged the desert for remnants of broken and depleted units, as divisional commanders plugged gaps in the defensive system with weary and exhausted troops, Rommel struck again. Under cover of a *khamseen*, he hurled 15th Panzer Division against 18th Indian Brigade in Deir El Shein. The Indian troops, without armour, were outclassed. The Gurkhas, Sikhs and Essex fought gallantly but hopelessly all day and were finally overrun.

The way was almost open for the Afrika Korps to break through on Ruweisat Ridge, roll up the 1st South African Division to their north and head for Alexandria. The tactical situation at this time is best described by Lieutenant Colonel G.R. Stevens in his book, *Fourth Indian Division*:

'Deep in the desert, where under the blinding glare of midsummer the horizon dances all day with mirages, the tough New Zealanders blocked the enemy's line of advance along the black cliffs of the Qattara Depression. Between the Kiwis and the Springboks, a gap of 15 miles intervened. In the centre of this gap, a long finger of high ground rose gradually out of the west until it overlooked both the sea coast and the deep desert. At its eastern extremity, this ridge – Ruweisat on the map – ended in an abrupt promontory. It was the key to the battlefield. Unless Ruweisat was firmly held, the Alamein defensive system was untenable.'

The lost 'E' Troop was reformed with surviving gunners and equipment that had been salvaged from regiments that had been destroyed in the recent fighting in Libya and around Mersa Matruh. Two officers, one warrant officer and 38 British Other Ranks from 164 Field Regiment and one officer and seven British Other Ranks from 32 Field Regiment were posted to the 11th Field Regiment. The regiment obtained five 25-pounders and the 265th Anti-Tank Battery was attached to the regiment. This latter unit was equipped with the new six-pounder anti-tank guns which had been used very effectively by the 2nd New Zealand Division at Mersa Matruh.

Later in the day the regiment moved west in desert formation along the Ruweisat Ridge towards the advancing Afrika Korps. The guns were ordered into action in area 482891 with observation posts at Point 96. As darkness descended all batteries formed a close leaguer on 'D' Troop's position.

Early in the morning of 2nd July, we were incorporated into another battle group by Brigadier Claude Eastman CRA, 50th Division. Our infantry component was 'C' Company of the 1/4 Essex with a few heavy machine guns of the Northumberland Fusiliers and a small number of Gurkhas who had survived the disaster in the Deir El Shein. Air cover was provided by 113 LAA Battery. The group which had been formed around the guns of the 11th Field Regiment was commanded by Brigadier Rob Waller CRA, 10th Indian Division and was aptly named ROBCOL. Orders to the battle group were to stop and throw back any attempt by the enemy to exploit the gap on the Ruweisat Ridge between the South Africans and the 2nd New Zealand Division.

At 09.00 hours on 2nd July ROBCOL advanced against the enemy on a bearing of 260°. Enemy infantry were reported in area 877292. At 11.30 hours a large enemy leaguer was observed north of the ridge in the Deir El Shein. The guns were ordered into action and effective fire was put down on a MT concentration. Towards noon a strong infantry attack developed against the gun positions which had an infantry shield almost under the gun muzzles. This attack appeared to be a move to test the strength of our blocking force. It was easily repulsed by 'D' Troop guns supported by infantry machine gun fire. 'E' Troop continued to engage the MT, now withdrawing west.

OP officers watched intently for any movement by the Afrika Korps panzers. A major concern of Lieutenant Colonel McCarthy at this point was the possible development of a *khamseen*. Rommel had been known to order his panzers to attack in a dust storm. The 18th Indian Brigade had been overrun in the Deir El Shein in a dust storm. With the gunners blinded the panzers commanders would be fully prepared to accept the risks in order to break through the flimsy Eighth Army defences.

It was hoped that the high-speed firing of the 25-pounders would create uncertainty in the German commander as to the strength of the battle group and in particular the number of guns.

Both field batteries and the anti-tank battery now came under heavy and accurate shell fire directed from an enemy OP on the Tel El Eisa feature. The heavier fire appeared to be directed onto the position held by 83/85 Battery which seemed to lie across the enemy's axis of advance.

At 15.00 hours hostile tanks were observed approaching from the west. The panzers halted at 3000 yards and 'D' Troop was ordered to engage with HE Charge III Cap on. Two tanks were destroyed but two of 'D' Troop's guns sustained direct hits from shellfire. As the afternoon wore on and the blistering summer sun moved slowly towards the west, casualties commenced to mount. At 18.30 hours 'D' Troop, all ammunition expended, was pulled out of action. The panzers advanced 1000 yards towards the position. 'E' Troop was ordered to engage. Again they stopped, taking hull down positions. Again they moved forward. The flashes from the 75mm guns on the Mark IVs were easily visible. By 19.00 hours 'E' Troop had only two guns in action. As the range decreased 265 Battery brought their six-pounders into action. Three more tanks had now been either destroyed or put out of action. As tank crews evacuated their burning panzers Northumberland machine gunners mercilessly cut them down. Under heavy attack the South Africans had pulled back their defences, seriously weakening and exposing ROBCOL's right flank. The position was saved when Major Geoff Armstrong brought up six guns of 'A' Battery Royal Horse Artillery and engaged the enemy firing over 600 rounds of high explosives.

At 20.00 hours the panzers were observed withdrawing into the west. Half an hour later, as darkness settled over the desert, the regiment moved back into leaguer at Point 96.

The casualties had been heavy. Five British Other Ranks killed. These included Bombardier Ecclston, who died in agony behind his gun, his stomach torn open by a piece of shell casing, and Bombardier Johnston, who sacrificed his life by continuing to lay and fire his gun with his left arm shot off. Eighty Other Ranks were wounded; some slightly but many seriously. Six officers were wounded, including Captains W.J. Clements and L.L. Boyd and Lieutenant W.E. Slight, who destroyed an abandoned 25-pounder with his last two rounds. Also Lieutenants L.P. Sturdee, A.M. McGregor and P. Curry. On 3rd July the ration strength of 83/85 Battery was down to 87 gunners and seven officers.

During the night fitters and artificers went to work on the guns. Only one 25-pounder of 83/85 Battery was found to be serviceable and this gun was transferred to 78/84 Battery on 3rd July. In addition one troop of anti-tank guns was unfit for service and was withdrawn to workshops.

Early in the morning of 3rd July, ROBCOL advanced westward. The guns were deployed 1000 yards south of Alam Baoshaza in an anti-tank role.

Soon after 06.00 hours the guns came under heavy shellfire which continued at varying intensities throughout the morning. Enemy tanks advanced into hull down positions during the day at a range of about 3000 yards. They were engaged by the guns of 78/84 Battery with HE. 'A' Troop of the RHA also brought down fire on the panzers. Soon after noon three of the guns of 83/85 Battery were returned to action.

During the afternoon Stuka dive bombers added their terrifying precision bombing to the shellfire, causing some casualties in both gun positions and wagon lines. In the face of British artillery fire the panzers made no further attempt to close. As the sun dipped towards the western horizon and the shadows lengthened OPs reported the withdrawal of the panzers opposite the regimental gun position.

For the first time since Rommel opened his offensive in Libya in late May, his victorious advance across the Western Desert and into Egypt had been brought to a halt. The Afrika Korps had been stopped by the guns of the 11th Field Regiment 60 miles from the ultimate objective, Alexandria and the Nile Delta.

It can truly be said that if Stalingrad and Alamein were the turning points of the Second World War, then the action on Ruweisat Ridge on 2nd and 3rd July was the turning point of Alamein and paved the way for Montgomery's victory in October of 1942.

Casualties on the second day of the artillery/tank battle on Ruweisat Ridge were again heavy with 32 Other Ranks killed, including Lieutenant Bombardier Watkins of the survey party who had escaped the trap at Sidi Haneish. ROBCOL did not withdraw that night but formed a defensive leaguer around the gun positions.

The following day ROBCOL and the 11th Field Regiment were in receipt of a message of congratulations from the Corps Commander and endorsed by the Commander in Chief General, Sir Claude Auchinleck.

The enemy continued to put down heavy counter battery fire on the ridge for the next few days, supplemented with Stuka bombing attacks resulting in further casualties – two gunners killed in action and eight gunners wounded. In a series of advance and withdrawals a truck with a number of Other Ranks became bogged down in soft sand and was captured.

After two more abortive attacks, the first on the 2nd New Zealand Division sector and the second on the South African Division front on the coast, the Afrika Korps went over to a defensive role. Rommel now needed time to rest his exhausted troops, repair and rebuild his armoured divisions, re-equip his infantry and bring forward supplies and ammunition. Although local action continued, the First Battle of Alamein ground to a halt about 15th July.

On 15th July, the 11th Field Regiment came under command of the 5th Indian Infantry Division and reverted to its customary role of close infantry support.

The action on Ruweisat Ridge on 2nd and 3rd July 1942 earned three awards for gallantry for the 11th Field Regiment. The first of these was to Captain Laurence Boyd RA who commanded 'E' Troop and earned the immediate award of the Military Cross. Captain Boyd's citation read as follows:

'On 2 July during the attack on his Coln near the Ruweisat Ridge this officer showed most conspicuous courage and devotion to duty. He fought his troop with success all day largely contributing to driving off an attack by infantry. When it was attacked by enemy MK III and IV tanks and heavily machine gunned and shelled he set a splendid example to all ranks by his complete disregard of danger. Although himself twice wounded he took command of a gun when the No. 1 was killed. He continued to fight his guns until two of them were put out of action and all his ammunition was expended.'

Sergeant John Keelan of 'E' Troop was given an immediate award of the Distinguished Service Medal. His citation reads:

'During the action on Ruweisat Ridge on 2 July this N.C.O. behaved with great coolness and showed an excellent example to his detachment. His Troop was shelled severely for several hours and finally attacked by enemy tanks. He controlled his detachment and supervised the fire of his gun with great steadiness and determination and set a splendid example to all around. When a shell killed four of his detachment he continued to fire his gun alone until the last round was expended. Although wounded and still under heavy fire from tank cannon and machine guns when the Troop was ordered to withdraw he brought his gun safely to the rear.'

The final award went to Sergeant George E. Wilkinson. His citation reads:

'This N.C.O. has set a very high example of courage and devotion to duty throughout the whole period of operations. On July 2nd South of Ruweisat Ridge when his Troop was attacked by tanks, BSM Wilkinson then No. 1 of a gun, was twice wounded. In spite of this he continued to direct the fire of his gun under heavy gun and MG fire until dark when he was ordered to withdraw. Although he had several opportunities of being evacuated with the other wounded he was in action with his gun on the following day and continued to command his gun efficiently again under heavy shell fire.'

Sergeant Wilkinson was awarded the Military Medal.

Ruweisat Ridge, El Alamein, 2nd July 1942
A Gunner's Story

Brushing away a cloud of flies trying to find a foothold on the rim of his mug, Max Pemberton hauled down a long draught of scalding hot tea, liberally blended with Carnation milk. Pushing his tin hat to the back of his head he squinted along the open sights of his 25-pounder gun. He tried to focus on the faint outline of a German tank hull down at an approximate range of 2000 yards. The shimmering heat haze obscured his vision and he turned away in disgust. Muttering a curse he pulled his hand away from the burning barrel of the gun. It was no joke that the African sun in midsummer could render metal capable of frying an egg.

It was after midday and the regiment was deployed on the western end of the Ridge. All morning the enemy had carefully and method-ically shelled the gun positions. Currently there was a lull in this counter-battery fire. The Afrikan Korps, after its almost non-stop advance from Libya, appeared eager to press on to its final objectives of Cairo and Alexandria. Rommel had selected the thinly defended Ruweisat Ridge with its firm going for his panzers to punch a hole through the Eighth Army's Alamein Line and roll up the South Africans to the north. The enemy axis of advance went right through the gun positions of the 83/85 Battery which, with 78/84 Battery, was the artillery component of a Desert Battle Group named ROBCOL. In order to better control the field of fire the guns were sited in terribly exposed positions on the slopes of the Ridge. Observation officers, standing in their armoured observation vehicles parked on the higher ground, maintained a constant watch to the west, binoculars jammed to their eyes. They knew that Rommel had selected the 15th Panzer Division, supported by the 90th Light Division, to lead the attack. British armour was almost non-existent at this time and placed in the battle and all that stood between the Afrika Korps and the Nile Delta were the guns of the 11th Field Regiment supported by a depleted company of infantry who were deployed in front of the guns.

Once more Max Pemberton looked along his open sights. He knew what the bastards were waiting for – the sun. It was now moving into the west and by 15.00 hours would be directly in the eyes of the gunner. All morning the gunners had waited for the dreaded *khamseen* to mount its fury but the wind remained calm with only an odd puff whipping up local sand movement. With the gunners blinded Rommel had often selected a *khamseen* in which to mount a panzer attack. The heat was now turning metal to skin blistering temperatures and drawing perspiration from sweating gunners crouched shadeless behind the guns.

Max Pemberton was a regular soldier. He was a Midlander and had enlisted in the artillery just prior to the outbreak of hostilities in 1939. Posted to India in November he had completed his training in Meerut. Max was your classic British regular, a confirmed grumbler and bitcher but reliable to the core and loyal to his mates. Occasionally he would glance to the north and note the Tel El Eisa feature. It was just a pimple on the desert but it was held by the enemy who had defended it aggressively against all attempts by the South Africans to recapture it. The enemy had established an OP on Tel El Eisa which effectively dominated the gun positions. Max could almost feel the eyes of the OP observer boring into his own.

The sun continued its slow but inexorable movement into the west. Gun numbers prepared ammunition and detachment commanders maintained a constant watch on both their front and the battery command post.

At 14.30 hours the prelude to the armoured attack commenced. The sickening whine of shellfire preceded the explosions across the gun position. Gunners were ordered into slit trenches already prepared behind the guns. The shelling continued. A command post NCO running towards the guns was caught in the open and disappeared in a cloud of smoke. Pemberton, clinging to the bottom of his slit trench that was much too shallow, wished that he had spent a little more time and dug deeper. He laughed ironically to himself as he remembered the comment of the recruiting sergeant when he enlisted and elected to join the gunners: 'Good choice, my boy, you'll stay 4–5000 yards behind the front line!'

Although the Warwickshire infantrymen had melted into the ground at the beginning of the shelling their Bren guns could be seen standing on the parapet of their weapon pits just a few hundred yards in front of the guns.

Across the sun-baked desert came that order, always electrifying when in action, 'Take Post!'

The gunners hurled themselves from their slit trenches and fell into their assigned positions on the guns. As the shelling recommenced a gunner on the next gun pitched headfirst into the sand and almost simultaneously No. 2 was hit square in the carriage. Three gunners were killed as the muzzle jerked skywards at a grotesque angle.

Max crouched low over his sights as he listened to the gun position officer follow his initial order: 'Enemy tanks approaching on your front,' followed by a short pause. Then 'HE, Charge Three, Cap On!' Detachment Commanders would now control fire upon an order from the GPO. Max heard No. 4 ram home the shell, followed by the cartridge and then the satisfying clunk as No. 2 slammed shut the breech. As he concentrated upon picking up his target he noticed Lieutenant Bill Slight moving out to the front and left of the guns. Damn fool he thought, must want to get himself killed. Max knew his No. 1, Sergeant Burroughs, was ready to throw the trail to the left or right if he gave the hand signal. Finally, through the shimmer of the heat haze, he saw his tank; it seemed to be coming straight for his gun but he knew that was just a visual illusion. It turned to the right as though avoiding an obstacle. Keeping the tank in his sights Max traversed left and lowered elevation. There appeared to be at least 30 panzers and possibly 40 rolling towards the gun position of 83/85 Battery which now had only six of its eight guns in action.

Suddenly there was the sharp crack of a 25-pounder as the gun to his right exploded into action. Good old Sergeant Norman Neal, Max thought, Nogger always had to be the first off the mark. He heard the range from the GPO repeated by his No. 1 – 'One thousand yards!' – and reflected upon the precision of the range and reckoned they must be using a rangefinder at the command post. He concentrated upon his target; it was a Panzer Mark III. He identified the number of bogeys and the short-barrelled 50 mm gun. Gun flashes along the line of advancing panzers indicated that they were firing into the gun positions. Max knew that he could wait no longer; there were too many tanks. He caught his quarry square in his sights and his right hand swept down and back on the firing lever. As the barrel came back on the buffer-recuperator and the proximity of the explosion temporarily blanked the enemy gunfire No. 2 had the breech open before the barrel returned to the firing position and the empty cartridge clattered across the trail. Max was brought back to reality by Sergeant

Burroughs shouting above the din, 'We got him, we got the bastard!' As he traversed right to pick up another target he could see the crew scrambling out of the turret, now skewed at a bizarre angle. Now the infantry heavy machine guns opened up, mercilessly cutting down survivors of striken tanks as they tried to escape and find safety from possible explosions and the tank crew's nightmare, fire. The gun was reloaded as fast as a well trained crew could do it and Max laid and fired on another target. Another gun was put out of action by a well-aimed round from a Mark IV Special and yet another gun, its crew all killed by shellfire, was being fought by its No. 1, Sergeant John Keelan, singlehandedly. At 600 yards the panzers found a *nullah* and went into hull down positions. They maintained their fire into the gun positions and enemy shellfire intensified.

Because of depleted ammunition supplies detachment commanders were ordered not to fire on tanks in hull down positions and the OPs maintained a close watch for enemy movement. The battery was now reduced to four guns in action. At 18.00 hours shelling intensified again with the obvious intention of driving the gunners to ground. Again the battery was ordered into the slit trenches but almost immediately the order to 'Take Post' was given. Max traversed his gun left and right across his front and selected a Mark IV Special. At under 800 yards, as the panzers rolled across level ground, they ran into a solid wall of HE from the rapid firing 25-pounders. At this range the fire of the field guns was deadly and as tank after tank was hit the panzers went into reverse and withdrew to the safety of the *nullah*. German artillery officers often confessed that they were constantly surprised by the speed of firing of the 25-pounder field gun. In addition, at these lower ranges the regiment's anti-tank guns were brought into action. Although of much smaller calibre their high muzzle velocity compensated for this disadvantage. Max's gun was now reported out of action due to buffer-recuperator problems.

At 20.00 hours there was a loud cheer from the infantrymen as the panzers were observed withdrawing west into the setting sun. Little did the commander of the 15th Panzer Division realize that at that moment 83/85 Battery was reduced to only one gun in action.

Max Pemberton stretched himself out of his layer's seat and gratefully grabbed hold of the mug of tea thrust into his hands by his No. 5.

There would be another day of this battle and there would be more good men condemned to die on the rocky slopes of the Ruweisat Ridge but for now the gunners of the 11th Field Regiment could enjoy their tea, McConachie's stew and just maybe a fair night's sleep.

4   THE SECOND BATTLE OF ALAMEIN (ALAM EL HALFA)

During the early part of July 9th Australian Division had been moving up from the Delta. They had been allotted the coastal sector. This shortened the South African front which, in turn, shortened the Ruweisat sector. The 5th Indian Infantry Division now was made responsible for this sector and moved in two brigades: 9th and 161st Indian Infantry Brigades. On 15th July, 11th Field Regiment came under the command of the 5th Indian Division HQRA.

On 14th July we received orders and information covering an attack to be mounted that night in conjunction with a New Zealand brigade on our left. The attack on a brigade front would employ 3/10 Baluchis and 4/6 Rajputana Rifles. Objectives were Points 63 and 64 at the west end of Ruweisat Ridge. The fighting continued through that night and the following day. By nightfall we had taken nearly 1000 Italian prisoners. The Kiwi attack was held up by a strongpoint and was assisted by 1/4 Essex. That night the enemy counterattacked and over-ran a number of our forward positions and appeared to be prepared for a major attack. Support for the threatened sector was rushed forward. Six-pounder detachments from the Royal Northumberland Fusiliers were moved up with 149 Anti-Tank Regiment. Our guns, which had been supporting 20th Australian Brigade in the north, were swung around over 90 degrees to give support to the 5th Indian Brigade.

Through the afternoon of 16th July we were plastered with enemy artillery fire. Bombing attacks intensified. At 18.00 hours, with the sun in our eyes, the panzers moved in the Dier el Shein to the west and north west. They were less than 2000 yards from our forward defence lines. As they came into range they were engaged by our tanks who maintained a hull down position and by the six-pounders which had been dug in flush with the rim of the ridge. Our 25-pounders were sited further back. With the advantage of greater range we engaged the panzers by indirect fire, controlled by our forward observation officers. Finally, like dogs rushing furiously to attack huge bears, our light tanks, and even lightly armed armoured cars, drove forward to engage the panzers, depending upon superior speed to avoid enemy fire. All this went on over the infantry who were wisely keeping their heads down in slit trenches and weapon pits. The armour and artillery battle continued for over two hours. At 21.00 hours the enemy broke off the attack and withdrew.

Not until the sun came up the next day did we appreciate the extent of our victory. The battlefield was littered with broken and shot-up German armour. It was safe to assume that a fair number of lightly disabled tanks had been salvaged during the night. The Afrika Korps had developed tank salvage to a fine art. The counterattack had advanced to within 800 yards of our forward defence lines. In addition to Mark III and Mark IV tanks, they had employed self-propelled guns, 20 and 37 mm anti-tank guns and 88 mm guns. It was also safe to assume that there were substantial numbers of lorried infantry waiting in the rear, ready to exploit any armoured breakthrough.

Prior to this attack and counterattack, the Australian 9th Division launched a determined counterattack in the coastal sector. They recaptured the Tel El Eisa feature just south of the coast road at the point of the bayonet. Possession of this commanding feature gave them excellent observation west and south west.

In the morning of 19th July we sustained our first serious dive bomber attack. We had been informed about the German dive bomber back in the Delta by a desert veteran. His account was so dramatic that we decided our informant was suffering from desert madness or Deolali Tap, to use an Indian expression.

Over the relatively short period that the regiment had been in action we had become hardened. Shellfire, panzer fire, machine gun fire, and even conventional high-level bombing were all part of the business of warfare and the risk of death or injury was accepted as being part of the job. Those feelings were, in turn, supported by the usual youthful optimism, expressed as 'It will never be me, it will always be the other fellow who gets it.' How many men had gone to their death in action with those famous words, 'I'll be all right, Jack!' on their lips? It was all impersonal and remote, a game of fantasy in a world of unreality. Many of us had seen a mortally wounded comrade refusing to accept that he was seriously wounded even as his life's blood ebbed away.

The German dive bomber or Stuka evoked an entirely different reaction. Their near vertical dive, combined with their eerie scream, personalized the attack and battered the senses.

I watched as they came over in formation and then peeled away one by one, going into what appeared to be a near vertical dive. Initially, I watched fascinated, and then as that high-pitched scream penetrated my ear drums, like the wailing of a thousand banshees, I was seized by fear and terror. I grovelled in the bottom of my slit trench, my face pressed into the ground, oblivious of the sand in my eyes and mouth. They're going to get me, I thought, not the other fellow. Then the bombs dropped. Not until the last unearthly scream died away did I emerge, spitting sand.

The German Command believed that the damage to morale by the scream of the Stuka was at least equal to the damage caused by the bomb.

Two gunners and our CO Lieutenant Colonel A.O. McCarthy, were wounded in this attack, the latter seriously. Major P.R.M. Waterfield, RA assumed command of the 11th Field Regiment.

That evening, the guns were moved over three miles, south west of former gun positions. During this move an AOV of 78/84 Battery was blown up on a minefield. Either our new positions were under enemy observation or Jerry just decided to give us a warm welcome because, commencing at 08.30 hours next day, we came under heavy shellfire. By noon we had suffered six wounded gunners and one man killed. At 16.00 hours a heavy concentration came down on 78/84 Battery position: one gun was hit, 14 other ranks were wounded and Captain J. Evans-Lawrence RA and BSM Raw were seriously wounded. Four days later, Captain Evans-Lawrence died of wounds in hospital.

We were, at this time, one of three field artillery regiments supporting the 5th Indian Division. The other two were the 1st Field Regiment RA and the 32nd Field Regiment RA. Gunner Colley had returned from hospital and he and I were the only survivors of the original survey party.

Reinforcements, both officers and other ranks, commenced to reach the regiment about 20th July. Brigadier Watts, a Territorial Army man was posted to the survey party along with four gunner-surveyors. We were also blessed with our first survey officer, Lieutenant F.R. Miles RA.

A major event was the updating of our transport. Although our newly organized LAD had salvaged and repaired an older three-ton Bedford to carry our survey equipment, our remaining North American built Ford V-8 was almost useless in sandy going. Overpowered and with only two-wheel drive, it had poor traction. It was replaced by two Willys jeeps, equipped with four-wheel drive and a low-reduction gearbox. Although a bumpy ride, the jeep was a magnificent vehicle for desert travelling, able to adjust to varied conditions.

Apart from the daily allotment of shelling and dive bombing, soldiering in the desert was dominated by a number of important factors. The first of these was a shortage of water, which was tightly rationed. Bathing was unheard of and even washing became a luxury. We would apportion a small amount of our daily ration for shaving and cleaning teeth. The remainder was required for drinking and making tea. Survival was more important than personal hygiene.

However, commencing in mid-August, HQ arranged on a rotational basis a system of visits to the Med, about 30 miles behind the lines, for bathing and washing clothes. Another factor was the constant and monotonous daily burning heat. There was no shade in the desert. Some relief could be obtained by rigging a ground sheet over a well-dug slit trench, providing one could find a sandy area to dig in. We soon came to dread a terror of the desert more devastating than the daily cook-out caused by the heat of the sun. This was the hot wind that blew up from the south to southwest called the *khamseen*. The intense heat and dryness of this wind resembles blasts of hot air from some enormous oven. It picked up the dust and sand which rose high enough in the air to darken the sun. It forced this fine dust into every crack, crevice or opening. The *khamseen* brought all forms of military activity to a halt. Fortunately, it dispensed its misery equally on foe and friend. It was the common enemy that took precedence over all other dangers.

Finally, there were the flies. Flies were the scourge of the desert and the ultimate curse of Western Desert warfare. Breeding, multiplying, feeding and fattening on the filth, refuse and excreta left lying in the desert, the North African variety showed no respect for race or rank. They were fierce, determined and aggressive. Through three years of service in India and the Middle East, we were relatively inured to the ways of the common housefly. We were, however, shocked and terrorized by the ferocity and number of the North African variety.

After some time in the desert, a unique kinship developed between all ranks, crossing minor boundaries and races and even spreading from friend to foe. To a major degree it was based upon common trials, dangers and hardships. This kinship or camaraderie is well exemplified in the following piece entitled:

The Desert Code of Social Intercourse
1.   Your chief concern is not to endanger your comrade.
2.   Because of the risk that you may bring him, you do not light fires after sunset.
3.   You do not use his slit trench at any time. Neither do you park your vehicle near the hole in the ground in which he lives.
4.   You do not borrow from him and particularly you do not request those precious fluids, water and petrol.
5.   You do not give him compass bearings which you have not tested and of which you are not sure.
6.   You do not leave any mess behind that will breed flies.
7.   You do not ask him to convey your messages, your gear, or yourself unless it is his job to do so.
8.   You do not drink deeply of any man's bottles for they may not be replenished. You make sure he has many before you take his cigarette.
9.   You do not ask information beyond your job, for idle talk kills men.
10.   You do not grouse unduly, except concerning the folly of your own commanders. This is allowable. You criticize no other man's commanders.
11.   Of those things which you do, the first is to be hospitable

and the second is to be courteous. The day is long in the desert and there is time to be helpful to those who share your adventure. A cup of tea, therefore, is proffered to all comers – it is your handshake and your badge of association. Over the tea mugs the good-mannered guest transacts his business expeditiously, gossips shop for a little, and gets him gone.

This code is the sum of fellowship in the desert. It knows no rank or any exception.

Written by an Indian Army Officer in the Western Desert, 1941.

Now that the regimental survey party was restored to full strength, we commenced survey operations. It was evident that sooner or later a major offensive would be undertaken by the Eighth Army. The current static defensive situation would not continue indefinitely. Any major offensive would involve artillery support. This would cover counter battery fire plus the softening up of enemy strongpoints, concluding with a major barrage.

Through late July and into August we checked existing positions and, where possible, fixed new targets. Some of this work involved an element of danger. The Afrika Korps observers were not going to allow groups of happy-go-lucky surveyors to drive around in jeeps, raising clouds of dust and placing red and yellow flags like organizers of a village garden party. Inevitably, we drew enemy shellfire. This did not help to earn us brownie points with our own OP officers or forward infantry defences. One such incident became quite nasty and cooled our enthusiasm for survey in forward defensive areas. We believed, from our maps, that there was a trig point near the west end of the Ruweisat Ridge.

With Gunner-Surveyor Reeve I decided to check this out. Leaving our jeep well in the rear, we walked to the point, setting up a director over the trig point. We had completed levelling when the familiar whine of 88s cut through the relative quiet of the afternoon. Reeve dived in one direction and I the other. The fall of shot about 150 yards plus gave us a break. I decided not to wait for the next round. I had noticed a stone sanger a short distance away. Shouting to my colleague, I took off and dived inside just as the next shell arrived. I was immediately aware of and recognized the peculiar putrid odour of decomposing human bodies. Looking around, I realized that I had jumped into a well-built shelter inhabited by two very dead and decomposing Italian infantrymen. The flies swarmed at me in apparent frenzy. Unable to handle the twin attack of odour and flies, I scrambled out and ran. I decided I would prefer to take my chance with the enemy gunfire than to suffer the horrors of that charnel pit. Reeve now joined me and we retreated rapidly along the ridge, throwing our dignity and pride into the freshening *khamseen*. After sunset that evening we went back to recover our director only to find it blown to pieces. This display of gunnery skill evoked our professional respect and admiration.

As the front stabilized, the 5th Indian Infantry Division held a sector about five miles wide, running across the Ruweisat Ridge. On our right, we joined up with the 1st South African Division with the 9th Australian holding the rest of the front north to the Med. Our left flank was secured by the 2nd New Zealand Division. The rest of the front to the Qattara Depression was heavily mined and patrolled by the 7th Motor Brigade, the 4th Armoured Brigade and in reserve, the 7th Armoured Division. The last named were the famous Desert Rats, so called after their divisional sign, a jerboa. The 7th Armoured Division had been in Egypt since before the outbreak of hostilities.

The mine field had become a standard form of defence in the desert. They were used by both sides, and could vary in depth from just a few hundred yards to one mile or more. Most types of mine were designed to at least stop, if not totally destroy, most vehicles. They could certainly blow the track of a tank, which was all that was necessary for defensive purposes. A disabled tank in an exposed position could be easily destroyed by artillery fire.

Anti-personnel mines were also liberally distributed into barbed wire or across areas that would force enemy patrols to use selected paths of approach, these areas being covered by machine gun fire. By August of 1942, mine laying had become a highly developed and skilful art. Conversely, lifting and disarming enemy mines was a high-risk and usually a dangerous job. Even the highly trained sappers of the engineering companies often sustained heavy casualties. Before any major attack it was necessary to clear tracks through the mine-fields to facilitate the passage of armour and transport.

Infantry patrols by both sides continued through August. These patrols, in general, took one of two forms: fighting patrols or recce patrols. The former were exactly what the name suggests. The recce patrol was sent out to secure information or take prisoners for the same purpose.

The Gurkhas in the Indian Division were particularly good at this form of warfare. They had converted the art of the infantry patrol into a science. Gurkhas originated from Nepal on the borders of northern India and had served the British Raj with loyalty and distinction for over a hundred years. Although short in stature, they were natural born fighters with tremendous endurance and determination. The Gurkha was different from all other coloured soldiers in the British and Commonwealth forces. Under the old British system of class distinction, now happily defunct, the Gurkha was regarded as an equal of the British soldier in every respect. He enjoyed the freedom of British NCO and OR messes and canteens. He had been granted the honour of carrying his personal weapon, the *kukri*, on parade and into battle. The *kukri* was a short curved sword with a single razor sharp edge. It has been claimed that a Gurkha could take the head off an ox at 30 paces with his *kukri*. Whatever the truth of this claim, he certainly terrorized the enemy in close quarter combat. On night patrol, the Gurkhas had no equal.

Most of us were now familiar with the twin terrors of the panzer division, the Mark III and Mark IV tanks. They were both easily identified by the number of bogeys. The Mark III had six either side and the Mark IV eight. The former was armed with a 50 mm gun. There was later an improved version of the Mark III fitted with a long 50 mm gun. The Mark IV had eight bogeys either side and was equipped with a short 75 mm gun. It was superseded by the Mark IV special fitted with a long 75 mm gun.

By mid-August it became apparent that Rommel was preparing for a major attack. The likely date would be decided by the next full moon, around 26th August. The real question was where?

On 20th August we learned that General Alexander had been appointed Commander-in-Chief of the Middle East Command and Lieutenant General Bernard Montgomery had assumed command of the Eighth Army. General Auchinleck had been replaced and there was regret and genuine sympathy throughout many formations. General Auchinleck, or the Auk as he was termed, was very popular with all Indian troops and the general feeling was that he had been shafted. The foregoing appointments were effective from 18th August. Full moon came and passed on 26th August. On 29th August there were reports of enemy concentrations of armour in the area of Quaret el Abd and Gebal Kalakh, 10 to 15 miles south west of our sector. It would appear that Rommel planned to attack on a relatively narrow front just north of the Qattara Depression. This sector was defended by only deep minefields.

On the night of 30th August Rommel unleashed the Afrika Korps. Air observation placed the number of tanks involved at between 350 and 400, of which 200 were panzer Mark IIIs and IVs. They were moving east and slightly south. It appeared to be a repeat of a right hook around our southern flank with the intention of rolling up our front. The difference this time was that the Qattara Depression was forcing the Afrika Korps to go through our minefields. The 5th Indian Division front was fiercely attacked the same night by Ramcke's parachutists. It was obviously a diversionary attack, but they overran one of our British units attached to the 5th Indian Division. The 2nd West Yorks lost a complete company.

The following day, the 15th and 21st Panzer Divisions broke through our minefields and wheeled north as expected with elements of the 90th Light Division on the inside of the wheel. They were on a course that would take them behind the 2nd New Zealand Division and in addition roll over the rear of the 5th Indian Division. We would be facing the Afrika Korps on two fronts. Alternate gun positions were set out for the 11th Field Regiment. These would allow a field of fire of between 90 and 180 degrees.

On the night of 1st August, I was detailed for OP duty the following day. Training in India had stressed the importance of every man being able to handle at least two functions. Gunners were trained to handle every position of the detachment, including No. 1. Signallers were trained in all aspects of both telephone and wireless (radio) communications.

Surveyors, in addition to field survey, were oriented to handle battery command post duties and also to assist observation post officers or OP ack for short. These latter duties were particularly important. The very nature of artillery observation, the eyes of the guns, made it necessary for the observation post to be up front with

49

the infantry, often placed in an exposed location. The casualty rate of OP personnel was relatively high. In the event of the death or wounding of the OP officer, the OP ack would be expected to control and direct the fire of the guns.

At that time in the desert campaign we were equipped with what could be described as an open armoured car. The official artillery description was armoured observation vehicle (AOV). It was armoured sufficiently to give protection against small arms fire, but little more. It was equipped with four-wheel drive. In addition to the OP officer, a captain and myself, the crew was completed with a signaller and the driver.

We moved off shortly after 06.00 hours in a south easterly direction towards the Alam el Halfa Ridge. We moved rapidly over the stony ground, coming to the high ground of the ridge in about 30 minutes. The Alam el Halfa feature was about 12 miles long, running east and west. It was about two to three miles wide. The British (Home Counties) 44th Division had taken up defensive positions along the ridge. They were supported by their divisional field artillery, and were screened by a number of the new six pounder anti-tank guns. These guns had been given their baptism of fire in a counterattack on the Ruweisat Ridge on 14th July. They had proved themselves to be effective against Mark IIIs and IVs when properly handled. The 8th Armoured Brigade was placed at the east end of the Ridge with the 22nd Armoured Brigade at the west end. We took up an observation position close to Point 102, our driver manoeuvring our vehicle into a hull down position. Point 102 was another of those British pre-war survey points. The 23rd Armoured Brigade, to which we were attached, was in reserve. We scanned the front, noting the tanks of the 22nd Armoured Brigade. I noted the familiar silhouette of the American Grant tanks with their distinctive high turrets, equipped with the stubby 75 mm gun. An excellent gun but with no more than a 10 degree traverse. The wind was freshening from the south into a *khamseen*. By noon it had developed into a stinging, howling fury. The horizon was obscured by a deepening rim of dust. Then the sun went out, obscured by a towering wall of sand and dust. We stopped all conversation because an open mouth invited an entry of gritty dust. Even the aggressive desert fly went to ground in order to survive. As an OP, we were useless so we drew some comfort from the fact that

Rommel's armour would be forced into inaction.

Information coming through to us in the early afternoon confirmed that the 15th and 21st Panzer Divisions had wheeled to their left and north. They were on a course that would bring them up against the west end of the Alam el Halfa Ridge. On the inside of this wheel units of the 90th Light Division defended their left flank and a strong recce group maintained a position on their right. The afternoon wore on and the wind gradually diminished. The barrier of dust commenced to recede. We swept the desert to our south with our binoculars, watching and listening. Suddenly the Grant tanks of the County of London Yeomanry started firing. Then out of the receding pall of dust we saw them – panzers!

As they began to take shape I noted the long barrelled 75 mm guns of the Mark IV Specials. They were now clear of the dust but were trailing their own mini-dust clouds. Now came the flash of the 75 mm guns, followed by the report punctuated by the sharp crack of our six pounder anti-tank guns. A Grant tank just exploded in front of us, two more burst into flames, then another was hit. I could see a man trying to drag himself clear from an open turret – he fell back into the flaming inferno. Another man crawled clear of his tank, clothes flaming, then collapsed into a burning heap, motionless. We watched, helpless, knowing there was nothing we could do. The Grant tanks, with their high turrets and dangerous levels of static electricity, and fuelled by high-octane aviation spirits, had earned the reputation of being metal coffins. The 21st Panzer Division methodically continued the destruction of the 22nd Armoured Brigade. The remnants retired behind the ridge, covered by a squadron of RTR and gunfire from the 44th British Divisional artillery.

The German armour was beyond the range of our guns on Ruweisat Ridge. Darkness quickly came, terminating the action. The panzers, as was their custom, went into leaguer. We turned and headed back to the regimental positions, the burning Grants illuminating the night sky behind us.

The Desert Air Force was active that night. How much damage they inflicted I do not know but they would prevent the panzer crews from getting much sleep.

The battle continued for the next two days. All efforts by the Afrika Korps to turn the flank of Alam el Halfa and break through into the rear of the main Alamein defence was frustrated and the panzers turned back. Accurate and heroic action by the crews of the six pounder anti-tank guns, coupled to concentrated artillery fire by our field guns, plus almost continuous bombing by the Desert Air Force, decided the battle. By late afternoon on 3rd September the panzer army was observed withdrawing south. It was a controlled, defensive withdrawal. An abortive attempt was made to cut off the retreating panzers. The 90th Light Division was just too good and the 132nd Infantry Brigade sustained heavy casualties.

Dive bomber attacks increased during this period of the battle, reaching a peak on 3 September. The Stuka pilots appeared to vent most of their fury on the 44th British Division, holding Alam el Halfa Ridge. This division had only arrived in Egypt in August, fresh out from England. They had been deployed less than 10 days before the attack commenced. Inexperience and unfamiliarity with the desert contributed to fairly high casualties.

Early afternoon on 4th September we were preparing to close down our OP in this position for the last time. The battlefield in front of us, so recently a maelstrom of destruction and death, was now deserted and peaceful. Here and there an exploded or burnt-out British or German tank broke the flat monotony of the desert landscape. Making a final sweep of the horizon with my binoculars, I noted a sudden puff of black smoke. It appeared to come from a panzer Mark III. It was unusual because, to the best of our knowledge, all Axis forces had now withdrawn from this sector. We decided to investigate.

Arriving at the location of the smoke, we discovered a German tank. Disabled the previous night, it had been set on fire by its crew. Two men walked towards us from the tank, their arms raised in surrender. The commander, an officer, was lying on the ground seriously wounded. The officer spoke excellent English. His tank had developed engine trouble during the withdrawal and in the confusion they had been left behind. After trying to repair their tank without success, he had given orders for it to be destroyed. They had run out of water the previous evening and gratefully accepted one of our chaguls. We transported them back to our lines, handing them over to the military police of Divisional HQ.

The Afrika Korps completed their withdrawal by 7th September.

Although harrassed by the Desert Air Force and pounded by our artillery, they sustained relatively little damage. Montgomery decided not to release the 7th Armoured Division in pursuit. The bottom line of the battle was that a major and well-planned attack by the Afrika Korps had been defeated by the Eighth Army. Rommel had gambled and lost. The outcome of the engagement gave a valuable boost to our morale.

On 5th September the following interesting entry appeared in the 11th Field Regiment War Diary: 'Threat from south considered to have ceased. OPs will be withdrawn and guns pointed westwards – orders by HQRA 5 Ind. Div.'

Thus ended the Second Battle of El Alamein, sometimes called the Battle of Alam el Halfa.

Ref Op Order No 2   Copy No ....

CONCENTRATION TASKS – A, D, E Tps ONLY

Z	3 rds GF	871570	281980				
Z	3 rds GF	871570	281980				
Z plus 5	2 " "	"	"	Less	30'	Add	300 yds
Z " 8	1 " "	"	"	Less	10'	Drop	100 "
Z " 10	2 " "	"	"	More	40'	Add	400 "
Z " 16	3 " "	"	"	More	1°	Add	300 "
Z " 19	2 " "	"	"	More	2°	Add	200 "
Z " 22	3 " "	"	"	Less	1°	Drop	300 "
Z " 27	3 " "	"	"			Drop	500 "
Z " 32	1 " "	"	"	Less	20'	Add	200 "
Z " 34	2 " "	"	"	More	40'	Add	400 "
Z " 40	3 " "	"	"	Less	2°	Drop	200 "
Z " 45	3 " "	"	"	More	20'	Add	400 "
Z " 49	2 " "	"	"	More	10'		
Z " 52	1 " "	"	"	More	10'	Drop	100 "
Z " 57	3 " "	"	"	More	1°	Add	400 "
Z " 59	1 " "	"	"	Less	3°	Drop	100 "
Z " 66	2 " "	"	"	Less	1°	Add	200 "
Z " 71	5 " "	"	"	More	2°	Add	200 "
Z " 75	1 " "	"	"	More	1°	Drop	400 "
Z " 84	2 " "	"	"	Less	50'	Add	100 "
Z " 92	3 " "	"	"	More	1°	Add	100 "
Z " 100	2 " "	"	"	Less	2°	Drop	200 "
Z " 105	1 " "	"	"	More	1°	Add	100 "
Z " 114	1 " "	"	"	More	1°	Add	100 "
Z " 120	3 " "	"	"	Less	1°	Add	100 "

All switches and ADD and DROP in range refer to the initial co-ordinate.
ZERO   HOUR   0400 hours.

Field
26 July 1942   (Signed)
        Capt. RA
        ADJ

Distribution:

78/84 Bty	Copy no 1 – 4
83/85 Bty	" " 5
File	" " 6 and 7

Actual artillery fire plan 11 Fd Regt. R.A. on Ruweisat
Ridge, El Alamein, Egypt. July 26, 1942

TASK TABLES – 11 Fd Regt RA   SECRET

Ref Op Order No 2   Copy No ....

HARASSING FIRE TASKS – B Tp ONLY

Co-Ords B Tp Old Posn 880010 275710 calculations based on these Co-Ords will be fired commencing 0001 hrs 27 July 1942

Time							
0001	1 rd	GF	275700	281200			
0004	1 "	"	Less 3	Add 1400 yds		9500 yds	
0009	1 "	1 gun	More 2	30'	Drop 2500 yds	7000	"
0018	1 "	GF	More 8			7000	"
0022	1 "	"	Less 10		Add 1600 yds	8600	"
0026	1 "	"	More 6	30'		8600	"
0031	1 "	salvo	More 1	30'	Drop 1850 yds	6750	"
0035	1 "	"	Less 8	30'	Add 2250 yds	9000	"
0041	1 "	1 gun	More 5	30'	Drop 600 yds	8400	"
0047	1 "	GF			Drop 1200 yds	7200	"
0052	1 "	"	Less 3		Add 1800 yds	9000	"
0054	1 "	"	More 5		Drop 1700 yds	7300	"
0059	1 "	"	Less 5		Add 1200 yds	8500	"
0101	1 "	salvo	More 11		Drop 1700 yds	6800	"
0107	1 "	GF	Less 15		Add 2500 yds	9300	"
0119	2 "	"	More 6	30'	Drop 3000 yds	9000	"
0122	1 "	1 gun			Drop 1500 yds	7500	"
0127	1 "	GF	Less 2		Drop 300 yds	7200	"
0130	1 "	"			Add 1400 yds	8600	"
0135	1 "	salvo	More 8	30'	Drop 1800 yds	6800	"
0142	1 "	GF	Less 11		Add 2500 yds	9300	"
0148	1 "	1 gun	More 8		Drop 2400 yds	6900	"
0151	1 "	GF	Less 3		Add 2400 yds	9300	"
0156	1 "	"	More 1	30'	Drop 2500 yds	6800	"
0200	1 "	"			Add 1100 yds	7900	"

Field
26 July 1942   (Signed)
                                               Capt. RA
                                               ADJ
Distribution:
_____

78/84 Bty   Copy no 1 and 2
83/85 Bty   "   " 3
File   "   " 4
_____

Actual artillery fire plan 11 Fd Regt. R.A. on Ruweisat Ridge, El Alamein, Egypt. July 26, 1942

55

5 ALAMEIN AND AFTERMATH

For it's Tommy this an' Tommy that, an' "chuck 'im out the brute!" But
it's "Saviour of 'is country" when the guns begin to shoot;
An' it's Tommy this, an' Tommy that an' anything you please;
An' Tommy ain't a blooming fool — you bet that Tommy sees!

Rudyard Kipling

Lieutenant Colonel McCarthy, our CO, although eventually
recovering from wounds sustained in a Stuka raid, did not return to
the regiment. Lieutenant Colonel A.H.E. Howell RA had now
assumed command of the 11th Field Regiment. He was formally CO2
104 RHA. On 20th September our CO2 Major P. R. M. Waterfield RA
was posted to HQRA 8th Armoured Division. He was replaced by
Major J. F. B. Huntley RA.

However, the really big changes in leadership at that time were the
replacement of General Sir Claude Auchinleck by General Sir Harold
Alexander as Commander in Chief, Middle East and Lieutenant
General Bernard Law Montgomery as Commander of the Eighth
Army. Although General Auchinleck had done a tremendous job personally, his choice of army commanders was open to question. A
major criticism of the Auk was excessive loyalty to subordinates. His
appointment of Ritchie as Commander of the Eighth Army proved
eventually to be a serious mistake. His subsequent failure to replace
him when his incompetence became obvious was a grievous error.
Auchinleck was respected and loved by all the Commonwealth troops
that constituted the Eighth Army at that time and there was genuine
regret at his departure.

On 8th September the 5th Indian Division was relieved by the 4th Indian Division. Divisional Artillery remained in place. As a result, we came under command of the 4th Indian Division. Towards the end of September, our support of the 161st Indian Brigade was terminated and the 11th Field Regiment was assigned to support of 4/16 Punjab Battalion of the 7th Indian Brigade.

Even at that relatively early point in the war the 4th Indian Division had earned for itself a proud reputation. It had played a major role in the successful conclusion of the hostilities in Eritrea with Italian forces and had spent over one and one half years in the Western Desert. It had served under the legendary Lieutenant General O'Connor, the first Commander of the Eighth Army who was taken prisoner at Tobruk. The divisional sign was the Red Eagle, often irreverently referred to as the shitehawk! In the course of time, the Red Eagle shoulder flash became a passport commanding instant respect throughout the Middle East, North Africa and Italy.

On 27th September we fired a major concentration into one of our favourite targets, Deir El Shein. It is of interest to note that 70 rounds per gun were fired over a 43-minute period or close to two rounds per gun per minute.

In early October, the 2nd New Zealand Division, which had held positions on Bare Ridge to our south since 30th June, moved north taking over part of the line from the 1st South African Division. It was replaced by the 50th British Division which had a Greek Brigade under command. Further south, the 44th British Division moved west from its former positions on Alam el Halfa into the main Alamein line. The First Free French, a highly mobile formation commanded by General Leclerc, was placed between the 44th British Division and the Qattara Depression. Finally, the 51st Highland Division moved up from the Delta into the northern sector taking over part of the line from the 9th Australian Division.

Our armoured formations had been increased to a total of over 1000 tanks. What was more important, we now had over 250 of the new American Shermans. The Sherman was considered the equal of the German Mark IV in all respects. Considerable time was spent in late September and early October in calibrating the guns. Even the magnificent 25-pounder wasn't perfect. Individual guns could be firing plus or minus of the ranging gun. It was important that these 'errors' be noted and adjusted.

By 10th October we learned the role that the 4th Indian Division would play in the forthcoming battle. We would hold Ruweisat Ridge and send in diversionary attacks. Divisional artillery, in addition to supporting these attacks, would take part in the counter-battery program and be available to give support as and where required.

In spite of rigid secrecy it was difficult to disguise the general sector in which the attack would take place. It was obvious that Montgomery had planned his major thrust in the north. It had become common knowledge that Monty 'favoured' certain divisions, formations, and commanders. He had great faith in both the 9th Australian Division under General Morshead and the 2nd New Zealand Division commanded by General Freyberg V.C. This, of course, was not without good reason, but the fact was a pointer to the area of action.

On 20th October we were given a trace of the big barrage, which indicated the role of the 4th Division artillery and thence down to regiments and finally batteries. Calculations for bearing and range were computed by two men working separately. Any variation, however slight, had to be rechecked and then cross-checked with the gun position officers. There is nothing worse for artillerymen than to end up shelling their own advancing infantry. Unfortunately, in spite of all precautions, it can happen.

The date of the attack was now set: 23rd October 1942.

Shortly before the battle commenced, General Montgomery's Order of the Day was distributed to all ranks. It read as follows:

'Personal Message to Officers and Men of Eighth Army
1.   When I assumed command of the Eighth Army I said that the mandate was to destroy Rommel and his Army, and that it would be done as soon as we were ready.
2.   We are ready NOW. The battle which is now about to begin will be one of the decisive battles of history. It will be the turning point of the war. The eyes of the whole world will be on us, watching anxiously which way the battle will swing. We can give them their answer at once: it will swing our way.
3.   We have first class equipment, good tanks, good anti-tank guns, plenty of artillery and plenty of ammunition, and we are backed by the finest air striking force in the world. All that is necessary is that each one of us, every officer and man, should enter this battle with the deter-

mination to see it through – to fight and to kill – and finally to win. If we all do this, there can be only one result – together we will hit the enemy for six, right out of North Africa.

4.   The sooner we win this battle, which will be the turning point of the war, the sooner we shall all get back home to our families.

5.   Therefore, let every officer and man enter the battle with a stout heart, and with the determination to do his duty so long as he has breath in his body. And let no man surrender so long as he is unwounded and can fight.

Let us all pray that the Lord Mighty in battle will give us the victory.

B.L. Montgomery.
Lieut. General G.O.C. in C
Eighth Army
Middle East Forces
23-10-42'

As 23rd October drew closer an air of tension began to build up at the gun positions. Most of this was quite natural prior to any major battle. There was, however, an additional factor: older units and desert-hardened veterans of the Eighth Army were still mesmerized by Rommel's name. On the night of 23rd October many officers and men half expected to see German panzers burst out of the darkness, guns blazing, pre-empting Monty's offensive.

On the afternoon of 23rd October gunners and all available hands worked steadily at preparation and placement of ammunition. In addition to stocks close to the guns, further supplies were protected in pits to the rear. These pits had been camouflaged and were now opened. The time for secrecy was over.

Sufficient ammunition had been brought forward to provide each gun with 600 rounds of high explosive. Put in another way, each gun would have sufficient HE to hurl nearly seven tons into enemy positions or a total of 6000 tons for all field and medium guns to be employed in the battle. These figures do not include nearly 800 anti-tank guns at Alamein.

As we had anticipated, the attack had been set to synchronize with the full moon which could now be seen in the eastern sky.

Zero hour for Operation Lightfoot, the code word for the attack, had been set for 22.00 hours. The counter-battery program was set for zero minus 20 minutes or 21.40 hours. After 10 minutes on our CB target, the guns would change angle and elevation to the start line of the barrage. The barrage served two purposes: first and foremost, it gave protection to the advancing infantry walking behind. The infantry, maintaining a distance of about two to three yards between each man, would move at a carefully controlled speed of 100 yards in two minutes. Consequently the barrage would 'lift' or increase range by 100 yards each two minutes. Later in the fire plan this rate would be reduced to 100 yards every three minutes. The second purpose of the barrage was to at least neutralize and hopefully destroy enemy strongpoints. The term 'creeping barrage' was often used in respect of this type of fire plan. This was the classic First World War frontal infantry attack so beloved by generals who had learned their craft in the mud and massacres of Flanders.

At Alamein there was an additional complicating factor – the mine-field. The planning of the El Alamein offensive involved clearing 'roads' through the enemy minefields for the armour to follow the infantry. Very often, however, the infantry had to advance through barbed wire, rigged with booby traps in the form of anti-personnel mines and covered by enemy machine gun fire. The barrage, if suffi-ciently concentrated, would neutralize these hazards to a greater or lesser extent.

It was now 21.30 hours; 10 minutes left before the fire storm would commence.

Gun detachments took up their respective positions, having thrown off their overcoats. Layers rechecked their gunsights. Loading numbers, kneeling on one knee, supported a round of HE on the other. Detachment NCOs walked methodically around their guns, making last minute checks. Then came the initial order to load, followed by the metallic noise of breech blocks being slammed shut. An intense and almost unnatural silence settled over the desert, as if nature itself trembled silently in anticipation of the impending fury that was about to be unleashed.

We stood in the command post, eyes glued to synchronized watches as the seconds ticked away. The moment was approaching that would take the ordinary day of 23rd October 1942, engrave it forever in military history and record it for all time with the saga of Stalingrad as the turning point of the Second World War.

Then it came. 'Fire!' At 21.40 hours over 25 miles of the Eighth

Army Alamein Front exploded into a sheet of flame as nearly 900 guns thundered out in unison. It was awesome. It was devastating. The earth seemed to quiver and tremble as the initial crash changed to a continuing series of reports and flashes. Silhouetted against their own flashes, the guns rose and fell as the barrels came back on their buff-recuperators. Detachments loaded, line of fire and range was checked, readjusted and fired. The speed and accuracy that had earned the 25-pounder its legendary reputation could now be seen in its finest hour.

There were 834 25-pounder and 48 medium guns at the Battle of El Alamein, the largest concentration of artillery since 1918. We literally saturated the Afrika Korps gun positions with HE. It was calculated that there was an average ratio of 15 Eighth Army guns to each enemy gun. The effectiveness of our counter-battery programme may be judged from the fact that there was no serious response from Axis artillery until 04.00 hours on 24th October.

At 21.50 hours we ceased firing. It was necessary to break for 10 minutes to allow the guns to cool. Cold water was sponged over the breach blocks to accelerate the cooling. All guns were then reloaded on pre-selected targets on the enemy's forward defence zone. In this short period of intense silence we could faintly hear, floating on the still night air from the north, the wail of bagpipes of the 51st Highland Division. Exactly at 22.00 hours, the guns of the Eighth Army continued their symphony of death and destruction. Twenty minutes later, after a five minute cool-off, we relaid on the opening fire of the barrage. At 22.20 hours the artillery barrage commenced and the infantry moved off behind it. The attack had now begun.

A new development of gun control was introduced at the Battle of El Alamein. This was the establishment of a central artillery command post which was connected to divisional artillery command posts which, in turn, was in communication with all artillery units in that division. This made it possible to bring a massive concentration of guns onto any target in a period not exceeding 12 minutes. Artillery support could be increased or decreased or stopped entirely. Although each infantry and armoured division was supported by its own divisional artillery, the relatively narrow front made it possible for field artillery to switch support rapidly to other formations if required. At one point in the Battle of El Alamein, the guns of the 4th Indian Division were swung nearly 180 degrees in order to help neutralize an unexpected panzer counterattack.

Apart from the artillery action, the role of the 4th Indian Division in the battle was to hold their sector and create local diversionary attacks. This caused some bitterness in the higher echelons of the division. There was the impression that we were being treated as second class troops. To a division with a proud record like the 4th Indian Division, this amounted to a major insult. Inevitably, this anger and resentment was directed against General Montgomery. Postwar historians record that the situation was serious enough for General Tuker, our divisional commander, to write a personal letter of protest to the Commander in Chief Middle East Command, General Alexander. Although he made use of the 4th Indian Division late in the North African campaign, Montgomery was never popular with any of our Indian units. The 4th Indian Division, in particular, retained strong loyalties and affection for both General Wavell and General Auchinleck. It is significant that not until Montgomery relinquished command of the Eighth Army in Italy, were Indian troops used in a major role.

A major diversionary attack by the 4th Indian Division had been scheduled for the night of 23rd October. It was to be mounted against Point 62 at the extreme west end of the Ruweisat Ridge. It was timed to move off at 22.20 hours and would be mounted at brigade strength. The objective was heavily fortified with huge stone sangers surrounded by barbed wire entanglements, liberally rigged with antipersonnel mines and sundry devilish booby traps. We employed the 1/4 Essex and a battalion of Gurkhas.

The Essex had developed their own method of handling barbed wire. They sent forward four Bren gun carriers, with their infantry following behind. Each carrier was equipped with one or more huge grappling hooks which were thrown bodily over the wire. The carrier would then go into reverse, pulling the wire away and detonating the mines. Naturally, all this was done in the face of enemy fire and at considerable risk to the operators. Of the four carriers used in this attack, one was knocked out by enemy fire, one struck a mine, but the other two advanced to the wire, successfully hooked their grapples, pulled the wire clear and exploded the booby traps. Through the gap thus created charged the Essex and the Gurkhas with bayonet and *kukri*. Although the attack was successful, they were forced to withdraw later that night under the pressure of furious counterattacks.

During the succeeding days divisional artillery, including the 11th Field Regiment, was used on different targets supporting a variety of formations both infantry and armoured. As October slipped into November the battle continued to rage in the north and some senior commanders voiced the opinion that Monty had 'blown it'. Rommel had been on sick leave when our attack commenced but was now reported to be back and in personal command of the Afrika Korps. Information obtained later indeed confirmed that the initial attack, code name Lightfoot, had failed. Rommel, hopelessly outgunned and outnumbered, short of petrol and supplies, with less than 200 tanks against our 800, had indeed battled the Eighth Army and Montgomery to a standstill.

A new attack was now planned again in the northern sector. It was entitled Operation Supercharge. If all went well, we would finally break through the deep enemy defensive system, allowing our armour to move out into the open desert. Supercharge would commence in the early morning hours of 4th November. The 5th Infantry Brigade of the 4th Indian Division would be used in a pivotal role. The brigade would mount an attack at Kidney Ridge, south of a feature known as Tel el Aqqaqir, situated at the extreme north end of our divisional front. Our attack would be mounted by 1/4 Essex and 4/6 Raj Rifles with a Gurkha battalion in reserve. Four hundred guns were to be used in this attack on a front of only 800 yards or one gun for each two yards of front. It was of vital importance that we reach our objectives because the main attack with units of the 2nd New Zealand Division, 1st South African Division and 51st Highland Division could not move until we had done so.

The artillery programme commenced at 02.30 hours, shelling selected enemy strongpoints for over one hour. During this time, the infantry moved up to their start line. The barrage trace was in the shape of a chevron or wedge with the point in the direction of the enemy. At 04.00 hours, the guns opened up on the initial line of the barrage moving north west in increments of 100 yards at two minute intervals. Resting guns on an individual basis for cooling off, the barrage continued until 07.10 hours. The brigade reached all objectives. It was the classic set piece infantry advance behind a perfectly timed artillery barrage. At 08.00 hours Essex carriers went into action against the enemy moving west and at 09.00 hours our armour started moving through the gap. The break-out had commenced. The Afrika Korps was now in full retreat and the final Battle of El Alamein was drawing to a close.

Six weeks later, on leave with Jack Parker in Alexandria, we sat in a bar opposite a corporal of 1/4 Essex, enjoying a cool beer. Identified by our Red Eagle divisional shoulder flashes, we fell easily into conversation. Eventually the discussion moved to the attack by 5th Brigade across Kidney Ridge on 4th November. The corporal gazed reflectively into his beer, blew some suds away, hauled down a long draft and said, 'My God, that was something. I've never seen anything like it!'

'Was it that bad?' I asked apprehensively.

He looked up. 'Hell no!' he replied. 'It was just like we were taught in infantry training back in Blighty. That artillery fire came down like a solid moving wall in front of us. We really felt that we had protection.'

Feeling a little more confident now, I asked, 'What about rounds falling short?'

'That was the amazing thing. During the whole advance I never saw one,' came the reply. 'We got so bloody cocky that we closed up behind the barrage – really leaned on it. Those Eyeties kept their heads down so long that when they looked up all they saw was a bloody big Rajput poking a bayonet at their throat. Even the Jerries didn't have time to recover – we were on them so fast that they were still in shellshock – they came out of their holes with their hands in the air – all except one bastard.' He stopped.

'What happened?' Jack prompted.

He looked up, took another draft of beer and continued. 'This Jerry crawls out of a sanger with his hands up – there's an NCO behind him hiding a machine-pistol. He shoots my mate – so I shot them both – one bullet – right through their bellies. I walked on leaving the bastard to holler his guts out.'

He finished his beer and said, 'Hey, you chaps, I owe you a beer.'

Although we really didn't need it, for the honour of the regiment we gracefully accepted.

Rommel was now withdrawing rapidly but skilfully, pursued by all available armour. The 2nd New Zealand and the 51st Highland Division were being used as the infantry arm of the Eighth Army. The 13th Corps, of which we were a part, had been appointed to take charge of the battlefield. This involved mopping up isolated pockets of resistance, rounding up thousands of prisoners and locating and recovering wounded. Rommel, desperately short of transport and petrol, had given priority to German formations. As a result, prisoners were overwhelmingly Italian. These included elements of four Italian infantry divisions. Many of those troops were in a pitiable condition, having been left without food or water for several days. Instead of a round-up of prisoners, our efforts resembled a rescue operation. All field dressing stations of the 13th Corps were inundated with prisoners of war seeking help. It was sad to see the depths of deprivation and misery to which these unfortunate men had been reduced. Bewildered and suffering, hungry and parched, they were glad and relieved to pass into captivity and safety.

On 12th November, after over four months in the desert and four battles, the 11th Field Regiment was withdrawn to El Imiyid on the Mediterranean coast. At about this time my promotion to war substantive bombardier was posted.

Being able to swim in the Med every day and having clean underwear became pleasures of sheer luxury. Training and parades were resumed. Missing buttons and other uniform deficiencies were again noted at inspections and there was a definite tightening of military discipline. Ten-day leaves to Palestine were made available in late November. Jack Parker and I submitted our applications, which were granted, effective from 18th December for 10 days. Three years and two months had elapsed since my last leave in October of 1939.

We hitched a ride on a regimental HQ lorry going to RABD arriving in Cairo the same day. My immediate priority was a visit to a dentist. I had been delaying the necessary treatment for two broken front teeth with exposed nerves.

A substantial brass business plate at the entrance to a downtown office building informed me that a Dr Hede Wolff practised dentistry. Locating the office on the third floor, I entered with growing misgivings. I immediately discovered that Dr. Wolff was a woman. In those far-off, happy days before the tides of Women's Liberation rolled in, this was a surprise. I found that Dr Wolff was Austrian, had set up a practice in Cairo prior to commencement of hostilities and was now marooned in Egypt. After a short but thorough examination, she informed me that I had excellent teeth and there was nothing wrong that good nutrition couldn't correct. Because of a shortage of dental supplies she would be unable to give me the proper treatment for my two broken teeth. She added that it would be a pity to remove them and suggested withdrawing the nerves in order to neutralize the pain. I agreed. At this point her assistant, an enormous black gentleman standing over six feet high, entered the surgery. He stood behind the chair, placing his large hands on my shoulders. He was the anaesthetist, Egyptian wartime style. The nerves were removed quickly, but not painlessly. We then entered into a friendly argument over Dr Wolff's professional fee. I felt that ten Egyptian pounds was a little steep for a junior NCO and said so. We eventually made a deal. In return for my solemn assurance that the African campaign would be over by 1st May 1943, she agreed to reduce her fee to five pounds! We shook hands and she admonished me in a motherly fashion to look after myself.

The war in Africa ended officially on 13th May 1943. I hope Dr Wolff forgave me my 13-day error!

Two days later we arrived in Tel Aviv. During the North African campaign, Tel Aviv had become a popular leave centre for British and Commonwealth troops. We checked in at a small hotel which had been recommended to us. The hotel reminded me of the guest houses at popular English south coast resorts before the war. Our room, fitted with twin beds, was spotlessly clean and simply furnished. The accent appeared to be on utility rather than luxury. There was also a bathroom with a real bath!

After a shower, shave and change of clothes we went downstairs to inspect the amenities. The dining room was furnished with individual tables and we gazed in disbelief at white linen tablecloths and serviettes. It was still too early for the evening meal, so we located and entered the inevitable bar. It was small with a short bar counter, complemented by six bar stools. The barman, who was also the proprietor, greeted us from his station behind the bar. He was a big man in his early forties with dark greying hair with a bald patch on top. He was dark shaven with bushy eyebrows and was wearing a tight-fitting shirt which accentuated a muscular chest and shoulders. After some small talk, during which he carefully avoided mentioning the war, he asked, 'Gentlemen, what can I serve you?'

Now neither Jack nor I were seasoned drinkers. In fact, one might say, using an Irishism, that we were only two drinks short of being teetotallers. However, we were youthful, brash and feeling our oats. We were also woefully ignorant of the wartime selection of alcoholic beverages at a Jewish guest house.

'What's the best drink you've got in the house?' Jack replied, sounding like the Rajah of Hyderabad.

Out host eyed us patiently and benevolently. 'I have some genuine German pre-war kümmel,' he replied evenly.

Neither of us possessed a clue regarding the merits of German kümmel pre-war or otherwise, but it seemed to have the right sound. I nodded.

'Set 'em up,' ordered Jack.

Our host set out two glasses and filled them. We raised our drinks, trying to look like men of the world and downed them in one gulp.

'Fill 'em up again,' I ordered.

'Gentlemen, you will enjoy kümmel much more if you drink it slowly,' our friend offered tactfully. He refilled the glasses. We raised our glasses, looked at each other, then downed them again. In unison we said, 'Fill 'em up.'

Our host looked at us intently and asked for our room number, then refilled the glasses with an air of resignation. After the fourth drink, I was moved to express one of my Irish toasts

'Here's to the girl I love,
And may that one be she,
Who loves but one,
And may that one be me.'

I remembered nothing more until the following morning when I awoke in bed, fully clothed with my boots off. I looked across at the other bed and noted Jack was making sounds of protest. The bedroom door was ajar and just then our host appeared.

Trying desperately to orient my vision, I asked, 'What happened?'

He fastened me with a fatherly look and replied, 'Well, after your sixth kümmel, I just walked around the bar and stood behind the pair of you. I caught you as you flopped off the bar stools and hauled you both to bed, and took off your boots. By the way, here are your wallets.'

Placing the wallets on the night table, he walked back to the door.

Pausing, he turned and said, 'By the way, my wife likes your Irish poetry. She would like you to write out the words of *Kathleen Mavourneen* for her.'

He turned and left the room. I have never forgotten the simple honesty and common sense of that hotel keeper. We decided that in future we would stay with beer.

After an excellent breakfast, we took a brisk walk along the seafront in order to clear our heads. We spent the rest of the day sightseeing in Tel Aviv. After supper that evening the lady of the house informed us about the excellent facilities operated and managed by the Tel Aviv Hospitality Committee. The members of this committee were mostly wives of Jewish professionals in Tel Aviv. I believe the leave centre was supported entirely by the Jewish population of Tel Aviv. It included reading, writing and games rooms and an excellent cafeteria. A number of services were also provided, some of them quite unusual. There was a uniform washing, cleaning and pressing service, including uniform repair. One could even have socks darned and boots repaired. The ladies also provided a 'write home' service in a variety of languages.

A unique service that was widely appreciated was gift buying for wives, girlfriends or family back home. In view of the fact that proprietors of gift shops in the Middle East took outrageous advantage of soldiers of all nations who were buying gifts, this saved British and Commonwealth troops thousands of pounds. A form was provided on which you indicated the type of gift required and approximately how much money you could afford to pay. The Jewish ladies performed the shopping at no charge. Jack Parker arranged for this department to buy two sets of silk underwear for his girlfriend, although he had a problem in deciding sizes! In addition to the foregoing the ladies would gift wrap and parcel ready for mailing.

On Christmas day, 1942 the Hospitality Committee provided a magnificent Christmas dinner. We learned later that four sittings were required to meet the demand. We sat down to dinner, a truly remarkable mixture of men from all parts of the British Empire – English, Scots, and Irish, Aussies, Kiwis and Springboks with a fair number of Gurkhas and an odd turban. Finally, there was representation from our Free French and Greek allies.

The menu cards were illustrated with the Ark of the Covenant and were individually hand-painted. They were inscribed with the fifteenth verse of the ninth chapter of the Book of Genesis:

'And I will remember my covenant, which is between me and you and every living creature of all flesh; and the waters shall no more become a flood to destroy all flesh.'

The menu was printed in English and Hebrew and featured:

Cream of Vegetable Soup
Fried Fish
Turkey or Chicken
Cauliflower
Baked Potatoes
Tomato Salad
Christmas Pudding
Vanilla Sauce
Tangerines
Coffee and Wine

None of this might seem very wonderful unless it is remembered that this meal was provided and served by a people who do not celebrate Christmas.

The following day, in response to a personal invitation, Jack and I were entertained to dinner by a charming German Jewish couple at their apartment. They had been fortunate in being able to escape from Nazi Germany prior to the war. They were both doctors. However, at the time of our visit the wife was supporting the family. Her husband had not yet obtained a licence to practice in Palestine. They recounted a fascinating story of how they had escaped from Germany, made their way across Europe, finally entering and settling in Palestine.

Palestine, at that time, was still peaceful and pleasant, Jew and Arab living side by side in relative harmony under the firm discipline of the British Mandate. But this situation was changing.

Increasing numbers of European Jews, fleeing from the fury of the Holocaust, were entering Palestine. The British authorities, under the terms of their Mandate, were trying to limit the number of Jews entering the mandated territory. As a result, they were caught between two fires. On the one hand was the Palestinian Arab who, alarmed by the possible loss of his land, was resisting the increasing Jewish influx. On the other hand were the Jewish terrorists, whose objective was to terminate the British Mandate and establish an independent Jewish state – Israel. The Jewish terrorists had formed themselves into groups like the Stern Gang and Irgun. Those gangs, representing a tiny minority of Jewish people in Palestine, were savage, vicious, and utterly committed to their objective. They showed little remorse in regard to ambushing and killing British soldiers. In one particularly unpleasant incident they captured and hanged a British sergeant.

The next day we bade a sad but grateful farewell to the Jewish ladies of the Hospitality Committee and started our journey back to Egypt.

Postscript to Alamein

When two armies with the combined size of the German Afrika Korps and the British Eighth Army have been engaged in mortal combat for over 14 days a lot of battlefield salvage is necessary. This necessity introduces the expression 'cleaning up the battlefield'. From burnt-out tanks and broken guns down to small arms and mines and from the bodies of soldiers killed in action to wounded men a tremendous amount of cleaning up must be undertaken. The 4th Indian Division was one of those units delegated by Montgomery to clean up the El Alamein battlefield.

The first order of business and the one with the highest priority was to locate and render first aid to wounded soldiers regardless of nationality. Eventually these men, or the majority of them, would have to be recovered by field ambulance. Some wounded could be brought in by vehicles improvised to carry 'walking wounded'.

Even as the last of the Eighth Army formations disappeared in the west on the Egyptian coast road in pursuit of the retreating Afrika Korps sappers and engineers were busy lifting minefields or clearing lanes through them to allow rescue personnel to search former enemy lines for wounded men.

The following morning I was detailed by the adjutant to report to Brigade HQ. I was instructed to make myself available with my jeep to drive a medical officer attached to a rescue group. At Brigade HQ my jeep was loaded with additional petrol, food, water and medical supplies. A grinning Johnny Gurkha fixed a solid looking Red Cross flag to the rear of the jeep. We got away soon after 09.00 hours following a Bren carrier manned by a detachment of armed Gurkhas. When

I queried the MO about this apparent anomaly the Indian doctor explained that there had been instances of wounded German soldiers half-crazed with pain and exposure shooting their rescuers. Two field ambulances brought up the rear of our little column.

Passing through the former brigade front we checked a number of strongpoints and weapon pits for wounded men. They were free of survivors. There were a number of bodies in the No Man's Land area; some were Indian, some Italian and some British. Finally we moved into the enemy front line. This sector had been held by the Italian Brescia Division. However, we knew that Rommel, having little faith in his Italian allies, had reinforced this sector with Ramcke's parachutists.

Approaching a former enemy strongpoint my nostrils were assailed by the pungent and unmistakable odour of decomposing human bodies. Italian infantry spent a lot of time and ingenuity strengthening their defensive positions. This one was no exception. In addition to being built up at the front and sides with heavy rocks and stones an enormous slab of stone over eight feet long had been placed on top. The MO and I moved to the open front and looked in. We were greeted by that scourge of the desert, a swarm of flies. Overcoming the intense smell of rotting flesh we peered inside what I thought must be a corner of hell on earth. My initial observation was that we were looking at eight very dead Italian infantrymen until one of the 'bodies' raised an arm in a weak imploring gesture. We called for help from our Gurkha escort who quickly hitched their Bren carrier to the huge stone and pulled it clear. There were two live wounded soldiers, whom we lifted clear of the strongpoint. After examining the first man the MO looked at me and shook his head, then moved to assist the second soldier. I made the dying man as comfortable as possible, arranging some shade with a groundsheet and two rifles. The MO had administered a shot of morphine. I knelt beside the unfortunate man, holding a water bottle to his lips, and lit a cigarette for him. He could barely inhale and I knew he was in his final minutes of his life. He tried to recover something from an inside pocket but couldn't. I reached in and withdrew an envelope and a photograph. The latter showed a pretty young woman and two little girls, about eight to ten years' old, in a garden background. The sealed letter carried an address in Rome. The man couldn't speak but his eyes transmitted the obvious message.

I nodded my head. He smiled in response and expired. Two stretcher bearers came up and I gave them the thumbs down sign and walked away. Although we located several more wounded soldiers that day, both Italian and German, none of them affected me more than the young Italian soldier who gave me his last letter home.

Italian soldiers seemed to be in the more serious condition. As we found out later Rommel, faced with a serious shortage of both supplies and transport, had given priority to German units and had, to all intents and purposes deserted his Italian allies. Many units were left without food or water. As the Afrika Korps retreated westwards Italian soldiers walked eastwards, surrendering to any Eighth Army units that would accept them. The greatest sufferers were seriously wounded soldiers who, unable to walk even with assistance, were deserted and left to die on the battlefield without water or medical assistance. They suffered the twin tortures of their wounds and thirst.

At about 13.00 hours the British officer commanding our group called a break for 'brew-up' and I took the opportunity to scan the battlefield with my binoculars. An area which only seven days earlier was a seething maelstrom of tanks and anti-tank guns, dotted with strongpoints manned by infantry armed with machine guns and mortars, was now a lonely deserted wasteland and an armoured graveyard. Here and there could be seen small groups of Arabs scavenging the battlefield for which they often paid the price in the form of an exploding booby trap or mine. It was a sad and depressing sight.

The final days of the battle of El Alamein were marked by torrential downpours of rain. These rains were a major factor in the inability of British armour to react quickly to Rommel's withdrawal. These heavy rains increased the misery of many wounded soldiers left to their fate in their trenches and semi-underground defensive positions. Soaked to the skin nearly freezing by night and burnt by the daytime sun, they suffered the tortures of the damned. As we alternated between pulling and lifting these unfortunate men from their holes, infested with worms and insects, under constant attack by flies and often forced to lie in their own human waste, we felt that we had plumbed the lowest depths of human misery. Dispensing water, shooting morphine, applying field dressings and lighting cigarettes, we did our best to alleviate pain and suffering. Ambulances would soon pick them up for conveyance to field hospitals. For them the war was over, whether they died or went into captivity.

It was late afternoon when the rattle of a German machine pistol made the MO and I hit the ground. Cautiously looking across towards our Gurkha escort I saw a Gurkha NCO direct a single shot into a slit trench. Apparently a wounded German had decided to go out fighting.

At our final stop, while the MO was treating a wounded panzer driver whom the Gurkhas had recovered from his wrecked tank, I walked across the former No Man's Land and stopped by the body of a British soldier. He was lying on his back and looked as if he had just laid down to rest. Unfortunately he was very dead and it appeared that he had been killed while advancing. His rifle with fixed bayonet lay beside him. Bareheaded, he looked so young, no more than eighteen years. His shoulder flash identified him as belonging to the 51st Highland Division.

The winter sun was just dipping below the horizon when we arrived back at Brigade HQ. After saying goodbye to the MO I returned to Regimental HQ and reported to the adjutant. Later in the evening, having enjoyed an ample if somewhat unsavoury supper, I lit my pipe and thought about the events of the day. I remembered the letter and photograph entrusted to me by the young Italian soldier. For a brief moment I considered keeping the letter and mailing it after the war but quickly decided that this was ridiculous. I might have reconsidered my decision if I could have foreseen later events.

In July of 1944 the regiment passed through Rome in its continuing support of the 4th Indian Division. The following morning I obtained a sturdy envelope from RHQ and after printing the Rome address on the outside I sealed both letter and photo inside, along with a short note describing the circumstances of its dispatch. The adjutant assured me that it would be transmitted to the Red Cross who would be responsible for its delivery.

Although I had included my home address with my note I never received any acknowledgement after the war.

6 ALAMEIN TO TRIPOLI

> In the day of Armageddon, at the last great fight of all,
> That our House stand together and the pillars do not fall
> Draw now the threefold knot firm on the ninefold bands,
> And the Law that ye make shall be the law after the rule of your lands,
> This for the waxen Heath, and that for the Wattlebloom,
> This for the Maple-leaf, and that for the southern Broom.
> *Rudyard Kipling*

We reported back to the base depot as per leave instructions and were informed that 4th Divisional artillery had moved to Libya. There was nothing to do but wait for a ride with a convoy going west to Tobruk.

New Year's Day, 1943, came and passed quietly. Matt Colley was no longer with the regiment, leaving me the sole survivor of the regimental survey party that had celebrated New Year's Day, 1942, in Northern Iraq. The events, too, of that year had passed into the pages of military history, taking with them the Battle of El Alamein and Stalingrad. We were aware, I believe, that not only had we witnessed one of the truly great battles of all wars, on a par with Waterloo, Trafalgar and Gettysburg, but each one of us had made his own contribution to final victory. However, in early January of 1943, it was a long way to Tunis and longer still to the end of the war, which stretched endlessly ahead into the mists of time.

What originally motivated Jack Parker and I to apply for a weekend pass to Alexandria, I do not know. We had visited and photographed the pyramids. We had suffered through the traditional camel rides. We

74

had sailed on the Nile and we had sampled both the delights and horrors of Cairo. It seemed fitting and proper that we 'do' Alexandria.

By 7 p.m. we had expended all our interest and exhausted most of our energy on the sights and sounds of Alex. Finding a convenient bar, which were in ample supply, we entered. The waiter who came to our table informed us that beer was not available.

'The war, gentlemen, it's the war,' he intoned as he rolled his eyes in feigned despair from the ceiling to the floor and back again. Any problem relating to civil supply or service in Egypt at this time was blamed on the war. Against our best judgement we settled for wine. Neither of us were seasoned drinkers and before long an eavesdropper would have noticed a deterioration in the subject matter of our conversation. We were scraping the bottom of the barrel when our discussion turned to No. 7 Sister's Street.

This famous or infamous address was the location of the Commonwealth Forces approved brothel in Alexandria during the Second World War. Kings' Rules and Regulations (KRRs) decreed that venereal disease was a self-inflicted wound and therefore subject to loss of pay, plus other disciplinary measures. However, by making use of approved facilities such as 7 Sister's Street, where the ladies and the premises were regularly checked and inspected by army medical officers, such loss and punishment could be avoided.

Like lambs to the slaughter, we made our way to No. 7 Sister's Street. It appeared to be a four-storey building fronted by iron railings in dire need of a paint job. We entered through the open doorway and were immediately assailed by a most odious odour, an awful combination of sweat, sex and sickly scent. As my vision penetrated the gloom of the large foyer I noticed a military policeman sitting behind a table near the bottom of a wide stairway. He gazed at us dispassionately, without reaction or emotion. The interaction of that terrible odour, blending with the aftermath of the cheap wine, was now blunting our earlier reckless resolve – we both wanted out, but who would be the first to risk being called 'chicken'.

The MP turned a massive heavily bound ledger in our direction and said, in a matter of fact voice, 'Fill in your number, rank, name and regiment and sign here.' He jerked a thumb over his shoulder and added, 'OK, up you go,' as if he were sending little boys to bed.

We stumbled up the stairs and were greeted at the top by a madam; her appearance was not calculated to stimulate romantic interest. The horror of the situation, coupled to my drunken nausea, had by now eliminated all sexual feeling. I was aware of passing over a sum of money and then being almost forcibly propelled towards a door which was pushed open. I entered. Trying desperately to focus my blurred vision, I perceived a dark-skinned young woman lying on a bed, smoking a cigarette and reading a book. As I entered she looked briefly at me without welcome or expression. Deliberately stubbing out her cigarette, she stood up, dropping her one and only garment, a kimono, to the floor. Then she lay back on the bed, her legs parted, complete resignation written on her face. I was possessed by a sudden wave of utter revulsion. My stomach heaved. This was the final straw. Turning abruptly, I took off for the stairway and almost plunged down the stairs. I went past the astounded MP without explanation or comment and out through the still open doorway. Then, clutching the rusty railings for support, I retched violently and painfully.

Chastened and sobered, we returned to our hotel. By mutual consent, discussion of the incident was dropped. Some wartime experiences were best allowed to slide softly into the limbo of the past without post-mortem analysis.

A few days later we left base depot on a convoy going to Tobruk. There was a number of 11th Field Regiment personnel on this same convoy. Some, like us, had returned from leave; a number were returning from hospital and there were a few reinforcements. Most of the latter were not long out from England. We passed through Burg el Arab and El Hamman, both major staging areas prior to the battle. We reached El Alamein in the early afternoon and halted for conveniences and brew-up. I walked out into the desert for a short distance, scanning the area in the direction of Ruweisat Ridge. There was little change since we evacuated our gun positions the previous November. From the high ground where I stood there was an excellent view south and south west over the desert.

The only signs of life were a few native Egyptians, combing the area for anything of value. Because of the ever-present danger of unexploded mines, they were taking awful risks. All of the Eighth Army and Afrika Korps disabled tanks had been recovered but here and there were the remains of a burnt-out or exploded tank, mute testimony to the passage of war. I returned to the convoy and eagerly gulped down the hot sweet tea.

The battlefield receded as we resumed our journey. My last visual recollection of that scene of carnage and human sacrifice was a German soldier's grave about 100 yards off the road. At one end a marker in the form of his rifle was embedded, muzzle down with his helmet sitting on the butt. It looked lonely and forlorn as a slight breeze whipped dusty sand around the stones.

Passing El Daba and Fuka, we came again to Mersa Matruh. Bypassing the town or what was left of it, we continued our journey on the coast road. This was the scene of General Ritchie's last stand. This was where Rommel took the Eighth Army to pieces and then shredded them.

We drove through the ruins of Sidi Barrani and the next day we crossed the Egyptian frontier and entered Libya. Reaching Bardia late in the afternoon, the officer commanding the convoy called a halt and ordered the formation of a leaguer. This order set off considerable grumbling. In spite of our victories and the fact that the current action was hundreds of miles away, British junior commanders still suffered from Rommelitis.

The leaguer was a temporary form of defensive encampment, used quite often in desert warfare and generally at night halts. The league, followed the same pattern as the old American wagon trains of the eighteenth and nineteenth centuries, and for the same reason – defence. A circle was formed. The outer circle consisted of armoured vehicles and machine gun posts with anti-tank guns and/or field guns placed strategically. 'Soft' vehicles were placed in the centre of the ring. Sentries and look-outs were posted.

A number of interesting leaguer stories came out of the Desert War. One of the best and possibly the most hilarious concerned elements of the 9th Australian Division at the final Battle of Alamein. Apparently, in the later stages of the battle, the Aussies made such a determined and furious bayonet charge that they overran the Italian unit opposing them. Deciding to keep on going, they captured an Italian leaguer, protecting an Italian comfort station. The ladies decided not to resist! The Australian advance came to an abrupt halt. It was reported that when the incident was brought to General Montgomery's attention he was not amused!

Another story concerned the 2nd New Zealand Division south of Mersa Matruh in June of 1942. A brigade of Kiwis found a German leaguer barring their withdrawal. Fixing bayonets, they 'rushed' the leaguer at night, sounding horns with the Maori infantrymen shouting wild native war cries. They went across the leaguer, causing indescribable confusion amongst the enemy and out the other side, hell-bent for Alamein and safety. General Erwin Rommel's comments about this incident are not available. However, in letters to his wife published after the war, he stated that of all the formations in the Eighth Army, he considered the 2nd New Zealand to be the finest infantry division.

However, for sheer uncompromising determination, it would be difficult to beat the story of the Gurkhas of our own 4th Indian Division. The Gurkhas excelled at night patrolling. Finding an enemy leaguer, they would remove their boots and, armed only with their *kukris*, would crawl inside the leaguer. Moving from group to group of sleeping soldiers, they would cleanly sever the head of one here or two there, using only their *kukris*. They would leave as silently as they came. The demoralizing effect of this type of action may well be imagined.

The following day we reached Tobruk and rejoined the regiment in camp a short distance outside the town. It was good to be 'home' again. The survey party was engaged in intensive survey retraining and I found myself enroled on an OP ack's course.

On 30th January we commenced a move from Tobruk to the Benghazi area. For training purposes, the move was completed in a series of night marches. The regiment went into camp at Er Regina.

Er Regina was the centre of an agricultural colonization area. It was created by the Italian Government before 1939 to encourage land-hungry Italian farmers to emigrate and settle in one of the new Italian colonies. There were many such agricultural settlements in North Africa. The vast majority, buffeted and pulverized by the ebb and flow of foreign armies, were now deserted and neglected. The land was parched and dusty from lack of the artificial irrigation that had made it fertile. The farmhouses, schoolhouses and churches were broken, pillaged and desecrated by successive attacks and numerous defensive actions. The area was now a melancholy memorial to Mussolini's dream of empire.

My Irish background had imbued me with a love of the land, the growing of crops and the eternal recycling of nature year after year. It was a sad experience to walk through these farms and smallholdings and see the work of years of toil and sacrifice blown away by successive *khamseens*; to stand in what had once been a neat whitewashed bungalow, a family home, and see the filth and damage left by occupying troops of many nations.

As expected, Rommel did not attempt to defend Tripoli. Fighting a series of skilful delaying actions, he continued his controlled retreat west to the Mareth Line. Tripoli was occupied by the Eighth Army in January 1943 without any fighting.

Shortly afterwards we heard the announcement that General Montgomery had decided to hold a victory parade. Whether this was intended to impress the local population or to boost the morale of the homefront in England, we did not know. We know that Monty attached a lot of importance to public relations, so it may have been possible that he wished to boost his personal image. We were not impressed and our sympathy was extended to 4/6 Rajputana Rifles and 3/10 Baluchis who were selected to represent the 4th Indian Division in the parade.

We spent the last week of January and three weeks of February training with the 5th Indian Infantry Brigade. Survey operations took us out into the desert south of Tobruk. It was in this area that the violent tank battles of the previous year had taken place. Most of the knocked-out German tanks had been salvaged. The panzer maintenance crews brought tank salvage to a fine art in the Desert War. The burnt-out or exploded hulks of British Crusaders, Grants and Valentines still littered the landscape; mute evidence of those terrible tank battles.

Investigating one of the British tanks, a Grant, we discovered the remains of the driver, bony fingers still gripping the steering levers. There was no identification. I had Gunners Roberts and Reeve with me. We excavated a grave with some difficulty in the stony ground and committed what was left of the unfortunate man to his last resting place. Into a piece of wood I recovered from our vehicle, I notched the words 'A British soldier lies here'. We hammered this into the grave, placing a salvaged tin hat on top.

There was little enthusiasm for field training amongst other ranks. Four months in action had bred such a degree of self-confidence that, like the alcoholic, we craved more. However, a notice to all ranks over the CO's signature brought us back to earth.

The composition of the 4th Indian Division at this time was built around two infantry brigades, the 5th and the 7th. We had 'lost' a brigade during the reorganization prior to Alamein. Major General Tuker, our divisional commander, was actively campaigning to recover this lost brigade. Divisional artillery still included the 1st, 11th and 31st Field Regiments plus 149th Anti-Tank Regiment.

Training came to a welcome end by 28th February and soon after we were on the road to Tripoli. In the afternoon of the first day's march, we passed through Marsa Brega. Beda Fomm, not far from here, was the scene of General O'Connor's stunning victory in 1941. With slender forces, he had force-marched across the desert, following a supposedly impossible route. He then cut off and totally destroyed an Italian army. It has been said of General O'Connor that he and his forces were deficient in all respects, except determination and audacity.

There was a gradual but noticeable change of scenery on the third day of our journey to Tripoli. Rocky desert and parched sandy wastes began to give way to sandy dunes and moist wadis. Here and there could be seen grass – real grass. It was sparse, scrubby and pale, but it was grass.

I felt myself caught up in a euphoria of sheer pleasure. In spite of all the death and destruction, suffering and misery that I had witnessed and experienced, a real normal world still existed. If grass grew then plants and trees grew. If trees grew, then birds flew and animal life still thrived. God was still in His Heaven even if His world was in poor shape.

On the final day of our journey to Tripoli we broke leaguer earlier than usual. Our speed had been increased slightly due in part to better road surface. The scenery continued to improve. We were passing through fertile farmland. Citrus fruits and olive groves appeared plentiful. Small, neat farmhouses became more numerous. From time to time we would pass a farm family watching us from outside their farmhouse. Small children, clean and well-dressed, would hold the hands of their parents. They would wave, weakly as if not sure if their salutation would be welcome. We would wave in return. I only regretted that I had neither chocolate nor confectionery, the international standard of currency for children of all races and colours. We passed Mussolini's magnificent Arch of Empire, built to mark the establishment of the Italian North African Empire. It now presided over its dissolution. We completed a fast run into Tripoli, arriving at a well prepared camping area before darkness fell.

The 7th Indian Infantry Brigade had already taken over garrison duties in Tripoli. The 5th Brigade and the remainder of divisional troops remained outside the town. A few days later I went into town with Jack Parker. It was sightseeing only, with maybe a cup of coffee. Military police were very much in evidence, ready to enforce the tight no-fraternizing regulations. Tripoli was a clean, pretty town and the war had left little evidence of its passage. Its chief value to the Eighth Army was its excellent port facilities. Although partially demolished by the Afrika Korps before they evacuated the town, it had been restored to 80 per cent capacity when we arrived.

However, the major question was when and where would the 4th Indian Division be called back into action? The American forces and the British First Army were fighting their way slowly but surely through central Tunisia. It appeared logical that as long as Montgomery could keep the Afrika Korps on the run with his armour, we would not be required. All indicators pointed to a major defensive action at Mareth on the Gulf of Gabes.

In early March, in anticipation of a major counter-attack by Rommel, Montgomery had disposed Eighth Army formations running south east from the Mediterranean in the north to Medinine in the south. These positions were carefully selected to give defensive advantage, 51st Highland Division on the right with 2nd New Zealand Division around Medinine and an armoured brigade holding the centre ground. In addition to the divisional field artillery, the position was defended by 500 anti-tank guns. The majority of those guns were the relatively new and very effective six-pounders. A small number of these guns had been deployed by the 2nd New Zealand Division and the 5th Indian Division at the First Battle of Alamein with excellent results. Well-trained crews, assisted by cool nerves, made these guns extremely effective.

On 5th March General Rommel directed an 'Eve of Battle' address to his panzer troops, exhorting every man to fight to his limit – that this would be their last chance to rout Eighth Army. The following morning the Afrika Korps attacked. There were three panzer divisions: 15th in the north moving south east on the Medinine-Gabes road, 21st in the centre attacking east and 10th coming out of the Matmata Hills and striking north east against the Kiwis. The three divisions employed a total of 400 tanks. The battle raged all that day but the panzers were unable to make any appreciable advance into Eighth Army positions. After losing 52 tanks, principally to the deadly fire of our six-pounder anti-tank guns, Rommel withdrew behind the Mareth Line. Our casualties were relatively light. Thus ended the Battle of Medinine, gateway to Tunisia.

Our divisional commander, General Tuker, had gone forward to the Medinine area and established Divisional HQ.

Three days after our Medinine victory, movement orders came in. The 4th Indian Division had been ordered forward to the Mareth Lines. The great armoured race across North Africa had now ended and from now on Monty would have to lean increasingly on his poor bloody infantrymen. We moved up to Medinine, passing through Ben Gardane. My mileage recorder, still working, showed me we had covered slightly over 200 miles from Tripoli. We took up gun positions opposite the Mareth Line.

The need to conduct limited survey operations gave me the opportunity to assess the overall topography of the Mareth Front. This was made easier by moving into the lower levels of the Matmata Hills on our left. The Mareth Line ran roughly north east to south west from the Med to a point close to the village of Toujane, a distance of 22 miles. It lay behind a natural barrier, the formidable Wadi Zigzaou.

This wadi was deep and impassable to either wheeled or tracked vehicles without bridging. The Wadi Zigzaou was the king of all wadis. It was a massive natural feature with a depth of 20 feet and up to 200 feet across. Rommel had turned this feature into an almost impregnable defensive zone. Barbed wire entanglements had been erected, tripped with the inevitable anti-personnel mines. Machine-gun posts were located at strategic points, giving wide fields of fire covering the wadi. Behind these fortifications lay two panzer divisions, ready to react to any major thrust across the wadi.

The question of outflanking or turning the Mareth Line had been considered by Montgomery. Maps indicated that this could be accomplished to the south west. It would involve a drive of over 200 miles over rough and broken country with no water supply. This road or track bypassed the Matmata mountain block on which the Mareth Line was hinged. A report obtained from the French was not optimistic. Earlier in the year, our Long Range Desert Group (LRDG) had negotiated this difficult approach operating behind the Afrika Korps. They claimed that in spite of the many problems involved, the route was passable. Naturally, ample supplies of those two precious liquids – petrol and water – would have to be carried. The purpose of this flanking approach was to get behind the Axis defence at Mareth. The column would come out on the plain at El Hamma near Gabes. Hopefully, Rommel would be forced to pull back his panzers from Mareth and commit them to battle. The plan of battle for Mareth called for a frontal attack across the Wadi Zigzaou, employing 50th British Division and 4th Indian Division. This would constitute Monty's right jab. The 2nd New Zealand Division, reinforced to corps strength with additional armour under General Freyberg, would undertake the flanking approach march. This force would represent the left hook. Prior to the opening of the battle, Freyberg's Battle Group commenced its 200-mile flanking march. They headed south out of Medinine towards Foum Tatahouine. Here they would wheel west where the track cut through a pass in the Matmata Hills, coming to Bir Zoltane where the corps would swing north to El Hamma. It was a wild gamble, fraught with many natural dangers.

Our divisional artillery had been sited to give maximum support to the frontal assault. In addition to counter-battery fire, we were involved in a heavy barrage.

It was interesting to study the various battle plans used by General Montgomery in North Africa, Sicily and Italy. He appeared to favour the old First World War strategy of frontal infantry assault, preceded and supported by massive artillery fire. This appeared to be a weakness of the many British field commanders who had learned their craft in the First World War. German field commanders, on the other hand, were totally committed to panzers and fast movement, supported by mobile infantry and artillery. Comparing the two commanders, Montgomery and Rommel, the former preferred the set piece battle with a clear superiority in troops and equipment. Rommel was the master of mobile tactics and improvisation. He allowed and encouraged his junior commanders to use their own initiative in the field within an overall plan. With Rommel, the very best of plans was never engraved in stone.

One of the very few British commanders in Africa who used the German system with astonishing success was General O'Connor. With relatively small forces and inferior armour but employing surprise, audacity and imagination, he achieved phenomenal success. It is regrettable that General O'Connor was never accorded the credit due to him for his exploits in the early years of the North African campaign. His loss as a prisoner-of-war was a severe blow to the Eighth Army.

Sergeant Neal's Story

Sergeant Norman Neal stubbed out his cigarette.

He stood up in front of the tractor which was hitched to an ammunition limber and a 25-pounder gun-howitzer and called his detachment to order. The battery sergeant major called the battery to attention as the battery commander drove up in his jeep. Standing up in his vehicle Major Douglas ordered the assembly to stand easy.

Normal Neal, or Nogger as he was usually called, was a pre-war regular soldier and had been posted to the regiment in India in 1937 when it was a horsed unit, a survivor in its original form from the First World War. Nogger had enjoyed soldiering in India as a horse driver in a six-horse gun team. However, like everyone else he had accepted the mechanization of the regiment in 1940 and its conversion from 18-pounders and 4.5 howitzers to the 25-pounder gun-howitzer.

Three days previously the 11th Field Regiment, along with its sister regiments, the 1st Field and the 32nd Field, had supported the 4th Indian Division in its attempt to cross the Wadi Zigzaou on the Mareth Line. The wadi was deep, wide and swollen with water from the recent rains which had turned the bottom into a mass of muddy gumbo. The divisional sappers and miners had performed feats of indescribable heroism in trying to construct a bridge under heavy enemy fire to facilitate the movement of armour to give some protection to the infantry. Although a small bridgehead had been established it soon ran out of supplies and was forced to retire when heavily attacked by units of the German 90th Light Division.

Rather than continue the assault and risk heavy casualties Field Marshal Bernard Montgomery decided to switch the Eighth Army from a frontal attack to an outflanking one. The Long Range Desert Group had reconnoitred a route through the Matmata Hills. The 2nd New Zealand Division with its armoured brigade was already on the move to exploit this route and hopefully cut off the Afrika Korps behind the Mareth Line. The 4th Division had also been withdrawn from the Mareth Front and were now awaiting orders for redeployment.

It had been a nightmare extricating the guns from their mud holes in their Mareth gun positions in a steady downpour of rain. In spite of four-wheel drive and heavily cleated tyres many detachments had to resort to winching supplemented by raw manpower. The regiment was now assembled on the lower slopes of the Matmata Hills.

Major Douglas, commanding 83/85 Battery, enjoyed a comfortable relationship with the rank and file of his battery. Confident and decisive, efficient and fair, he exhibited an empathy with and a deep understanding of the concerns, problems and fears of junior officers and other ranks. One of his most appreciated practices was to keep all ranks informed of the general tactical situation and what was expected of the battery.

Morning sunlight was cutting through the dark grey clouds scudding over the mountain peaks, breaking and racing away eastwards. It glinted and sparkled off the broken waters of the Mediterranean 30 miles to the north and finally it neutralized the damp chilling cold, replacing it with an almost balmy warmth.

Pushing his service cap to the back of his head the battery commander addressed the assembly: 'The Commander-in-Chief has decided to abort further frontal action on the Mareth Line not because it could not succeed but because the probable cost in casualties is not acceptable. The 2nd New Zealand Division is already on their way around the Matmata Mountains with the objective of outflanking the enemy and cutting off his retreat from the Mareth Line. The 4th Indian Division will go through the mountains. The 5th Indian Brigade will go through a reconnoitred mountain pass. The 7th Brigade will go *over* the mountains. The 11th Field Regiment will continue to support 7th Brigade with the same objective. I must warn you that the decision to take this route poses a calculated risk because of the difficulty of getting the guns through the mountains and negotiating a very narrow road. The enemy has destroyed sections of this road and it is expected that suicide patrols will attack our column in the mountains. Engineers covered by infantry will move ahead of the guns to effect repairs and the major hazard will be negotiating the narrow road with the guns. It is going to be very difficult but I know that I can depend on you all. Remember, the 83/85 Battery stopped the Rommel's panzers at Alamein last July. Let us do it again at Mareth. Troop and detachment commanders will attend a separate briefing before we move. Thank you, gentlemen.'

At the briefing Nogger learned the details of the outflanking movement. Because the brigade advance was limited to just one road the infantry would take the lead with units of the Bombay and Madras Sappers and Miners close behind them and indeed were already on the move. They were being followed by Divisional HQ and Signals. Eleventh Field Regiment HQ would then take the road followed by 78/84 Battery and then 83/85 Battery.

The road, if such it could be called, went up into the mountains and in places was literally carved out of solid rock cut into the cliff face with drops of up to 1000 feet on the down side at the higher elevations. The decision to launch the artillery along this road had been highly controversial. It would be a fearful foray attended with enormous risk.

Dawn was breaking the following morning as that early morning quiet was broken by the noise of tractor engines. The guns moved out with NCOs directing their drivers into their place in the snakelike column.

Maintaining a road speed of 20 mph the regiment moved rapidly through the foothills and by mid-morning were entering the mountain pass. All detachment commanders were standing in their quads watching the road ahead, ready to pass directions to their drivers whose range of vision was more limited. The gradient rapidly increased from one in 15 to one in 10 and then one in seven. Gearboxes were moved into four-wheel drive and then low reduction. At 1500 feet the rock face ascended almost vertically on their right and the left shoulder fell away in a sharp drop to the valley floor over 1000 feet below, barely visible through a pall of misty cloud.

As his driver concentrated upon keeping his front wheels close to the rock face on his right side Nogger alternated his watch from the limber and gun behind him and the left front wheel which was now moving perilously close to the edge and he drew his breath sharply as from time to time the tyre appeared to be rolling on air space. Finally he gave the signal to the driver to stop. He ordered the detachment out of the quad and told them to march ahead of the tractor. Nogger thought, We may lose a gun but I'm damned if I'm going to lose six gunners. He tied back the driver's door and ordered him to be prepared to jump clear if he felt the tractor was going to take off the road.

After negotiating a short 'safe' area they entered another constricted section. Nogger started walking backwards, guiding the driver. He kept his eyes on the gun and limber wheels running along the edge of the road. There were frequent stops as vehicles ahead were forced to halt. At one of these stops the left gun wheel dropped off the edge and was only prevented from dropping to eternity by Nogger shouting to the driver to slam on all brakes. Nogger went back and checked the wheel. It was tricky. Although safe, providing there was no movement, there was a real danger that any attempt to move gun either back or forward would drop the wheel clear of the road. Nogger ordered the detachment to recover one of the ropes that were used to apply manpower to the gun wheels and they attached it to the hook provided. With the detachment pulling the wheel towards the rockface the driver moved cautiously forwards. The gun wheel came clear onto solid road. Another 10 feet and the emergency ended.

It was well past midday when 83/85 Battery crested the top of the pass and commenced the long and tortuous descent. Shortly afterwards the order that warmed the heart of every British soldier came rippling down the column. 'Brew Up!'

As the detachment started the fire with petrol in a cutaway four gallon petrol can Nogger lay back on a flat rock nicely warmed by the sun and admired the view. The imposing peak of Mount Cairo was clearly visible and to the east the sun could be seen reflected off the Mediterranean Sea.

It wasn't long before the start-up signal came back from the vehicle in front. As the tractor roared into life the detachment climbed aboard and the column moved forward.

In recounting the story of the crossing of the Matmata Mountains at later dates Nogger was never quite sure which was more nerve-racking, the ascent or the descent. He finally decided that looking downwards into the valley with a limber and gun weighing one and one half tons trying to push you into oblivion induced more pure terror than gazing upwards into the sky. On the way down they crossed a major road break which had been repaired by the infantry working under the direction of the divisional engineers. It was reported later that Brigadier Lovett was observed assisting in the repairs.

The natural exhilaration induced by the successful crossing was leavened and dissipated by the news that the wily Rommel had anticipated or/and observed the outflanking movements by the New Zealand Division and the 4th Indian Division and had withdrawn the Afrika Korps from the Mareth defensive positions. However, Montgomery's major objective had been achieved: to force Rommel to withdraw from the strong positions he held behind the Wadi Zigzaou. Thus the heavy casualties which almost certainly attended a frontal attack were avoided.

An important benefit arising from this action was the ability of the 4th Indian Division to move guns and heavy equipment through mountainous country. Major General Tuker was complimented by the Commander-in-Chief who observed that this action augured well for the fighting that lay ahead through the mountainous Tunisian terrain.

7   THE TUNISIAN CAMPAIGN

SCREW-GUNS (Mountain Guns of the Royal Artillery)
Smokin' my pipe on the mountings, sniffin' the mornin'-cool,
I walks in my old brown gaiters along o' my old brown mule,
With seventy gunners be'ind me, an' never a beggar forgets
It's only the pick of the Army that handles the dear little pets.
Rudyard Kipling

At 23.00 hours on 20th March, Eighth Army artillery thundered over
the Mareth Line. There was a brilliant full moon as 50th Division
forced the wadi, supported by our 5th Indian Infantry Brigade. A
tenuous bridgehead was established. It became obvious that this
bridgehead could not be held unless additional reinforcements were
moved across. The Afrika Korps were reacting furiously to our
attack. Under murderous machine-gun fire, a temporary bridge was
completed. Across this bridge we moved some Valentine tanks. The
bridge collapsed under the weight. Coupled to heavy rain the following day, which turned the floor of the wadi into a morass of mud, 50th
Division was isolated. Support by the Desert Air Force was substantially reduced by the weather conditions. On 23rd March Rommel put
in a fierce counter attack composed of units of the 90th Light Division
and the 15th Panzer Division. They recaptured most of the bridgehead, in spite of gallant resistance by the Tynesiders, who managed
to retain a toehold. The 4th Indian Division were again called upon
for support. Madrassi and Sikh Sappers and Miners were brought up.
They commenced construction of a heavier bridge. Operating under

fierce German fire, they worked away as if they were operating in India on a civil project. In spite of their gallant efforts, the combination of the Wadi Zagzaou, the elements and the Afrika Korps was just too much. The Eighth Army withdrew to its start line.

General Montgomery now decided to call a halt to the frontal attack across the Wadi Zagzaou. The casualty cost was proving too high. He would hold the Mareth Front, employing local minor attacks and fighting patrols. He decided to switch the main attack to his left hook. The Kiwis had made excellent progress in their approach march, outflanking the Matmata Hills. They were also able to report that although the going was difficult they had not encountered any major problems. The 1st Armoured Division was dispatched to supply additional support.

A third plan was now developed. General Tuker, using information obtained by 1/2 Gurkhas, prepared his plan. The Gurkhas had penetrated deep into the Matmata Hills on recce patrols. Expressed in its simplest form, this plan called for the 4th Indian Division to turn the Mareth Line by literally going over the mountains. The Matmata Hills rose to a height of over 2000 feet. Mount Cairo was just over 1500 feet and Mount Delhi was 2000 feet.

The plan was approved by General Montgomery.

It required two days to reassemble the 4th Indian Division in its concentration area. Brigades and various support units, including divisional artillery, had to be reclaimed from the 50th Division and the 7th Armoured Division. We limbered our guns, cleaned up our gun positions and moved back to our assembly area. An air of expectancy and excitement pervaded the regiment. Mountain warfare, supporting infantry with our gun howitzers, would prove to be an interesting change of pace.

By the night of 24th–25th March we were ready to go. The division was divided so that we would make two separate thrusts. The 7th Brigade was sent south to move around the main mountain features, passing through the Khordache Gap and then swinging north through Technine and Beni Zeltan into the Gabes plain. The 5th Brigade was to force the Hallouf Pass.

Information obtained by 1/2 Gurkhas indicated that this pass was heavily defended. Roads had been expertly mined, particularly at critical points where the mined areas were difficult to avoid. Negotiating these roads with quad tractors, limbers and 25-pounder guns was in itself difficult enough. Some sections of these narrow roadways or tracks just clung to the side of the mountain, with a sheer drop to one side. In places the road had crumbled away. From time to time the detachment commander would order the gun crew out of the tractor; then, walking in front of the tractor, he would guide and direct the driver by hand signals. It was alleged later, but hotly denied, that some drivers had tied their doors open, ready to jump should their tractor and gun decide to take off for the valley floor.

Stubborn resistance by small pockets of the enemy made it necessary to provide continuous artillery support. In order to maintain the advance behind the infantry, this was achieved by leapfrogging troops within each battery, two troops in action and two troops moving.

Captain R.B. Dickson RA, acting as OP Officer for 78/84 Battery, conducted an excellent 'shoot' on 26th March. He knocked out a field gun and neutralized a machine gun emplacement. As a result, 30 Italian defenders surrendered to our infantry. The following day, Captain F.R. Jephson RA, supported by his OP crew, took 15 prisoners. On the same day, Captain N. Roach-Rooke RA and his OP crew had a remarkable escape. Operating with 2/9 Gurkhas, a 75 mm shell landed in their armoured OV but failed to explode.

The combination of close infantry support, sudden and frequent calls for artillery support, difficult gun deployment and high mountain peaks presented many difficult gunnery problems. Most, but not all, were solved.

Detachments of the Madras Sappers and Miners, the divisional engineers, operated at the head of each column with the infantry. They checked for and cleared mines. They repaired roads sufficiently to render them passable. On the evening of 27th March 11th Field Regiment reached the top of the pass in the Beni Zeltan defile. We were forced to stop because stretches of these stone abutments supporting the road had collapsed. Our sappers, with labour supplied by 1/2 Gurkhas, had been working on the road since midday. A lot of the work was old-fashioned manual labour, carrying stones and packing them in under the direction of the sappers to support the road above. Everyone pitched in at this work – sappers, infantrymen and gunners. Even Brigadier Lovett, 7th Brigade commander, was seen doing his bit. There was, at this point, a great air of excitement amongst all arms and all ranks. If only we could get out of the mountains fast enough we could race across the plain below and hopefully cut off the retreating Afrika Korps. Early in the afternoon of 28th March we started down the defile behind our infantry. It was a tricky descent. Upon reaching the mouth of the defile infantry patrols had gone forward to establish contact with the enemy. We were too late. On the morning of the previous day, 2nd New Zealand Division had made contact with the Afrika Korps. Rommel was too fast. Again, he earned his name, Desert Fox. Realizing that he was being outflanked, he made a fast withdrawal west, then north. The Battle of Mareth was over. The bottom line for 4th Indian Division was that we had taken 460 prisoners and had sustained about 100 casualties, mostly from mines. We had also demonstrated to Eighth Army HQ that the 4th Indian Division had an aptitude for mountain warfare.

The following day we moved out of the Matmata Hills and went into leaguer at El Midou. Shortly afterwards we were in receipt of a message to all ranks of the 4th Indian Division from the Corps Commander. It read as follows:

'I write to congratulate you and all ranks of the Fourth Indian Division on your splendid work in the mountains during the Mareth Battle.

You were called upon to carry out a difficult task at immediate notice. You were very short of MT and you had no time to collect mountain warfare equipment. Nevertheless, you accomplished your task with complete success, crossing difficult mountainous country, clearing extensive mined areas, and driving in strong enemy resistance.

Your advance turned the southern extremity of the Mareth Line and contributed strongly to the enemy's enforced withdrawal, a withdrawal which by a few hours only robbed your Division of a large haul of enemy personnel and equipment.

I am very pleased once again to have Fourth Indian Division in 30 Corps, and I congratulate all ranks on an outstanding performance – which could only have been carried out by troops highly trained in mountain warfare.'

Rommel and the Afrika Korps were now being forced back into the jaws of a giant pincer movement. The Eighth Army was pushing him north towards Tunis and the British First Army with US II Corps were squeezing him from the west. He knew he must keep those two jaws from closing. Consequently, he retreated only 20 miles north to Gabes. He had strengthened a position here that has gone into military history as the Wadi Akarit.

The Wadi Akarit position was a natural defensive combination of physical features. Commencing at a point less than 15 miles from where the Mediterranean Sea cut into the African land mass to form the Gulf of Gabes, was the impassable Fedjadi salt marsh. This marsh extended inland for about 120 miles. This 15-mile gap was protected for about two-thirds of its length by a high ridge system known as Dyebel Zemlet el Beida. Between the eastern end of this feature and the sea there was a deep *nullah* known as Wadi Akarit, providing in itself a serious obstacle. About five miles inland stood a saddle back about one mile in length and rising to a height of over 500 feet. The map showed this feature as being named Roumana. Continuing west from Roumana, a series of rolling hills extended for about two miles rising up finally to form a fearsome feature known as Fatnassa. This conglomeration of high ground appeared to be a geographical freak. It seemed to be a monstrous figment of a mad artist's imagination. But it was real, very, very real. Crests formed pinnacles then falling to create escarpments, counter-escarpments, ravines, crevasses, corridors and rocky outcrops of all shapes and sizes. Rommel had improved these positions in several ways. He had constructed an anti-tank ditch which extended the natural obstacle of the *nullah* by an additional two miles. In addition, German engineers had built in machine gun emplacements at critical points and placed a number of their deadly 88s in position that would threaten a tank approach. The German commander must have really believed that he now held an impregnable defensive position with a secure flank.

General Montgomery's final plan of battle for the assault on the Wadi Akarit bore the stamp of General Tuker's contribution. The 51st Highland Division was to attack across the wadi on the right. The 50th Division was to attack frontally against the anti-tank ditch and the rolling ground west of Roumana. The 4th Indian Division would attack through the mountains with both brigades.

The attack by the 50th and 51st Divisions was set to go in at 04.30 hours on 6th April. The 4th Division Artillery had taken up their gun positions several days earlier. Regimental Survey was actively engaged in 'fixing' geographical points and features that could prove useful if infantry support was necessary. There would not be any pre-attack artillery bombardment. General Tuker wished to retain the element of surprise for as long as possible. The Gurkhas were always more effective when attacking in silence. Instead of the old American maxim of 'not shooting until you can see the whites of their eyes', the Gurkha never raised his *kukri* until he could cut the enemy's throat.

The 5th and 7th Indian Infantry Brigades commenced their approach march immediately after darkness fell on 5th April, 1/2 Gurkhas going off in front, leading the attack and aiming for the key Fatnassa features. The objective of the 1st Royal Sussex was to seize the Meida Kopje at the west end of the anti-tank ditch; 1/9 Gurkhas were to move along a ravine or valley between two of the main counter features.

Platoons of Rajputana Rifles machine gun battalions would go forward to support infantry units. At 02.30 hours, we were called upon for crash shoots to neutralize strongpoints holding up the advance, while 1/2 Gurkhas reported that they were on their first objective at 01.30 hours. Further gunfire was brought down on the El Meida feature. Within an hour the Sussex captured El Meida at the point of the bayonet.

The 4/16 Punjabis, which were being held in reserve, were now released. Their axis of advance was on the extreme left along the high ground, overlooking a military road running north west.

By dawn the battle was raging along a 10-mile front. The 51st Division had broken into the enemy positions across the wadi. The 50th Division was running into problems attacking across the anti-tank ditch. Before dawn 1/9 Gurkhas, moving rapidly along the crest of a mountain block, were heading for the rear of the Fatnassa feature. They stormed ridge after ridge, defended by elements of the 90th Light Division. Wielding their *kukris* with deadly effect, they broke the morale of the defenders. The mad rush of the 1/9 Gurkhas carried them over one and one half miles into the enemy defences. They took over 2000 prisoners. The 4/6 Rajputana Rifles were following close behind. Passing behind the 1st Sussex position on El Meida, they forced their way into the enemy rear behind the anti-tank ditch. Penetrating nearly half way onto the Roumana feature, they took over 1000 prisoners, mostly Italians. One infantry officer reported that white surrender flags were being waved profusely.

At 08.45 hours General Tuker sent a message to Commander 10 Corps that we had broken the enemy and the way was clear for 10

Corps to go through. Shortly afterwards, Eighth Army tank columns started moving over the divisional crossing at the anti-tank ditch.

By midday on 6th April the battle was over. However, elements of the stubborn and gallant 90th Light Division continued their tenacious resistance behind crests and in the fissures of Fatnassa. 1/2 Gurkhas ran out of ammunition. They fell back on their favourite method of attack, the *kukri* charge. They even resorted to climbing up above enemy strongpoints and throwing rocks. Our forward OP officers with the infantry called for gunfire from time to time in order to dislodge or at least neutralize the stubborn resistance. The 90th Light battled gallantly but hopelessly. By first light on 7th April the Afrika Korps was in full retreat.

Later that afternoon a Gurkha patrol led by Subedar Major Marbahadur Gurung drove northwest along the military road, secured by the Punjabis and met a jeep with American scouts. The Eighth Army had joined up with US II Corps to form a continuous front.

The trap had closed on the Afrika Korps.

Considering the scope and difficulty of this battle, the casualties of the 4th Indian Division were remarkably light. There was a total of less than 400.

Casualties of the 11th Field Regiment were relatively light: five gunners wounded and two killed in action. One of the two men killed was the CO's driver. On 5th April Major D.N.E. O'Halloran RA, commanding 78/84 Battery, was killed. He had been moving forward to reconnoitre new gun positions at Wadi Akarit when his AOV exploded a Teller mine. His driver, Gunner T. Walker, was wounded but recovered. Major O'Halloran was a capable and popular officer and well liked by his men.

This account of the Battle of Wadi Akarit cannot be closed without the story of Subedar Lalbahadur Thapa. This amazing man, a Gurkha NCO, almost single-handedly opened the way for the 5th Brigade to advance to Fatnassa. It is also typical of many other hand to hand battles waged by individual Gurkha soldiers in this engagement. This account is taken from *Fourth Indian Division* by Lt. Col. GR Stevens:

'The dense darkness of that boulder-studded ravine hid a great feat of arms. Under command of Subedar Lalbahadur Thapa, two sections of Gurkhas had moved forward to secure the only pathway which led over the escarpment at the upper end of the rocky chimney. This trail reached the top of the hill through a narrow cleft thickly studded with enemy posts. Anti-tank guns and machine guns covered every foot of the way, while across the canyon, where the cliffs rose steeply for some 200 feet, the crests were swarming with automatic gunners and mortar teams. Subedar Lalbahadur Thapa reached the first enemy sanger without challenge. His section cut down its garrison with the kukri. Immediately, every post along the twisty pathway opened fire. Without pause, the intrepid Subedar, with no room to manoeuvre, dashed forward at the head of his men through a curtain of machine gun fire, grenades and mortar bombs. He leapt inside a machine gun post and killed four gunners single-handed, two with the kukri, two with pistol. Man after man of his section were stricken until only two were left. Rushing on, he clambered up the last few yards of the defile through where the pathway snaked over the crest of the escarpment. He flung himself single-handed on the garrison of the last sanger covering the pathway, striking two enemies dead with his kukri. This terrible foe was too much; the remainder of the detachment fled with wild screams for safety. The chimney between the escarpments was now open and with it the corridor through which 5 Brigade might pass. It is scarcely too much to say that the battle for Wadi Akarit had been won singlehanded several hours before the formal battle began.'

Lalbahadur Thapa was immediately recommended for the Military Cross by his commanding officer. When General Montgomery (now a Field Marshal) read the citation, he recommended Lalbahadur Thapa for the Victoria Cross, the supreme award for valour.

General Tuker, 4th Indian Division Commander, expressed his opinion after the Battle of Wadi Akarit that had he been given his third Brigade, so often requested by him, the 4th Indian Division could have prevented the escape of the Afrika Korps. This would have shortened the Tunisian Campaign by a full month and saved the Allies thousands of casualties. At any rate, the accomplishment of the 4th Indian Division at both Mareth and Wadi Akarit had placed India on the map in the Second World War.

We had hardly enough time to service the guns before the division was ordered forward in pursuit of the fleeing Afrika Korps. Rommel was retreating north and was expected to turn and fight again at Enfidaville. As we moved away from Wadi Akarit the terrain changed to a large plain which surrounded the large towns of Sfax and Sousse, both of which were indefensible. This plain continued for about 200 miles north. At Enfidaville, the ground changed to hilly country rising to a height of over 1000 feet.

As we drove along the improved highways with the Mediterranean on our right, we marvelled at the pleasant farm scenery and the pastoral beauty of the countryside. There was little sign of the normal devastation indicated by war. Spring had come to Tunisia and the countryside was a riot of wild flowers. We rolled past several small fishing villages facing the waterfront with boats pulled up clear of the water, almost to the cottage doors. Passing through Sfax we moved back into the country. The palm trees added a dash of the tropics to the countryside. We came to El Djem. Here survived the ruins of a magnificent Roman amphitheatre. It represented the ancient Kingdom of Carthage and demonstrated the extent of the far-flung Roman Empire. Some divisional units turned left and passed through the holy Moslem city of Kairouan. Kairouan was reputed to have in excess of 150 mosques. With its myriads of domed mosques, it looked like the creation of a Disney cartoon artist. So we came to Sousse, the largest town in southern Tunisia. As we drove through the town, the road was lined with the civilian population, watching us with open curiosity. Older men with greying hair stood next to generously busted matrons and charming young ladies, blowing kisses in profusion. There were, too, the inevitable children, running beside the vehicles, trying vainly to keep up, with arms outstretched in supplication. Once more, I lost my lunch for the day. We were now less than 25 miles from Enfidaville. As we drove north west away from Sousse, the mountains ahead could be clearly seen. They swung west in a broad semi-circle. On 16th April 11th Field Regiment went into camp in a pleasant grassy area amidst dense olive groves.

The Afrika Korps had withdrawn to its final defensive positions. These covered over 100 miles of mountainous country. This area covered the north west section of Tunisia, from Enfidaville in the south to Bizerta in the north and from Medjez el Bab in the west to Tunis and the Cap Bon peninsula in the east. It was rumoured at this time that Rommel had been flown back to Germany, seriously ill, and that General Von Arnim had taken over command of all Axis forces in Tunisia.

US II Corps was holding the northern sector at Sedjenane facing Bizerta and the British First Army was holding the centre at Medjez el Bab, facing Tunis.

The Eighth Army was now but a shadow of the massive military machine that had faced the Afrika Korps at El Alamein in October of the previous year. The 9th Australian Division, 1st South African Division and 44th British Division had all been withdrawn. The 50th and 51st Divisions were in the process of withdrawal to Tripoli in order to prepare for the Sicily landings. This left the 2nd New Zealand Division, 4th Indian Division, 7th Armoured Division and 201st Guards Brigade, plus some assorted armour.

The Afrika Korps had fortified two major features facing the Eighth Army. Takrouna on the left was a promontory of high ground, capped by a village three miles west of Enfidaville. The capture of this feature was allotted to the 2nd New Zealand Division. The second fortified area which denied our advance was called Djebal Garci which had been given to the 4th Indian Division.

Djebal Garci was a spade-shaped promontory projecting south into the plain and rising to a height of 1000 feet at its rear. It fell away to low ground either side. General Le Clerc's Free French Brigade had occupied and secured high ground to our left. Although they nominally came under command of the 4th Indian Division, they were non-operational at this point in the campaign.

The main road from Enfidaville passed Takrouna in a northwesterly direction, going through the small town of Pont du Fahs, where a railway line crossed the highway then turning north to Tunis.

Vigorous patrolling by 1/4 Essex yielded seven Italian prisoners on 17th April. They provided valuable information about the defences.

The divisional attack opened on the night of 19th April at 21.00 hours. It was led by 1/4 Essex and 4/6 Rajputana Rifles; 1/9 Gurkhas followed almost immediately afterwards. The going was very rough and at times they were reduced to crawling. It was another rock climbing experience, reminiscent of Wadi Akarit. As they moved deeper into the German defences, the enemy reacted savagely. A description of the action that followed is extracted from *Fourth Indian Division*:

'In the darkness, men grappled and slew each other. The survivors went to earth as bombs burst about them, rose and rushed forward in the dust and smoke and fastened upon other enemies. For four hours, the Rajputana Rifles battled their way forward in one of the bitterest encounters of the war. Every gain drew a counter-attack from desperate men pledged to hold the heights at all costs. Yard by yard the assailants worked upwards, around rocky knolls, across mountain wadis, surging over crests to face other crests from which mortar and small arms fire swept down incessantly upon them.'

It was man fighting man reduced to its rawest form. It was an individual action, one on one, the winner moving forward a few yards to set up another one on one. It was attack and counterattack followed by attack and counterattack. No quarter was asked, there was no surrender and there were no prisoners.

Artillery observers following closely behind the leading edge of attacking infantry called for gunfire to neutralize the upper slopes. Divisional artillery opened up, thundering over and above this indescribable confusion and began to pulverize the higher mountain strongpoints previously registered.

From our gun positions on the level ground we gazed up at Garci mountain covered in a pall of smoke as the morning light increased. Our infantrymen were now trying to dig in and consolidate their positions in the face of enemy mortar fire. All through that day fighting continued as we battled to hold our positions on the lower slopes of the Garci feature. The Kiwis to our right had run into the same fierce resistance. Although they had overcome some Italian units with little difficulty, elements of their old friends, the 90th Light Division, had reacted violently and ferociously to every yard of the advance. It became obvious the enemy was prepared to make us pay dearly for every yard. The cost in casualties was too much. The advance came to a halt. At this point our CRA, Brigadier Dimoline, was instructed to take over the battle and bring down massed artillery fire.

At the gun positions in the early afternoon of 20th April we were informed that divisional artillery would be supplemented by an additional four field regiments coming under our direct command, 51st, 64th and 69th Medium Regiments would also be on call. With additional emergency assistance from flanking formations, our divisional artillery under Brigadier Dimoline could call on 300 guns. The relatively narrow width and depth of the fighting front would allow a powerful concentration of available artillery. We could use the recently developed system of artillery fire control. It was first used at the Battle of El Alamein. Since then, practice and better communications had improved our effectiveness. We could now switch massed artillery fire from one target to another in less than five minutes instead of twelve. This form of artillery fire was far more effective than the old creeping barrage. The barrage tended to waste a high percentage of shellfire on open ground where the shells exploded harmlessly clear of any specific target. These sudden concentrations of artillery fire, on the other hand, placed an extremely high percentage of shells right on the target and in addition to the material results, they affected the enemy psychologically. Infantrymen and artillery OP officers have reported seeing an odd defender running wildly from the shelter of his slit trench to escape the murderous shellfire only to be cut down before he had covered more than a few steps.

We calculated that the total artillery force at Garci could deliver shell at the rate of eight tons per minute. Put another way, we averaged 640 rounds per gun over the three days of battle. Although Erwin Von Rommel never lived long enough to write his memoirs, his son completed the work, based to a major extent on letters to his wife during the war. In a number of instances, he commented on the high concentrations, accuracy and ability of Eighth Army artillery to switch from target to target.

However, in spite of this mass of gunnery power, the advance was continuing to be costly in terms of killed and wounded. It was becoming evident that Monty had miscalculated the strength and determination of the Afrika Korps at Garci and Takrouna. On the night of 22nd–23rd April the Essex, Rajputana Rifles and Gurkhas were relieved and moved back for a rest south west of Enfidaville.

The 56th London Division was placed under our command and plans were made to attack at Tabage in the coastal area. On the morning of 30th April German units, following a successful counterattack against the 56th Division the night before and in the absence of reserve positions, pushed forward in an aggressive advance. This advance, finding no opposition, came within 2000 yards of a high concentration of field artillery in the orchards south west of Enfidaville. It was indeed fortunate for the gunners that 4/16 Punjabis and 1/2 Gurkhas were covering that area. Although their officers were all absent at a conference, the NCOs reacted with coolness and assurance. They organized their men, took command of sections, platoons and companies and counterattacked. They pinned down the enemy, forced him back and restored the situation.

It was a magnificent example of Indian warrant officers and NCOs rallying and organizing their men in the absence of all their officers and staging a successful counterattack against a determined enemy.

Apart from artillery fire the Garci-Takrouna battle had now ground to a halt. Post-war historians reveal that at about this time General Alexander visited General Montgomery at Eighth Army HQ. What passed between them is not recorded. We do know that both General Tuker commanding the 4th Indian Division and General Freyberg commanding the 2nd New Zealand Division were both opposed to Monty's plan of battle on this front but were overruled. They had recommended that the drive to Tunis be concentrated on the First Army front at Medjez el Bab. Here, a breakout through the Axis defences would provide access to open flat country, ideal for deployment of armour.

Shortly before noon on 30th April we received movement orders from Divisional HQ. The 4th Indian Division with the 7th Armoured Division and 201st Guards Brigade would leave the Eighth Army immediately and commence the journey to join the First Army at Medjez el Bab. We would lead the final drive for Tunis.

The Divisional Commander's order of the day made interesting reading:

'Fourth Indian Division is now moving over to First Army. The name of our division stands at the very top of Eighth Army, mainly because of the great dash and courage of our fighting men and our refusal, ever, to give an inch of ground that we have won, even if we have had to fight with fists and stones.

Let us now place our Division at the very top of First Army. We shall probably meet the Hermann Goering Division very soon. They are the people who shot British prisoners in cold blood. Let us of Fourth Indian Division teach them a lesson once and for all.'

The division moved off the same afternoon with Divisional HQ in the lead, followed by the 5th Brigade, then the three field artillery regiments, 1st, 11th and 31st with 7th Brigade bringing up the rear.

Previous detachments had already gone ahead to organize traffic at critical points and avoid confusion. Even as we moved off, the 7th Brigade was still in the process of disengagement.

We headed south, passing through Kairouan after dark. Headlights were allowed but the rigours of months of desert warfare had reduced the effectiveness of this relatively useless piece of equipment to almost zero. This was the first time I could remember being on a line of march during the hours of darkness. Heading west, then north west, we passed through the old Roman town of Sbeitla. Driving all night, we passed Sheiba and entered the fertile agricultural country of Central Tunisia. Grazing sheep were in evidence and struck a strangely peaceful chord. At dawn we halted for calls of nature and, of course, to brew up. Civilian density increased as we proceeded and American soldiers waved to us as we passed. They gazed with some astonishment at the wide variety of nationalities and ethnic origins in our division. There were bearded Sikhs and Rajputs, Jats, Punjabis and Gurkhas in their distinctive headgear, all mixed in with sundry British types. We passed through Le Kef and Le Krib and the picturesque town of Teboursouk, perched on the side of a hill, drawing closer to Medjez el Bab, the gateway to Tunis.

Arriving at the First Army's front, we went into camp in the rear. On 3rd May we moved into our pre-selected gun positions. The guns were laid out for the last time in the North African campaign. I went up front with our survey officer to appraise the situation.

Apparently General Tuker had persuaded the corps commander to open the offensive with a night attack on a narrow front, spearheaded by the 4th Indian Division. The 1st British Division would attack on our left. We had 400 field guns plus a 17-pounder and an additional six-pounder anti-tank regiment. Our attack would also be supported by 20 squadrons of fighter-bombers! How times had changed from the early days of the Western Desert when the sight of just three British planes would justify a rousing cheer.

The Medjez el Bab position could best be described as a gap between hills and broken ground on either side. The German positions had been strongly fortified and their artillery, including a high proportion of the deadly 88s, had been carefully sited for maximum effect. However, there was open ground behind this formidable defensive wall, not more mountains as at Akarit and Garci. The task of the

4th Indian Division was to punch a hole in a narrow front through this wall, then secure and hold the opening. The infantry would be supported by a massive concentration of guns. The 7th Armoured Division would then pass through this hole, fanning out on the far side, hopefully non-stop to Tunis, about 30 miles away.

As darkness fell on 5th May, following a mass bombardment from 400 guns, the 1st British Division stormed Bou Huaker. They secured their objectives, holding the left flank of the 4th Indian Division. The 5th Brigade commenced their advance at 23.00 hours and 7th Brigade followed. Each brigade had been given three objectives. As the infantry arrived on their start line, all the guns of the corps, including mediums, were switched to the barrage. The original ammunition allotment for the attack had been 450 rounds per gun. General Tuker had demanded that this figure be increased to 1000 rounds per gun. General Tuker got his way. Neutralized and demoralized by this tremendous concentration and accuracy of our artillery fire, the enemy resistance weakened. Our infantry moved forward with 1/9 Gurkhas in the lead, followed by 4/6 Rajputana Rifles and 1/4 Essex. Then came the 7th Brigade with 1/2 Gurkhas leading, followed by the 1st Royal Sussex and 4/16 Punjabis. Shortly after 03.00 hours the rumble and clanking of tanks were heard. First light was barely 30 minutes' old when the fighter-bombers were heard. They went over our gun positions, coming in low on their bomb run out of the south over the infantry, dropping their bombs with apparent rehearsed precision. Then up and away they went. Never had we witnessed such supportive accuracy.

At 07.30 hours 7th Armoured Division, the Desert Rats, began to roll and at 08.45 hours they reported that they were on 4th Indian Division objectives. One hour late they were authorized to 'go as fast and as far as they liked.'

The German lines had broken and the defenders were in full retreat. Here and there German gun detachments put up stubborn individual resistance but the end was inevitable. It was all over. At a cost of about 150 casualties the 4th Indian Division had punched the hole. The road to Tunis was open. After the frustration of Mareth, the dogged and vicious hand to hand fighting at the Wadi Akarit and the costly advance at Djabel Garci, Medjez el Bab was the classic victory.

Later that day, the 7th Armoured Division entered Tunis led by 11th Hussars. A fitting end to the North African campaign for a division that had justly earned the honour. General Von Arnim had wisely decided not to try to defend the town.

On 11th May we joined in the round up of prisoners in Cap Bon peninsula. Our Regimental HQ was established adjacent to Divisional HQ at Ein el Asker. On 12th May the total Superga Division surrendered to a Rajputana Rifles carrier patrol. The remnants of the 10th Panzer Division totalling 3000 men surrendered to the 1st Royal Sussex. On this date, the 5th Indian Brigade met with Free French forces advancing from Pont du Fahs.

General Von Arnim, supreme commander of German-Italian forces in Tunisia since Rommel's return to Germany, had sent an emissary to offer to surrender all German forces under his direct command to General Tuker's HQ. However, before negotiations could be completed, 1/2 Gurkhas, who had been mopping up in the area, stumbled upon General Von Arnim's HQ. Lieutenant Colonel Showers, the battalion commander, accompanied by his orderly, Rifleman Sargahana Limba, accepted the surrender. The CO posted guards over the HQ and waited for General Tuker. What ensued is neatly described by General Tuker in *Fourth Indian Division*:

'The senior German staff officers then formed up outside the commander's caravan, and the two generals walked down the line saying good-bye. A salute, a hail and a handshake – but no mention of Hitler was heard. The two generals, their chiefs of staff, ADCs and a German interpreter got into their cars and drove away slowly under a guard of the Royal Sussex. Von Arnim stood up in the front seat of his car as it passed down the track between groups of Germans who were standing in their lines to say farewell to the commander of all Axis forces in Africa. They raised a cheer as he passed and slowly formed into a long column to follow him into captivity.'

The other general mentioned in this quotation was General Kram, commander of the 5th Panzer Army.

All organized resistance ceased on that day. There were about 250,000 prisoners, although the final tally was expected to be much higher. The fierce 90th Light Infantry Division which had stubbornly

104

resisted the Eighth Army from Alamein to Tunis surrendered very fittingly to the 2nd New Zealand Division at Enfidaville.

As a point of interest, General Tuker claimed Von Arnim's caravan on behalf of the 4th Indian Division. It was eventually presented to the Indian Government.

8 RETURN TO THE DELTA

The battle of El Alamein was now complete. The struggle that had commenced on 23rd October 1942 at El Alamein in Egypt finally ended on 13th May 1943 in Tunisia. General Montgomery's promise to destroy all Axis forces in Africa, as outlined in his message to all ranks, was not completed until the latter date.

The final destruction in Tunisia of the Axis forces truly ranks along with Stalingrad as the turning point of the Second World War.

It would be unfair to draw comparisons between the many formations, divisions and battle groups that had been welded together to form the magnificent Eighth Army. However, without casting any reflections on any other division, infantry or armoured, it would be reasonable to claim that the 7th Armoured and 4th Indian Divisions played a major role in the final victory. These two formations had shared the tragedies and the triumphs of the North African campaign from its beginnings on the Egyptian border in 1940 until final victory in Tunisia in 1943.

Our regimental noticeboard overflowed with copies of messages of congratulations from all over the world to the 4th Indian Division. The one we liked best and in which we took professional pride came over the signature of General Freyberg, V.C. on behalf of the 2nd New Zealand Division. It was directed to General Tuker and the 4th Indian Division. It read 'We count it an honour and a privilege to have served beside you and trust that such will be our fortune again.' It can truly be said that recognition by one's peers is the sweetest praise of all. The final accolade was extracted from Field Marshal Bernard Law Montgomery himself. At a conference for senior officers in Tripoli

106

on 3rd June he was questioned concerning instructions from Field Marshal Alexander to transfer formations to British First Army in late April. His reply was: 'I gave them my best 7th Armoured and 4th Indian Divisions.'

Fourth Indian Division Administration Order No. 8 dated 3rd May 1943, read as follows: 'COs will ensure that the French ownership of all houses, barns, etc., occupied by troops under their command is scrupulously respected. Where buildings are already deserted by their owners, particular care will be taken not to increase the damage or remove or destroy furniture or other property.

Farm implements and tools will, under no circumstances, be destroyed or misappropriated and only for the most urgent operational necessity will implements be used. When used, the necessary arrangements for hire or compensation will be made with the owner or, in his absence, with the local French Authority.

All ranks will be made to appreciate that the welfare of the local inhabitants and their attitude to the Allied Forces for many months to come depends upon the extent to which they can recover their property as far as possible intact after enemy occupation.'

We had been warned that our time in the Tunis area would be limited. Arrangements were made for all ranks to visit Tunis on a rotational basis. Jack Parker and I squeezed into one visiting group. As mentioned earlier, the German Military Commander of Tunis had decided not to defend the city. As a result, Tunis was spared the horrors of war.

Jack and I spent a pleasant day sightseeing, took a few photographs and enjoyed coffee and delicious French pastries.

On 17th May our regimental advance party joined Divisional HQ and pulled out to prepare our next location somewhere in the area of Tripoli. Fifth and 7th Brigades left in the next three days. On 20th May Divisional Artillery, including the 11th Field Regiment, took the road south to Gabes and Tripoli.

It was an uneventful journey.

As we crossed Wadi Akarit I took a last look westwards at the towering Fatnassa feature. It stood, grim and foreboding, its faint purple eminence silhouetted against the setting sun: no longer a fortress, it would possibly become a rock climber's paradise in the future.

One week later we reached our destination, Misurata, located 120 miles east of Tripoli on the Mediterranean coast. Our advance party had completed preparation for our arrival with their usual efficiency. RHQ and battery areas had been marked out, allowing a generous allotment of space. The site was clean and level and close to the sea.

Divisional Command had ordered two weeks' complete rest for all units. Duties to be kept to an irreducible minimum. It was a pleasant two weeks. We swam in the warm waters of the Med, relaxing on the sandy beach. There was time also for those personal chores like washing clothes, repairing uniforms and darning socks. The mail caught up with us finally at Misurata so writing letters home became a priority.

Early June brought news of an important impending parade. There was a sudden availability of khaki drill shirts and shorts. Boots had to be polished and even blanco became fashionable to restore the appearance of webbing belts. Grumbling rose from the normal average to a shrill crescendo. Questions and enquiries became numerous. Where was this parade? What idiot would dare ask men who have soldiered from Alamein to Tunis to polish boots and starch shirts? Warrant Officers were tight lipped and non-committal. Senior NCOs were obviously no better informed than the rank and file. The regimental noticeboard was scrutinized daily and even hourly. The news broke on or about 15th June. Fourth Indian Division was to be inspected and reviewed by His Majesty King George VI.

The date of the review had been set for 18th June 1943. It would be held in Tripoli. The average British soldier took his share of royalty with nonchalance and the familiar 'who cares' attitude. However, to our Indian troops, this was the most important day of their military careers.

On the morning of 18th June the division formed up, in brilliant sunshine. The Royal Regiment of Artillery enjoyed its traditional place of honour on the 'Right of the Line.' It was a scene reminiscent of the best of pre-war military pomp and ceremony.

Subedar Narinder Singh of 4th Field Company, Sappers and Miners and Subedar-Major Narbahadur Gurung were both introduced to His Majesty. He also presented the Victoria Cross to Subedar Lalbahadur Thapa, hero of the Battle of Wadi Akarit.

Later that evening, in the NAAFI, Jack Parker and I drank tea with a group of Gurkha infantrymen of 1/2 Gurkhas. The presentation of the Victoria Cross by the King Emperor to one of their own had made

108

a deep impression. They told us that the events of that day would be told to their children and grandchildren and passed on to their great grandchildren. Their only regret was that so many fallen comrades had not lived to witness this great honour. They dismissed their own accomplishments as merely doing their duty, but were effusive in their praise for our artillery support. A soldier could never ask for a more loyal friend than Johnny Gurkha: neither would he fear a more deadly enemy.

There was considerable disappointment throughout the division when it was learned that we would not participate in the Sicily Campaign. The formations to be used in the Sicily landings had long since been withdrawn from the Tunisian Campaign. They were currently undergoing extensive training and re-equipping. Fourth Indian Division would return to Egypt and the Delta.

Elements of the division began moving east on 22nd June. A few days later the 11th Field Regiment rolled out of Misurata on the coast road. We took up the now familiar line of march: Regimental HQ in the lead, followed by 78/84 Battery, then 83/85 Battery with the Light Aid Department bringing up the rear. By this time our transport was well below strength. We were reduced to only two vehicles in the survey party – one jeep and one 15-cwt Chevvy. Sergeant Watts took the jeep and I rode the Chevvy.

We rolled east, every day enveloped in the burning June sunshine and the dust. With our backs to the Tunisian battlefields we said goodbye to the rich fertile agricultural settlements of Tripolitania. Entering the dusty desert of the Libyan Plateau, we passed through Agheila, Benghazi, Cyrene, Derna and Torimi. Looking south into the dancing desert heat-haze, I fancied I could see British Valentine tanks, outgunned by the German Panzers, fighting a desperate but losing battle.

There too were the 25-pounders, gunners stripped to the waist, barrels horizontal, breech-blocks burning holding back the advancing panzers. Then, floating on the winds of the *khamseen*, came the shouts of the Aussie infantrymen and the war cries of the New Zealand Maoris as they charged the enemy behind the long British bayonet. All that now remained was the rusting hulk of the occasional derelict tank relieving the monotony of the desert landscape.

We passed Tobruk. Once it had been the symbol of Eighth Army resistance to the Afrika Korps. Now it stood, quiet and peaceful, its bullet-chipped white plaster buildings reflecting the rays of the setting sun. Two days later we skirted the battlefield of Mersa Matruh.

Exactly one year ago we had terminated our forced march from Iraq in this area. One year ago: it seemed a lifetime, so many experiences and so many good men no longer with us.

We came to El Alamein for the last time. From the high ground of Tel El Eisa the saddleback at Ruweisat Ridge could easily be identified. Ruweisat Ridge, where in the first week of July 1942 Rommel's panzers finally foundered against the guns of the 11th Field Regiment. It now lay quiet and deserted. Even the spirits of the Alamein dead had fled this parched and barren wasteland.

On 7th July our long and nostalgic journey from Misurta came to an end. On a hot and humid afternoon we arrived back in the Delta and set up camp. Once again we slipped into the daily round and common task of a life that seemed to be evenly split between the spit and polish of peacetime soldiering and the exigencies of active service.

We followed the progress of the Sicilian Campaign, wishing we were there. We cursed the heat and humidity of the Delta and we cursed the eternal flies. We railed against authority and the perceived stupidity of our commanders. We wrote letters to home and tried to drown our exasperation in gallons of strong hot tea.

It might be noted that at this time over 70 per cent of the regiment had not seen England, home or family for over four years. The war had stopped the normal recycling of personnel between the UK and overseas military stations. Many of us had lost close family in the savage German bombing of London and other areas in 1940 through 1943. Leaves, when available, were strictly local. The hard-pressed British Middle East Command, with transportation space at a premium, was forced to harden its heart to consideration of leave to the UK. Even applications for compassionate leave were moved to the back burner. It was the way of the war.

It was about this time that the rare arrival of a selection of British newspapers triggered a wave of anger and deep resentment throughout the regiment. It was an anger that, were it not for the restraining power of British military discipline, might even have initiated a minor mutiny. The *Daily Mirror*, a London tabloid, carried a front page picture of a group of Canadian servicemen arm in arm with a number of English girls sitting at a table in a dance hall. The table was exhibiting unmistakable evidence of alcoholic refreshments. It is not known if the matter was brought to the attention of our CO Lieutenant Colonel Howell, but from that date on British newspapers were no longer available.

The Sicilian Campaign came to an end on 17th August. Once again, as at Alamein, the German commander successfully withdrew the bulk of his forces. Complete victory had again eluded Montgomery.

In early September the regiment became the recipient of a series of invitations from a wealthy Egyptian businessman. The invitations were properly directed to the CO. They requested the pleasure of the company of six other ranks to include junior NCOs to dinner at his estate near Alexandria. Officers and senior NCOs were excluded from these invitations. I placed my name on the list of applications, along with Jack Parker.

Two weeks later, dressed in immaculate khaki drill, our group of six men arrived at the imposing entrance to our host's estate in the early afternoon. The initial air of mystery that had surrounded these invitations had by now been dispelled. Our host, an Egyptian and a Moslem, had been educated in England at Oxford and the London School of Economics. In addition to Arabic he spoke fluent English and French. His sympathies in regard to the war were firmly behind the Allies. This was in sharp contrast to many of his wealthy contemporaries who made no secret of their Nazi support. He claimed that his hospitality represented his small contribution to the Allied war effort.

Following the winding driveway, we passed between palm trees, manicured shrubs and formal flower borders, arriving at the front entrance. The house was a magnificent white stucco residence, modelled in the style of a French château. Uniformed servants appeared and we where shown in through the main entrance hall into a large reception room. I was reminded of the formal drawing rooms in the old Dublin Georgian houses. It was decorated and luxuriously furnished in the European style. The French accent was unmistakable.

Our host was waiting for us and came forward as we were shown in. He was a tall man, broad shoulders and without the pot belly one often sees in Egyptians of his class. His mouth, broad and generous, revealed very white teeth. He had a long prominent nose, dark eyes and was clean-shaven. Although dressed in a European lounge suit, he acknowledged his Egyptian nationality by wearing a red fez. He greeted each one of us with a firm handshake. We introduced ourselves by giving our rank, name and regiment as per instructions from our RSM, covering deportment and behaviour. We were served with iced fruit drinks which were definitely non-alcoholic. Our host informed us that all the facilities of the estate were available for our use. These included an Olympic-size outdoor swimming pool, tennis courts, a miniature golf course and riding stables. Servants would be available to assist us. He then took his leave, saying he would join us for dinner at 7 p.m.

Jack and I made our way to the stables. A groom saddled and bridled two horses, giving us detailed advice on how to handle a horse. His relief was evident when we mounted and he noted we had some equestrian experience. After a pleasant ride around the estate we returned our mounts to a grateful groom. Finding the remaining four members of our party in the swimming pool, we joined them. A servant brought us swim shorts and towels. It seemed our host thought of everything.

We enjoyed an excellent meal in an imposing dining room. As I appraised the silver, cut glass, expensive china and table linen, I was reminded of a scene from the *Arabian Nights*. It would have been difficult to construct a more vivid contrast: from desert dust and flies, McConachies stew and tea laced liberally with petrol to the extreme heights of European cuisine and service.

After dinner we joined our host in the library for drinks and cigars. I noted our host neither smoked nor consumed alcohol. Over a bottle of genuine pre-war Johnnie Walker scotch, we slipped easily into conversation.

Complying with instructions not to discuss military matters was made easy by our host: he obligingly led the discussion into comparisons between Western and Middle East cultures. Sipping from a glass of soda water, he made a point. 'Take, for example, the institution of marriage. I believe we are well ahead of Western practice,' he stated with a faint smile.

Jack cut in immediately. 'I don't see how you can say that when you take four wives and we devote our lives to one.'

Our host smiled and replied, 'Ah, the idealism of youth. It would seem you have a point but consider – when the Western bride says

'I do' at the altar and signs her name, she has signed a contract, because that is what it is. By your own admission, this contract is for life without reservations or conditions of any kind. With only two words and a signature, she has agreed, for life mind you, to love and obey her husband, to look after his emotional and material wants, to bear his children, to bring them up, to comfort and to nurture them, and to look after and be responsible for the multitude of duties associated with running a household. Finally, to be available when needed and to be out of the way when her presence might be inconvenient. Now all this without any commitment from the husband in regard to remuneration.'

'There may be some truth in what you say,' Jack replied, 'but your people have to be even worse because the Middle East husband would inflict all this misery on four wives.'

Our host looked at us patiently and said, 'We may have a slight misunderstanding here. Moslem law, it is true, allows a man to have four wives, but only if he can afford to keep them in a manner relative to their station in life. For example, when the young Moslem businessman asks a lady to be his wife, she would enquire as to how many wives he can afford to keep. If he replied that his salary would only permit one wife, she would likely refuse to be made a slave, unless, of course, his future prospects were good.'

"What you are saying is that the Moslem girl can exercise free choice,' I cut in.

'The English, French or American girl has the same freedom of choice, so what does that prove?'

'Well, we really cannot prove anything, but gentlemen, you will agree that the right to have four wives would act as a powerful stimulant to success. In addition, the chores of the household are shared. This alone is an improvement over the Western system. Finally, the Moslem system allows a wife to employ her skills in a selected area of personal interest.'

We were not prepared to make any concession on an issue where we considered we were defending the superiority of Western civilization.

Jack said doggedly, 'There is no way you could persuade a Western wife to share her husband with another woman, let alone three.'

'I am sure you are right in that respect,' rejoined our host. 'And maybe that is one of the reasons why married infidelity and your divorce rate is much higher than ours.'

113

He obviously enjoyed making his final point, but we felt we had at least earned a draw.

After sincere expressions of thanks and appreciation, we took leave of our host. As we rolled away, following the winding driveway, Jack seemed pensive. Finally he turned to me and posed a question. 'In all the time we were there, did you notice anything unusual?'

I replied in the negative.

'Not once in all the time we spent on the property did we see a woman.'

It was an interesting fact and possibly the explanation was related to Moslem customs. We never found out.

Field training intensified and early October brought the news that the 4th Indian Division had commenced reassembling in the Delta preparatory to divisional training. On 14th October we pulled out of the Delta en route to Syria. Three weeks of mountain training with the division in the Lebanon lay ahead of us. Four days' line of march through the Sinai Peninsula and Palestine brought us into the selected training area. It was evident that the games of summer were now over.

We knew by now that we were moving back into action. Italy seemed the obvious answer but, as we were an Indian Division, a strong case could be made for a move to Burma where the situation was critical. There was, of course, the outside chance of being sent back to Northern Iraq. About this time the regimental rumour mill produced one of its classics. It went as follows: Winston Churchill, being highly suspicious of the post-war intentions of his friend and ally, Josef Stalin, with regard to Poland, had volunteered two British or Commonwealth divisions to fight on the Russian front. Fourth Indian Division would be one of these two divisions. We would move through Iraq and Iran, then north through the Caucasas and reinforce the Crimean front.

From information that became available after the war, the first part of this rumour was true. As to the second part, who knows? It remains an interesting line of conjecture if we use the question 'what if'?

Divisional training came to a successful conclusion in early November. On 4th November 11th Field Regiment commenced its trek back to Egypt, arriving in the Delta four days later. The Russian rumour was now put to bed by the news that we were going to Italy.

Preparations for our move proceeded at a hectic pace. We were

Above: Guns of 11th Field Regiment RA in action against 15th Panzer Division, 2 July 1942 on the Ruweisat Ridge. A painting by Cyril Mount

Left: General Sir Claude Auchinleck, Commander British Eighth Army, 1st Battle of Alamein. Copied from an original by Cyril Mount

Sgts Chamberlain and Turberfield relaying fire orders to the guns of 11th Field Regiment, R.A. 1st Battle of Alamein, July 1942

The 25-pounder gun-howitzer. Sgt Norman Noal and his detachment in Tunisia. April 1943

Capt L. Boyd R.A., 83/85 Battery at El Alamein, July 1942

A 25 pounder of 83/85 Battery which saw action in the 1st and Final Battles of El Alamein, now in the Imperial War Museum

11th Field Regiment. Observation Post on the Ruweisat Ridge, Alamein. Knocked-out Stuart tank in foreground. October 1942. By Cyril Mount.

11th Field Regiment. Observation Post on the Ruweisat Ridge, Alamein. Early morning tea. October 1942. By Cyril Mount.

Left: grave of an unknown British soldier on the shore of Alamein. September 1942

Below: British humour at Alamein, courtesy 51st Highland Division. November 1942

After Alamein. German Mark IV Panzer with 75mm gun. November 1942

After Alamein. British Sherman tank. November 1942

After Alamein. Italian 105mm field gun. November 1942

Sgt Burrows and two of his detachment, 83/85 Battery, R.A. November 1942

View of the front from an 11th Field Regiment Observation Post. July 1942. By Cyril Mount

Life in the desert. The summer of 1942 at El Alamein by Cyril Mount

brought up to our full war strength of 24 guns by the addition of a third battery, 187. Equipment and vehicles were replaced as necessary. Personnel, both commissioned and other ranks, were posted to the regiment. About this time Sergeant Watts left the regiment. His departure presented me with the opportunity for promotion to i/c Regimental Survey Party. However, in the absence of an officer, this position would justify the rank of sergeant and base was awash in surplus sergeants. The matter was settled before the end of November when Sergeant Tug Wilson was posted to the regiment and interposted to RHQ i.c. Regimental Survey Party.

I took an immediate liking to Sergeant Wilson. He was quiet and unassuming but efficient and conscientious. Over the following months we developed a satisfying relationship based on mutual trust and respect. At the end of November 1943 we rolled out of Royal Artillery Base Depot for the last time, completing the short journey north to Port Said the same day. The loading of guns, transport and equipment commenced immediately. On 3rd December 4th Indian Division, including divisional artillery, completed embarkation.

The convoy, under British naval escort, was scheduled to sail that night. A crisis developed on our ship when the firemen threw down their shovels and went on strike. The situation was both difficult and delicate. There was the very real danger of the strike spreading throughout the convoy. After a conference with the ship's officers, our CO called for volunteers from the ranks to stoke the boilers. There was an enthusiastic response from gunners and drivers of the 11th Field Regiment.

Our convoy sailed on schedule. The voyage was uneventful in spite of several threatening approaches by German aircraft. Four days after leaving Port Said, the high cone of Mount Etna was seen on the horizon and on 9th December we sailed into the Gulf of Taranto in southern Italy. Under overcast skies and a cold driving rain from the north west, we dropped anchor in Taranto Harbour.

The 11th Field Regiment had arrived in Italy.

9   WELCOME TO ITALY

Early on the morning of 10th December, standing on one of the lower decks of the ship, I viewed the Italian landscape. I was not impressed. In my mind the southern European coastline bordering the Mediterranean Sea was associated with sunshine, warmth and luxury. It was here that the gentry and the wealthy from Britain and northern Europe came, before the war, to escape the miserable, damp, cold winters. It was here that they could bask in the sunshine and winter warmth of the French and Italian Rivieras and the Greek islands.

The weather could hardly be much worse. It was cold and wet and the raw blustery wind out of the north stung the skin with iced rain drops. Visibility was limited and it was with difficulty that I could discern the opaque outline of Mount Etna. This was our welcome to Italy. The contrast with the warm winter sunshine we had left behind us in Egypt was stark, real and demoralizing. I was filled with foreboding for the future.

We disembarked later that day and moved into a temporary camp: some military humourist had placed the regimental camp in groves of olive trees.

A few days later we moved to the town of Pietrogalla, setting up camp in the high ground surrounding the town. It was wild, cheerless, broken country with few redeeming features: an almost unending vista of starved grass, rocks and stunted shrubs.

We began light training, designed more to occupy the time and maintain morale than to sharpen skills. Unloading and assembling the immense amount of divisional transport, weaponry and stores was proceeding at Taranto. Sergeant Tug Wilson and two gunners were detailed to return to the port to recover and bring to Pietrogalla regimental survey party transport and equipment.

The standard War Department one-man bivouac, issued originally in Egypt, took on a new significance. We had ignored them in the Middle East and North Africa, preferring to sleep under the stars. There were valid reasons for this rejection. The first probably was the bother and time involved in erecting the damn thing. More important, however, was the ingrained psychology of desert warfare: the combination of mobility, surprise, fast advances and even faster withdrawals maintained a constant readiness for surprise. To be caught unprepared by an enemy surprise attack was bad enough, but the ultimate horror was to be overrun while tangled in your bivvy without your pants! We had become accustomed to sleeping on open ground, fully dressed, making the one concession to civilized living by removing boots.

However, in the middle of an Italian winter with the northern winds coming off the snow-capped peaks of the Appenines, the Army issue bivvy assumed a new meaning. Some practice revealed how fast this little abortion could be erected. We found it was surprisingly well designed. The bivvy was six feet long, about three and one half feet high and just wide enough for one man. It was supported by two poles, each of which were constructed in two interlocking sections for ease of packing and was equipped with its own built-in ground sheet. In the absence of experience in utilizing the bivvy under European winter conditions, we resorted to trial and error. As always, experience is the best teacher. My final solution to the problem of maintaining maximum heat with protection from the elements was as follows: erect bivvy, lay ground sheet out flat, make up bed, interlocking the three army issue blankets to get three layers underneath the body, lay greatcoat lengthwise over the bed, tucking in the sides, finally lace up ground sheet with string (it was equipped with holes for this purpose). All this had to be done on hands and knees. If there was no snow on the ground it was easier to carry out the chore outside, then draw it carefully inside the bivvy. Getting inside this creation was, in itself, a triumph of physical dexterity. The limited height allowed only enough space for a sit-up position and little room for the removal of clothing. Regardless of weather conditions, we undressed outside the bivvy, then, with uniform neatly folded, we crawled inside.

117

Pants and jacket were placed for a pillow with a boot either side, then carefully one inched down into bed, drawing up the two ends of string under the chin. The bottom line of this military masterpiece was never, but never, be caught short in the middle of the night.

We spent Christmas of 1943 at Pietrogalla. In spite of the many limitations imposed by location and weather conditions, a gallant effort was made by Lieutenant (QM) A.G. Gough RA and our RQMS to provide Christmas cheer. New Year dawned with a forecast of worsening weather conditions.

Having now reoriented to the Italian Campaign from the Middle East, the current military situation became of more than passing interest. There were actually two separate fronts in the Italian Campaign, divided by the high mountain range of the Appenines. On the western side of this range, the Fifth Army, commanded by General Mark Clark, having occupied Naples in October, had reached the German Gustav Line where its west end was anchored on Monte Cassino. At the east end of this line, on the Adriatic Front, the Eighth Army, still commanded by Montgomery, had bumped the Gustav Line at Ortona and Orsogna. The overall direction of the Italian Campaign was controlled by Field Marshal Sir Harold Alexander. Shortly after we arrived Field Marshal Sir Bernard Montgomery was recalled to England to prepare for the opening of the Second Front under General Eisenhower. This was expected to open some time in 1944.

On 3rd January an unfortunate accident occurred. In a theatre of war, where men were being killed and wounded every day, it would be easy to trivialize this incident. Such was not the case. A 15-cwt truck of 78/84 Battery grazed a school gateway, dislodging a concrete pillar. The pillar crashed into the roadway, instantly killing two young Italian children. The chords of emotion initiated by this incident rippled through and saddened every man in the regiment. Those two children were so very young and innocent, victims of a conflict over which they had no control and no understanding. Their sudden and violent death came to symbolize to many of us all the Italian children who had suffered and would suffer because of the war in their country.

On 5th January we were hit by a major snowfall which developed into blizzard conditions. Vehicles were snowed in as the fierce winds built up massive drifts. Major Clements made an effort to convert a couple of tractors to snow ploughs but they too became bogged down in the snow. Eventually we fell back on manpower. Every man that could be spared from essential duties, regardless of rank or trade, was pressed into service. Shovels of all types were produced. The regimental sergeant major assumed overall command of the operation. Under the demanding direction of the battery sergeant majors we eventually dug ourselves out and cleared necessary roadways.

We were to endure many more snowstorms during the mountain warfare of the Italian Campaign in the winter of 1943–44. However, this particular snowfall administered our baptism by snow and, almost overnight, converted us into winter warfare veterans.

We were now under orders to move forward to occupy gun positions opposite the Gustav Line in the general area of Lanciano. Maintenance on vehicles, guns, and equipment was accelerated. The weather turned mild with the sun fighting furiously to penetrate the dense cloud cover that had persisted since we had landed in Italy. The warmer temperatures melted the snow, breaking the frost in the ground. We were now introduced to mud, the gunner's nightmare.

On 13th January we moved out, taking the road to Lanciano. The regimental and battery recce parties had preceded our move by one day. Reaching Urari about 16.00 hours, we laid over for the night, pushing on the next morning and arriving in Lanciano. Lanciano appeared to have escaped the more serious depredations of warfare and was fairly intact. Apparently it had not fitted into the German defensive plans for the Gustav Line. With the withdrawal of Italy from the war and her eventual capitulation the Axis Powers no longer existed.

The 7th Indian Infantry Brigade relieved the 5th New Zealand Brigade near Orsogna in a sector running down to the Avielli River. Four days later, the 5th Indian Infantry Brigade led by 1/4 Essex took up front line positions to the right of the 7th Brigade.

At 15.00 hours on 15th January 78/84 and 187 Batteries reported zero lines recorded and guns in action. The next day at 14.00 hours the same report came into RHQ from 83/85 Battery. On this date the guns of 78/84 and 187 Batteries fired the opening rounds by the 11th Field Regiment in the Italian Campaign. These first shoots were under the OP direction of Captain F.R. Miles RA who had been our survey officer in July and August 1942 at El Alamein. We were now supporting 1/2 Gurkhas and 1st Royal Sussex.

For the next six days we were involved in a major attack in the Orsogna sector. The attack was mounted by the 4th Indian Division and the 11th Canadian Brigade. Under heavy overcast skies, intermittent rain squalls and driving cold winds, the infantry advanced yard by yard and house by house in the ruins of the town. Again and again they were forced to give ground to the stubborn defenders and again they regrouped and moved forward. Often they were led by NCOs who had taken command when their officers were killed or wounded. It was house to house fighting and often attackers and defenders grappled in hand to hand combat to retain possession of a single floor. The Canadians were the acknowledged masters of this type of fighting. Italian downtown housing resembled the British system – wall to wall terrace style. The Canadians, having seized control of one house, would place a charge of explosive in the wall on an upper floor. After the explosion tore the wall open they would rush through the hole, using the bayonet on the survivors. Our Gurkhas, who liked close fighting, developed an affinity for this type of warfare but used the *kukri* instead of the bayonet.

Controlled by our OP officers working closely with forward infantry units, we brought down harassing fire on a wide variety of enemy targets throughout this attack. Sometimes we were supporting our own infantry, sometimes we were supporting the Canadians; often we were called to participate in a divisional fire plan under the direction of the CRA and 78/84 Battery carried out a number of shoots under the direction of the Air OP. These were declared successful. We had been introduced to this form of fire control in Tunisia and our initial shoots were something less than satisfactory. Practice in Syria had sharpened our skills and improved our technique.

Another nationality was now added to the wide variety of races and ethnic origins in the Italian Campaign. A Polish division moved into the Orsogna-Ortona sector in January. Their CRA, with his intelligence officer and an interpreter, came to visit with our CO. This meeting was followed by visits by Polish officers, NCOs and gunners to our command posts and gun positions. They were always accompanied by an interpreter because, with few exceptions, they spoke little or no English. They were obviously well-trained and their questions displayed a mastery of the art of field gunnery and its relation to infantry support.

I was particularly impressed by their friendliness towards us, which appeared to be over and above the usual camaraderie between allies in arms.

One day, whilst explaining our survey operations to an English-speaking Polish NCO, I posed a question in the form of a statement. 'Most of your chaps seem very friendly.'

He was a tall, good-looking man with a Douglas Fairbanks moustache and sombre, thoughtful eyes. He looked directly at me and smiled. 'We haven't forgotten that it was Britain and, of course, France that declared war on Germany when Hitler invaded Poland in 1939,' he said quietly.

'A fat lot of good that was to you – you were overrun anyway,' I replied.

'Ah! But you did take that action and we cannot forget.' He paused and continued. 'London is the home of our Polish Government in Exile and, as such, we are the guests of your British Government.'

'That's no big deal,' I said. 'London right now is home to half a dozen European governments in exile.'

He laughed in a good-natured fashion. 'We Polish soldiers without a country have been supported, trained and equipped by the British Government. My battledress is British, our guns are British.' He gazed out over the Appenines in a northerly direction and went on, 'Only with the help of Britain and the United States can we hope to return to a free Poland, providing they get there before the Russians'. He looked back at me and said, 'Now you understand our friendliness and gratitude towards Britain and British troops.'

After sharing a final mug of tea my friend expressed his thanks for my assistance and left. His name I have unfortunately forgotten. I can only hope that he survived the war and returned to his beloved Poland.

The offensive on the Adriatic Front was slowly grinding to a halt to be followed by the inevitable stalemate. Although our infantry had battled to the limit of human endurance and beyond, there comes a time when a wise commander knows by instinct when the time has arrived to call a halt. It never makes sense to sacrifice the lives of brave and highly trained men in a hopeless cause. Eighth Army commanders at all levels had good reason never to underestimate the bravery and fighting qualities of the German soldiers. However, they had miscalculated both the strength and the depth of the enemy defences at Ortona and Orsogna.

In late January we established liaison with 11th Canadian Brigade. Major A. Duncan RA commanding 187 Battery, established an OP in the area of the Irish Regiment of Canada. The infantry had now switched to a defensive role but maintained vigorous patrolling activity. Artillery action continued, mainly harassing fire tasks.

The rain continued, sometimes changing into wet snow or freezing rain. The latter phenomenon came as a shock to most of us. It was a new experience. Our Canadian friends claimed the weather reminded them of home. They were quite familiar with freezing rain!

Then there was the mud. Continuing traffic in the gun position area had churned up the ground and converted the area to a sticky, gooey mess. Clay soils are probably similar all over the world. Italian clay seemed to be able, under the right conditions, to develop its own peculiar and patented brand of stickiness. Bringing ammunition up to the guns became a major chore. Even tractors were unable to handle the problem. We fell back on manpower. It was a heavy back-breaking job. After completing a spell at this awful chore one day, those First World War pictures of Flanders mud passed before my eyes. I could see those poor bloody infantrymen carrying over 50 lb of equipment, slogging painfully through that awful mud. I could almost smell the sweat, feel the exhaustion and hear the panting agony of artillerymen manhandling their guns behind straining six-horse teams as they sunk lower and lower in that Flanders muck.

Finally, there was the damp. It was penetrating, it was persistent and it was capable of finding its way through all forms of clothing. It paused when it reached the skin and then moved into the bones. We lived, moved and had our being in a state of perpetual dampness. One could lie down in a cloying sensation of cold damp and awake in the pleasurable stickiness of warm damp. The only antidote was tea taken very hot, strong and sweet. About this time the RQMS decided to break out the rum ration, which, of course, went into the tea. Now I have never been able to develop an interest in liquor and of all liquors, rum had to be the vilest. It is even worse than Greek ouzo, Middle East arak or Irish potheen. Although I had no quarrel with those who liked the wretched stuff (after all we were fighting to defend democracy), why should good tea be ruined by adding rum?

The news that the 4th Indian Division had been ordered out of the Ortona-Orsogna sector and would cross the mountains to Cassino came as no surprise. Rumours had been circulating through the gun positions for several days.

Tug Wilson came to me one day with a bulky package of maps and suggested we retire to the shelter of the survey equipment truck. As we pored over the maps in the weak light of a hurricane lamp we gradually came to appreciate the overall picture of the Italian Front, from the Tyrrhenian Sea north of Naples to the Adriatic Sea near Ortona. With the information in our possession we were able to mark in the German Gustav or Winter Line and approximately the Allied positions. It was not a pleasant picture.

Italy represents a long, relatively narrow, neck of land jutting out from the European mainland into the Mediterranean Sea in roughly a south-easterly direction. A dorsal range of mountains, the Appenines, runs down the centre, forming a barrier rising to heights of from 2500 to 6000 feet. From this central spine a series of mountain blocks radiate laterally like the bones of a fish towards the coast on either side. Between these lateral ridges, there are deep valleys and rivers. The Gustav Line crossed Italy at its narrowest part and through its most mountainous region. The eastern half was anchored securely in the Maiellas, a mountain range which ran down to within a few miles of the Adriatic coast. In the west the German defence line followed a mountain range shown on the maps as the Aruncis, a towering mountain block which terminated at the Monte Cassino massif.

Monte Cassino was about 40 miles north of Naples and 70 miles south, south east of Rome. The road to Rome was Route 6. This route, after leaving Naples, passed around and to the north of Monte Trocchio, then, crossing the Rapido River, it went straight into the town of Cassino, situated at the base of Monte Cassino. It then detoured around the mountain, forming a half circle before continuing direct to Rome. There was an alternative road in the form of Route 7. This road crossed the Pontine marshes, reaching Rome along the foreshore. It passed through the low-lying marshes that were criss-crossed with canals and was built up above the marsh level. It crossed numerous bridges. From a military viewpoint, Route 7 was considered impassable; a few blown bridges and the road was useless. Route 6, running through firm terrain on either side, was the obvious choice. It was, however, under the constant observation of the enemy, firmly settled on Monte Cassino, 2000 feet above. Nothing could move on

Route 6 north of Monte Trocchio, across the Rapido valley, without being detected by German observers. Monte Cassino represented the classic example of domination of surrounding terrain by height.

Our survey experience enabled us to read these maps accurately and vividly. This was Garci in Tunisia, only twice as high, and many times more difficult. The enemy was successful at Garci, forcing the Allies to switch their main drive to Tunis to Medjez El Bab. There was no alternative on the road to Rome.

Even as orders came down to gun position officers to prepare to come out of action, the regimental recce party, with battery representatives, was on its way across the mountains to Monte Cassino. We understood that our Polish friends would be covering our withdrawal. We came out of action early in the morning of the last day of January. Gunners struggled in the sticky mud to limber up behind the tractors. Gun platforms, assisted by wide diameter tyres, minimized the problem but back-breaking manpower was still necessary. In many instances detachments were obliged to resort to winching. As the last gun was hooked to its limber the grey black clouds, scudding from over the mountains, slowly parted to reveal dashes of clear blue sky. Soon afterwards we were bathed in warm morning sunshine. Was it an omen for good fortune or a tantalizing invitation to disaster?

The regiment pulled out at 10.30 hours. It was a slow and torturous line of march. The road through the mountain passes was narrow and in poor repair. It curved and twisted, rose and fell in a dizzy fashion. At times it almost came back on itself in order to get over a sharp elevation. As we ascended we moved out of the pleasant sunshine and into low cloud which eventually submerged the column in damp mist. Several short halts were made for the usual reasons, but it became evident that we were under orders to push on. The 2nd New Zealand Division had preceded us by several days and the 78th British Division would soon be moving along the same route. Reaching our staging area on the San Severo-Lucera road, we parked for the night.

The continuous pattern of active service month in and month out without any relief, produced its own form of monotony. It was a monotony that looked desperately for any incident, no matter how trivial, that might provide relief, even if only temporary. Such an incident took place that evening.

News got around that Lieutenant (QM) A.G. Gough RA and a number of gunners, including NCOs, would be leaving the regiment on route to Foggia. They had been posted to the Home Establishment. The normal 'recycling' of regular soldiers in the British Army, who had completed their six years with the colours, had been terminated by the declaration of war in 1939. Consequently, many men had served over six years abroad without any form of home leave. They had seen almost continuous action for two years, from El Alamein to Cassino. Now they were returning to England, to Scotland, to Wales and even to Ireland; returning to family and to friends and could look forward to at least 28 days' leave. We were happy for them but sad to lose them. The bonds of friendship forged over many years, the sharing of hardships and danger would now be broken.

This event also presented many men with the opportunity to pass letters and messages to relatives and girlfriends at home, avoiding the scrutiny of the censor. Strictly illegal, of course, but it was done.

There was a party that evening and the wine flowed freely. Officers and warrant officers turned a blind eye and discreetly faded into the darkness. There are times when a smart CO will close the book on King's Rules and Regulations.

After another night's halt at Cancello we arrived at our immediate destination, the Divisional Artillery Concentration Area at Baia E Latino. We were about 25 miles north of Naples and 75 miles from Rome. As we moved into our allotted space in the concentration area the rain started again. It came slowly and deceptively, like an Irish drizzle coming from over the Connemara Mountains, then gradually increasing to a steady downpour. RHQ transport, blessed with reasonably firm ground, skidded wildly from side to side but were able to park without incident. Then came the guns. As the senior battery 78/84 came in first. As drivers engaged four-wheel drive and low gear, crawling and ploughing their way through deepening mud to their parking area, the ground was churned into a muddy morass. Most of the guns of the other two batteries were forced to unlimber and winch both limbers and guns into their parking areas. The rain changed to a wet snow as darkness fell, blotting out the whole miserable scene.

10   MONTE CASSINO (1)

Extending southwards from the Appenines were the Aruncis. Projecting from the Appenines, they ran to the coast, reaching the sea north of the Garigliano River and about 70 miles south of Rome. After rising to a height of over 5000 feet at Monte Cairo, the Aruncio projected to a spur at Monte Cassino, the central bastion of the Gustav Line.

The Cassino spur appeared to rise vertically from the plain below to a height of 1700 feet. It was a limestone block, a monstrous conglomeration of jagged stone, boulder strewn hog's backs and V-shaped ravines jutting out from the main range in a southerly direction. On the west side it dominated the Liri valley and on the other the Rapido Valley. The command of Monte Cassino over these two valleys and the road to Rome from the south has been likened to the control of the Strait of Gibraltar by the Rock.

Route 6 from Naples, after passing around Monte Trocchio and crossing the Rapido River, runs into the town of Cassino at the foot of the mountain. It then swings left, forming a rough semi-circle around the massif before entering the Liri valley and heading towards Rome.

Over the centuries since the birth of Christ, Monte Cassino has been the focal point of wars centred upon either the defence or the conquest of the Eternal City. It was seized by the Lombards in the seventh century and figured prominently in the Napoleonic Wars.

Nothing could move in this area without being detected by German observers on Monte Cassino. In a matter of seconds they could bring down accurate and devastating artillery fire.

The Allied Fifth Army, commanded by General Mark Clark, after landing at Salerno in early September, had battled their way north against fierce enemy resistance. They had entered Naples on 1st October. After crossing the Volturno River they had run into the forward defences of the Gustav Lines in November. The Fifth Army was composed of the British 5th, 46th and 56th Divisions and the American 3rd and 36th. They had forced the Mignano Gap after prolonged and bloody fighting and had broken through the Bernhard-Gustav Line. In early January of 1944, three corps of Fifth Army stood on the Gustav Line proper. The Gustav Line, after crossing the Appenines from the Adriatic, followed the Rapido River on the west side. After being firmly anchored on Monte Cassino, it followed the course of the Garigliano River to the Tyrrhenian Sea.

A massive attack had been mounted by General Clark in January. On the left, British 5th and 56th Divisions were to attack across the Garigliano. In the centre, British 46th Division was to cross the Garigliano south of the confluence between the Liri and Garigliano River and on the right, US 36th Division were to cross the Rapido River south of Cassino. The French Expeditionary Corps were also under the command of General Mark Clark. General Juin, their commander, was instructed to fight his way across the Matese massif to the north of Monte Cassino.

Although 10th British Corps forced a small bridgehead across the Garigliano at terrible cost, American units that succeeded in crossing the Rapido were annihilated by murderous fire from the Cassino defences. A second assault was mounted by US 34th Division, supported by a regiment from the heavily depleted 36th Division. They succeeded in crossing the Rapido and secured a foothold on Monte Cassino north of the town. From these precarious positions the Americans made a series of determined attempts to sweep over and seize Monte Cassino by storm. For three long weeks the gallant infantrymen of the 34th battled their way across the face of Monte Cassino. Under constant enemy fire, lashed by the elements, soaked by almost continuous rain, they moved painfully into the mountains. They captured Monte Castellone and secured a tenuous hold on Snakeshead Ridge. They captured Hill 445 which brought them to within 400 yards of the summit of Monte Cassino. Although the Free French captured Monte Belvedere, fierce enemy counterattacks brought the advance to a halt.

127

Lieutenant Colonel Stevens, in his book *Fourth Indian Division*, describes the situation:

> 'After gallantry beyond all praise, the American assault petered out on the bare hillsides. The survivors of 34 US Division clung grimly to their hard-won ground, buffeted day and night by the elements and by the foe. They had done all that men can do.'

The casualties sustained by the Fifth Army were out of all proportion to achievements. British 10th Corps lost 4000 men. US 36th Division lost nearly 2000 men in the initial assault across the Rapido and the fighting on Monte Cassino cost US 34th Division over 2200 men.

On 22nd January the ill-conceived and poorly executed Fifth Army amphibious landings had been made at Anzio. They went nowhere and contributed nothing to the Italian Campaign. The Anzio adventure became, in time, a liability. Military planning and decisions from early February on were influenced by the necessity of relieving the Anzio bridgehead. Finally, it provided an excellent killing ground of Allied soldiers for General Von Mackensen, the German commander charged with containing the bridgehead. In four weeks total Allied losses at Anzio were nearly 20,000 men. On 4th February the newly-formed New Zealand Corps, commanded by General Freyberg, V.C., held a planning conference. The broad objective of the corps was to seize and reduce the Cassino fortress. Expressed in its simplest form, the 4th Indian Division was to attack Monte Cassino from the rear. The division would advance on a thrust line that ran roughly between Monte Castellone and the village of Villa San Lucia, deploying in the foothills of Monte Cairo. A New Zealand brigade would be placed in a holding capacity around the base of Monte Cassino. The 4th New Zealand Armoured Brigade would concentrate in the area of Monte Trocchio, ready to exploit any success and break into the Liri valley. The third division in the New Zealand Corps, 78th British Division, would remain in reserve. An important factor underlying the development of the plan was to avoid a direct frontal attack on Monte Cassino. However, all of the military jargon in the battle plans could not conceal the fact that Monte Cassino would continue to be the infantryman's nightmare – flesh and blood against concrete, steel, lead, impossible terrain, and the winter elements.

128

Our divisional commander, General Tuker, was known to be deeply concerned about the attack plans on Cassino. In his efforts to obtain information about Monte Cassino and the monastery in particular, he found that Fifth Army Intelligence was surprisingly ignorant. On 12th February General Tuker sent a report to General Freyberg. This letter [found in *Fourth Indian Division*] read as follows:

'1. After considerable trouble and investigating many bookshops in Naples, I have at last found a book dated 1879 which gives certain details of the construction of the Monte Cassino Monastery.

2. The Monastery was converted into a fortress in the 19th Century. The Main Gate has massive timber branched in a low archway, consisting of large stone blocks 9 to 10 metres long. This Gate is the only means of entrance to the Monastery.

3. The walls are about 15 feet high, or more where there are monks cells against the walls. The walls are of solid masonry and at least 10 feet thick at the base.

4. Since the place was constructed as a fortress as late as the 19th Century, it stands to reason that the walls will be suitably pierced for loopholes and will be battlemented.

5. Monte Cassino is, therefore, a modern fortress and must be dealt with by modern means. No practicable means available within the capacity of field engineers can possibly cope with this place. It can only be directly dealt with by applying blockbuster bombs from the air, hoping thereby to render the garrison incapable of resistance. The 1000 lb. bomb would be next to useless.

6. Whether the Monastery is now occupied by a German garrison or not, it is certain that it will be held as a keep by the last remnants of the garrison of the position. It is, therefore, also essential that the building should be so demolished as to prevent its effective occupation at that time.

7. I would ask that you would give me definite information at once as to how this fortress will be dealt with as the means are not within the capacity of this Division.

8. I would point out that it has only been by investigation on the part of this Division with no help from 'I' sources outside that we have got any idea as to what this fortress comprises, although the fortress has been a thorn in our side for many weeks.

When a formation is called upon to reduce such a place, it should be apparent that the place is reducible by the means at the disposal of that Division or that the means are ready for it without having to go to the bookstalls of Naples to find out what should have been fully considered many weeks ago.'

Additional information obtained by General Tuker was of historical interest, if not of military value. The original abbey was built in the sixth century by a monk who was the founder of the Benedictine Order. It was sacked in the sixth century by the Lombards. After being rebuilt early in the seventh century, it was again destroyed by the Saracens in AD 884. It was again reduced by invading German forces in the thirteenth century and was the scene of fierce fighting in the Napoleonic Wars. Although the monastery was converted to a fortress in the nineteenth century, it was subsequently returned to the Benedictine Order.

General Tuker was in poor health at this time. A medical problem had finally forced him to accept the inevitable – hospitalization. On 4th February he surrendered command of the 4th Indian Division to the CRA Brigadier Dimoline. The enormity of the loss to the division of this wise, experienced leader with his ability to persuade senior commanders to accept his points of view could never be calculated.

In a final desperate attempt to save his Indian infantrymen from the massacre he could see developing, he directed the following appreciation to the corps commander before he entered hospital:

'1. It is apparent that the enemy are in concrete and steel emplacements on Monastery Hill.

From a wide experience of attacks in mountain areas, I know that infantry cannot 'jump' strong defences of this sort in the mountain. These defences have to be 'softened up' either by being cut off on all sides and starved out or else by continuous and heavy bombardment over a period of days. Even with the latter preparation, success will only be achieved, in my opinion, if a thorough and prolonged air bombardment is undertaken with really heavy bombs a good deal larger than Kittybomber missiles.

2. We have complete air superiority in this theatre of war but the softening of the Monastery Hill has not been started.

An attack cannot be undertaken till this softening process is complete.

Already, three attacks have been put in and have failed – at some considerable cost. Another attack without air 'softening' will only lead

130

to a similar result. The Monastery feature is a far more formidable obstacle than Takrouna and resembles the higher part of Garci, which was rightly deemed inaccessible to infantry attack once initial surprise had passed. At Garci, the enemy was in field defences and not in concrete emplacements.

3. If proper air 'softening' is not possible, then the alternative remains: to turn Monastery Hill and to isolate it.

This course I regard to be possible as the enemy is, I believe, still only in field defences in the mountain areas to the west and southwest of Monte Castellone. Using Monte Castellone and the area now held by the U.S. II Corps as a firm base, we can attack in fast, short jabs to the west and southwest of Monte Castellone and cut No. 6 Highway west of Monastery Hill. With this and an attack on Cassino to keep that place quiet, the river can (I feel) be crossed lower down and the crossing joined up with the cutting from the north of No. 6 Highway, thus isolating Monastery Hill.

4. To go direct for the Monastery Hill now without 'softening' it properly is only to hit one's head straight against the hardest part of the whole enemy position and to risk the failure of the whole operation.'

General Tuker had hardly departed from the battlefield when the original plan of attack was changed. New Zealand Corps Operation Instruction No. 4, dated 9th February 1944, described the task of 4th Indian Division as: 'Attack and capture Point 593; exploit south to cut Highway 6 and capture Cassino from the west.'

The scene was set for the destruction of the 4th Indian Division.

The first week of February continued cold with prolonged periods of rain or wet snow. The regimental survey party had been given an assignment that involved observation of Monte Cassino. On 8th February the morning broke clear and sunny. I went forward with Sergeant Tug Wilson and two gunner-surveyors to the Monte Trocchio area. Monte Trocchio was a pyramidal mountain, rising from the Rapido plain to the height of over 1000 feet.

Locating the trig point, we set up a director and range-finder. Below us, Route 6 wound its way around the base of the mountain with the terrain rising to the north. To our north and about two miles away, was the village of San Michele. The Rapido River valley showed as a vast slash in the mountain mass of the Aruncis with the village of San Elia five miles distant. To the north west the 5000-foot peak of Monte

Cairo could just be detected through the receding morning mist. However, it was Monte Cassino, with Route 6 pointing like an arrow towards its heart, that drew our observation like a magnet. It riveted our attention. It rose up almost sheer from the flatness of the flooded Rapido plain. The famous Benedictine monastery was perched on the top like a constantly revolving eye that could see everything in all directions. In spite of the much higher feature of Monte Cairo commanding the distant landscape, it was the 2000-foot height of Monte Cassino that dominated the area and hypnotized the observer. Projecting south and east from the Aruncis, Monte Cassino and its 'eye' cast its own peculiar spell over the Allied troops in the vicinity.

At this distance Monte Cassino appeared to be bare and even but the powerful lens of the range-finder revealed a different picture. The feature was a combination of varying ridges with sharp crests falling into hollows of unknown depth. It was possible even at our range of 5000 yards to see huge rough boulders and follow the irregular course of rocky escarpments. The higher slopes were relieved by what appeared to be small farms. Some orchards were visible. As the range-finder was moved slowly upward a heavy growth of wild bush and tangled scrub appeared. Finally, the massive walls of the monastery showed clearly in the lens. Holding the instrument steady on an aperture in the wall, I knew instinctively that I was looking into the eyes of the enemy.

We had barely completed our measurements when a familiar whistle announced the arrival of an enemy shell. It exploded plus. Grabbing our equipment, we scrambled into a crevice in the area of the shellburst, knowing that the next round would fall minus. It did. Then we waited for the inevitable round of gunfire. It never came. Tug Wilson and I looked at each other and as if on cue we broke into laughter.

Tug said softly but with emphasis, 'The cunning bastard. That bloody OP officer watched us scrambling away from the high ground and decided to save his ammunition.'

It was a minor but nonetheless powerful demonstration of the observation advantages of Monastery Hill.

Battery recce parties were busy checking and marking gun positions. On 10th February we received orders to move into action. At 04.00 hours the next day RHQ 78/84 Battery and 187 Battery pulled out of the concentration area. The guns moved into action under the shadows of Monte Trocchio. The density of mud and the depth of soft ground caused by the extraction of the first two batteries reduced 83/85 Battery to immobility. Work was begun in preparing an alternative exit.

At 09.00 hours the following morning the enemy welcomed us to Cassino. We were shelled accurately and heavily. Sergeant Leavesley and Gunner Bailey were wounded. At 14.30 hours we were caught in the open excavating gunpits with another severe shelling. One gun of 'B' Troop 78/84 Battery took a direct hit. Sergeant Keable, Brigadier Boon, Gunner Hewetson and Gunner Goodey were killed. Lieutenant J.P. Walker and five gunners were wounded and evacuated.

Three hours later the race to be the first battery ready for action was won by 187 Battery when the GPO reported: 'One eighty-seven battery, ready to fire!'

They were soon followed by their sister battery: 'Seventy-eight, eighty-four battery, ready to fire!'

Soon afterwards 83/85 Battery arrived at the regimental gun area and went into action. They were forced to leave some of their vehicles in the mud of Baia E Latina. The wrecked gun of 'B' Troop was replaced and a new detachment was made up by blending reinforcements with more experienced gunners.

Early in the morning of 14th February an unusual message came in from HQRA 4th Indian Division. A truce had been arranged between local commanders from 08.00 to 11.00 hours in area of square 82.25 in order to allow both sides to bring in dead and wounded. The incident shed an interesting sidelight on what some old British militarists might have called a civilized or a gentlemen's war!

Captain R. Bentham RA was wounded by intense gunfire at his OP on Monte Cairo. He was evacuated but later returned to the regiment.

The question of whether to bomb the Benedictine monastery on Monte Cassino had become highly controversial. There were international overtones. In spite of the German commander's statements to the neutral press that they had not occupied the monastery, Allied Command thought otherwise. In addition, any infantryman who was ever called upon to fight his way across that murderous mountain firmly believed it was occupied by the enemy. In early February of 1944 the die was cast: the monastery would be bombed.

At 09.30 hours on 15th February the first wave of Flying Fortresses came over and dropped their blockbusters from 18,000 feet. After four groups of Fortresses completed their bomb run Mitchell bombers came over and bombed from 10,000 feet with greater accuracy. Twelve bombs from the Fortresses had fallen on 7th Indian Brigade area and four had landed in 1/2 Gurkha 'B' Echelon lines. Finally, at 13.30 hours, Mitchells and Maraurders completed the bombing of the famous monastery.

It was a terrible scene to witness. No civilized person with any love or respect for beautiful buildings, ancient art, antiquity or history could view the awful destruction of the monastery on Monte Casino in 1944 without deep feelings of sorrow, dismay and regret.

There were two interesting footnotes to the bombing of the monastery. The first was that in spite of the massive weight and number of bombs the monastery ruins were used by the enemy as a fortress until the very end. Major junior infantry officers will swear it was of more tactical use to the German defences after it was bombed. Secondly, the only entrance as described by General Tucker remained completely undamaged.

Under the revised plan of attack General Freyberg decided to strike at Monte Cassino with a frontal attack by his New Zealanders from south of the town of Cassino. Fourth Indian Division would attack from the rear, starting from the former American positions on the ridge crests 1500 yards to the west of the monastery.

Perfect gun positions did not exist at Cassino and good gun positions were rare. As a result, all corps artillery was concentrated in a relatively small area around Monte Trocchio. In addition, there was a number of American batteries which were providing us with added support. Space was so limited that in places guns were in action almost wheel to wheel. At this location the guns of the New Zealand Corps presented an ideal counter battery target to enemy artillery.

The corps artillery symphony commenced on the night of 16th February. The monastery was pounded plus selected registered targets. The concentration of artillery lit up Monte Trocchio like flickering flood lighting. Across the valley of the Rapido shells could be seen bursting on the monastery and on the slopes of Monte Cassino. Here and there a flash followed by a fire would mark where a house had been hit. Jerry sent up white flares rising continuously above the mountain: lines of tracer criss-crossed across the face of the mountain – it was 4th July, Victoria Day and Guy Fawkes Day all rolled into one. Then, filtering through the rolling thunder of the guns came the distant crackle of small arms fire as the infantry went in.

The 7th Indian Infantry Brigade had run into problems getting to their start line. Under observation by enemy OP officers the previous day they were shelled heavily in their assembly area. Their attack was set back by 24 hours. Eleventh Field Regiment had fired an average of 450 rounds per gun on the opening night of the attack. Throughout the next day we struggled to replenish stocks of ammunition. Tractors, risking enemy artillery fire, brought ammunition close to the gun positions but again it was manpower. Every man available, regardless of rank or trade, was pressed into service. It was becoming a familiar routine, a feature of field gunnery in the Italian Campaign opposite the Gustav Line.

That night we fired in support of the 7th Brigade. Around 02.00 hours a shell exploded against the breech ring of No. 3 Gun, 'F' Troop, 187 Battery. Of the six-man detachment, three gunners were killed instantly. The other three were wounded and evacuated.

Enemy counter-battery fire was quick and accurate. Two American eight-in. howitzers, located only 400 yards from our RHQ received direct hits. An ammunition pit took a direct hit and blew up with a tremendous roar. A signal vehicle, operating in the rear of our gun positions, was struck. Corporal Coates of the Royal Corps of Signals was killed with two Kiwi signallers. The remaining signaller was seriously wounded. RHQ was struck twice and Gunner Keddy was wounded. Another pasting was taken by 78/84 Battery. One gun sustained a direct hit and was put out of action. Fortunately, the detachment had dived for slit trenches and there were no casualties. The battery finally moved to a new position 22nd February. This almost continual shelling was taking its toll upon all ranks beyond actual casualties. Two gunners were evacuated with shell shock.

In the early morning of 14th February the 4th Indian Division had finally relieved the remnants of US 34th Division. They were in a pitiable condition. For over two weeks, under enemy fire by day, freezing by night, soaked by almost continuous rain, with little or no food, they had dug in and held their precious piece of Monte Cassino. It was a piece that had cost their division 80 per cent casualties. Of the equivalent of a British brigade, only 200 men had survived. Of this number, 50 men were so exhausted they had to be carried down the mountain on stretchers.

A major problem facing military planning in any assault on Monte Cassino was the constant tug-of-war between operational and administration demands. A fighting soldier needs a constant supply of three things: weapons and ammunition, food and drink and first aid or, if necessary, evacuation.

The truck head stopped far short of the battle positions: from there it was mules (there were over 1500 assembled for the New Zealand Corps assault on Monte Cassino), and/or portering with manpack. Over 80 per cent of all movements could be observed by the enemy. The threat of hostile harassing shelling hung over the Cassino mule tracks like a sword of Damocles.

It was finally decided that a brigade group would represent the maximum force that could be deployed and maintained for effective action at a divisional level. At the time of the Cassino assault, the 4th Indian Division mustered only two brigades. The 7th Indian Brigade, commanded by Brigadier Lovett, was selected to make the assault. The 7th Brigade consisted of the Royal Sussex, 4/16 Punjabis and 1/2 Gurkhas. The 1/9 Gurkha Rifles and 4/6 Rajputana Rifles were added to Brigadier Lovett's command. Brigade strength was completed with the 12th Field Company, 'B' and 'C' Companies, Rajputana Machine Gun Battalion and one troop of 57 LAA Regiment RA. Two companies of 2/7 Gurkha Rifles were assigned to the brigade for portering duties.

Brigade Headquarters were located in the vicinity of Cairo village.

It was decided that Point 593 should be treated as a separate operation. No move would be made against the monastery until this high ground was either captured or neutralized. Point 593 was capped with an old Italian military fort which further assisted the defenders. The Royal Sussex had been assigned the task of capturing Point 593 and had taken up approach positions below. On their left 4/16 Punjabis were facing the monastery with 1/2 Gurkhas as brigade reserve further back on the ridge; 4/6 Rajputana Rifles were on call in the Cairo village area with 1/9 Gurkhas in San Michele.

On the evening of 16th February, the day following the bombing of the monastery, the Royal Sussex were observed in their forming-up area. Any hope of surprise was now lost. As they moved forward but still short of their start line, they found their way obstructed by a line of huge boulders. As they tried to outflank this obstacle, the enemy swept the area with intense machine-gun fire. The Sussex were forced to withdraw, having lost 20 men including two officers.

The following night the Sussex men renewed their assault. In spite of machine-gun fire from the defenders, secure in their sangers and slit-trenches, the Sussex worked their way around the boulders and secured a toehold on Point 593. Lieutenant D. Cox, after personally destroying two machine-gun nests, reached the walls of the fort severely wounded. His company commander, Captain H. Hawkes, also reached the fort badly wounded. Literally sheets of spandau fire and hand-grenades brought the Sussex to a halt. They were forced to fall back to their original jump-off positions. A company stretcher bearer went forward in the face of heavy fire and brought out Lieutenant Cox over his shoulders.

The attack cost the Royal Sussex seven officers and 63 men.

Assault plans were changing again. The revised plan called for the Rajputana Rifles with three companies of the Sussex under command to go for Point 593. Two hours later, 1/2 and 1/9 Gurkhas would go through on their left and attack the monastery and 1/4 Essex and 1/6 Rajputana Rifles would attack to the north of the town of Cassino. Finally, 2nd New Zealand Division would cross the Rapido and fight their way towards the entrance to the Liri valley. The assault had now moved from brigade to corps level. Although 1/2 Gurkhas had reached battle positions one day earlier, 4/6 Raj Rifles and 1/9 Gurkhas were again detected by the defenders moving up to their start line. Harassing fire caused heavy casualties and out of a total of 200 mules bringing supplies forward, only 20 animals reached the forward zone.

At 23.59 hours the Rajputs renewed the attack on Point 593. Major Markham-Lee led his gallant infantrymen in a mad rush for the crest. They were forced to go to ground in the face of devastating small-arms fire from inside the fort and sangers outside. Major Markham-Lee again and again led his men forward. At 01.40 hours divisional artillery put down a five-minute concentration on the summit. At 03.15 hours all three companies were pinned to the ground. Lieutenant Colonel Scott committed his last company at 04.30 hours. The German defenders stood firm and continued to deny the crest of Point 593 to the attackers.

After the final capture of Cassino the bodies of Major Markham-Lee and a number of Rajputana riflemen, including Jemadar Mara Ram were found inside the ruins of the fort. They had reached their objective but died in the centre of the enemy defences.

Rajputana Rifles casualties totalled 196 of all ranks. Only two British officers survived.

Early that morning 1/9 Gurkha Rifles moved forward from 4/16 Punjabis position towards the monastery. Moving now downhill, they approached Point 444, a small ridge about 300 yards from the rear walls of the monastery. They came under small arms fire from two sides. One stream of fire came from Point 593 where the defenders were covering that approach from their right and another from Point 450, a sharp crest about 500 yards to their left. Captain A. Bond of 'C' Company led a platoon rush across the slopes of Point 593 towards the monastery wall and disappeared from the main body. The fierce and unrelenting crossfire brought the assault to a halt and forced the attackers to ground.

The advance was turned back with the loss of 94 men of all ranks. Of the platoon, led in the rush by Captain Bond, one man, a signaller crawled back badly wounded. He reported that Captain Bond and the rest of the platoon had been killed charging a machine gun emplacement.

However, of the total litany of losses posted by the 7th Brigade on that miserable February night in 1944, the highest of all was sustained by 1/2 Gurkha Rifles. This battalion, which had distinguished itself at Alamein and throughout the Tunisian Campaign, suffered over 50 per cent casualties. Commanded by Lieutenant Colonel Showers, who had led them through Tunisia, they had been assigned a direct assault on the monastery from the north. Their immediate objective was a false crest. Aerial pictures had revealed a hollow with a tangled mass of wild undergrowth behind this crest just short of the monastery walls. This type of scrub had been proved negotiable so it wasn't considered to be a serious obstacle. However, what the aerial photographs hadn't shown were the enemy defences placed in and behind the bushes. Anti-personnel mines were planted throughout the thickets with trip wires threaded through the thorny bushes to booby traps. Behind this formidable obstacle were set machine guns at 50-yard intervals. Between the machine-gun posts fox holes and slit trenches concealed sub-machine gunners and bomb throwers. The German commander had correctly assessed his enemy's approach and placed his defences for maximum effect.

Although it wasn't incumbent upon him to do so, Lieutenant Colonel Showers had decided to lead his battalion personally. His orders to all ranks before the attack were clear, precise and to the point – we will close on the enemy at all costs.

As usual in all attacks on Monte Cassino, the 1/2 Gurkhas were detected approaching the false crest. The defenders held their fire and as the Gurkhas came over the crest they hurled a wave of hand grenades. The leading platoons dashed into the undergrowth and were blown up. As succeeding platoons came over the crest, they were wiped out by concentrated machine-gun fire. Colonel Showers, shouting encouragement to his men, went down, shot through the stomach. The leading company took 70 per cent of casualties in five minutes. Survivors battled on. Many were found later tangled in up to four trip wires. One NCO, Naik Birbahadier Thapa, badly wounded, forced his way through the mass of bush and trip wires into the middle of the defenders. He took down several storm-troopers with his *kukri* before being shot down with a machine pistol at close quarters. A stretcher bearer, Sherbahadur Tapahe, following the attack, made almost 20 trips across this deadly bullet swept ground carrying wounded men to safety. He was finally killed.

'B' and 'C' Companies were reduced to platoon strength. 'A' Company came forward to reinforce the survivors and Lieutenant Loftus-Tottenham was shot down leading a rush at a spandau post. The survivors of 'B' Company under Major Ramsey-Brown found a shallow *nullah* and attempted to dig in behind the deadly scrub. Major Ormsby of 'C' Company, who was wounded, went to ground. It was a hopeless situation. Even the courage and reckless bravery of Johnny Gurkha were of no avail against such impossible odds. They were ordered to withdraw.

Seven British officers, four Gurkha officers and 138 other ranks had fallen almost under the walls of the monastery. The words of General Tuker began to echo across Monte Cassino.

The 2nd New Zealand Division assault had gone in as planned on the evening of 19th February. They met with initial success, crossing the Rapido to the south of the town of Cassino. Their second objective, after crossing the river, was the area of the railroad station. This

139

was located about 1000 yards from the base of the mountain. The 28th Maori Battalion stormed and secured this position in spite of a desperate defence. Consolidation of this position would have opened the way into the Liri valley. However, unable to complete the crossing of the Rapido because of heavy enemy fire, the forward Maori companies were overrun the following day. After heavy artillery preparation the enemy counterattacked violently, using panzers. It was necessary to withdraw the survivors behind the river.

The first assault by the New Zealand Corps had now ended. With a few minor exceptions, we were back on our start lines.

11 MONTE CASSINO (2)

The month of March dawned cold and damp as I viewed the back of the monastery at Cassino from an OP in the grey darkness of early morning.

The previous day I had been detailed for OP duties. Our party consisted of Captain P.G. Francis RA, a signaller, and myself. Battalion Headquarters had provided us with a Gurkha guide. Because most of the track to the OP lay under direct enemy observation from the monastery, we had waited until darkness before commencing the two-mile march. Jerry had registered sections of this track and would send over a few rounds from time to time throughout the night. Within 500 yards of the OP, the first rounds came down. We went to ground, dispersing amongst a profusion of huge boulders. With a little luck in the selection of a shelter those rocks could provide excellent protection. The major risk was caused when a shell exploded on a boulder: flying chips of rock came away with tremendous velocity and could kill as surely as a bullet. Reaching the OP, we had been welcomed by the outgoing party. They had been glad to see us.

Our position projected slightly in front of the forward defence lines. The chief protection appeared to be the handiwork of a former occupant. He had crafted a solid breastwork using stones of various sizes and literally glued in place by the addition of chunks of mud and turf. His completed masterpiece would have earned him an instant membership in the Bricklayers Union.

As I searched the monastery ruins through binoculars, I was amazed to note how much of the massive walls had survived our air bombardment. The rising sun, breaking through morning mist, revealed the surviving windows in clear detail. It was an eerie feeling looking at those openings – there were eyes watching you as intently as you were watching them. I could now understand the feelings of the infantryman, lying all day throughout the hours of daylight in his shallow slit trench or behind a crude barrier of rocks, knowing that every move, even the necessary act to relieve nature, was observed by the enemy.

The Cassino front was static. We were floating in a calm between two storms.

The first New Zealand Corps assault had passed and the second was in its planning stage. We could expect a week of relative quiet.

Back at the gun positions ammunition was being brought up, allocated and prepared for the next assault. Ammunition conservation was in effect at this time. Divisional artillery was limited to 20 rounds per gun per day.

Fourth Indian Division Sappers and Miners were constructing a jeep track into the forward area. This track, coming from Cairo village, would allow entry to a narrow valley running almost up to the walls of the monastery. It was shielded from the view of enemy observers.

At 15.00 hours Jerry put down shellfire on our FDLs, including our OP. Two Indian other ranks were wounded and evacuated. A Gurkha officer informed us that, even in the absence of offensive action, divisional casualties averaged 30 to 40 men per day. Shell and mortar fire on FDLs and supply tracks were the principal causes of these losses. The all-seeing eyes of enemy observers saw everything and noted all movement.

My OP officer, Captain Francis, was a tall man, heavily built, dark-shaven with thinning hair and penetrating grey eyes. He was a quiet man but with a sense of humour. Confident and knowledgeable, he commanded respect and loyalty in both associates and subordinates. He maintained an all-night vigil during our first night at the OP. Early next morning, he told me to watch the front whilst he caught some sleep but to call him if anything happened.

Somewhere around 09.00 hours my attention was drawn to movement low down on the opposite slope. Fixing my glasses on the area, I watched intently for further movement. Then I saw the cause. A German soldier had emerged from what was obviously a well-camouflaged strongpoint. Why would the enemy reveal the location of a position they had taken such care to conceal? Then the truth dawned upon me. As he pulled down his pants it was apparent he had been caught short. Captain Francis was now up and I drew his attention to the situation. He swept the front with his glasses.

'Can I bring down a few rounds on that position?' I asked hopefully.

'Dammit, Oates, you know bloody well how we're fixed for ammo.'

He looked across the intervening space again and went on as though talking to himself. 'The bastard! Crapping in front of my OP.'

He swung around abruptly and barked at me. 'Grab your rifle and let him have a few rounds.'

I picked up my .303 Lee-Enfield. Releasing the safety, I laid it on the breastworks and sighted along the barrel. A white posterior, almost glistening in the morning sunlight, presented a clearly delineated target even at 450 yards. I squeezed the trigger. I missed but our friend went to ground, disappearing behind a pile of rocks. About five minutes elapsed before he appeared again. He obviously had a problem. I fired again but again I was wide. Once more he disappeared behind the rocks. Captain Francis nodded with approval. 'Good, let him crap in his own hole,' he said softly.

Watching intently, we saw our friend emerge for the third time. He was now carrying a large white cloth or shirt attached to a rifle which he placed upright between the pile of rocks. Facing us squarely across the narrow valley, he raised his arms in supplication then, continuing to face our direction, he proceeded with his business.

I turned to Captain Francis and asked, 'What now, sir?'

'OK,' he replied, 'Let it go. At least we made him turn his backside in the other direction. No one shits in the face of a British officer.'

The balance of our tour of duty at the OP was uneventful except for an incident on our last night. An enemy patrol got to within 50 yards of our position before they were detected by a Gurkha patrol and routed.

Three times during our return to Battalion HQ, we were at the receiving end of mortar fire. We arrived back unscathed but a carrying party, taking supplies to the infantry, sustained three casualties the same night.

On 6th March, during a heavy rainstorm, Jerry decided to plaster the gun positions north of Monte Trocchio with shellfire. An NCO in 187 Battery was wounded and evacuated.

Ammunition build-up for the forthcoming attack continued daily. Judging from the unusually high percentage of smoke shells it was evident that smoke-screens were to play an important part in the offensive.

The enemy was well aware that we were building up for another major assault and maintained well-planned harassing fire on concentration areas, gun positions and supply tracks. On 9th March three signalmen, returning from an OP, were caught by mortar bombs: Signallers Barber and Backlund of 78/84 Battery were wounded and evacuated. The next day six Stukas dive bombed the gun positions, one bomb falling only 150 yards from 78/84 Battery Command Post. Another OP party was caught by shellfire between the gun positions and Battalion HQ. Lieutenant Cullen RA and Lance Bombardier Wellbeloved were wounded and evacuated, the former with serious abdominal wounds.

Corps Command had finally recognized that any attacking force could not place sufficient men on a start line close enough to the summit of Monastery Hill to destroy the defenders. The basic concept to the new assault was designed to turn or bypass the monastery. The corps would strike southwards from the upper Rapido Valley. The 6th New Zealand Brigade would lead the assault on the town of Castle Hill. Castle Hill overlooked the town. It was about 350 feet high and derived its name from an old Italian castle that crowned the summit. Having seized the town, the Kiwis would then push forward and capture the railway station. If everything went according to plan, the New Zealand armoured brigade would be released to sweep around the base of Monte Cassino and advance north up the Liri valley. The corps would strike and hold Point 435. Point 435 was a rocky outcrop of Monastery Hill. It had a flat top and was only 250 yards from the walls of the monastery. It was known as Hangman's Hill. The name was derived from a concrete pylon in the shape of a gibbet surmounting the top. At one time it supported an aerial ropeway connecting the monastery with the town of Cassino.

Fourth Indian Division would also mount a diversionary attack on the opposite side of Monte Cassino, making use of the new jeep track named Cavendish Road.

General Freyberg planned on making maximum use of air and artillery power. Over 1500 tons of bombs would be dropped prior to the assault. A heavy barrage would move ahead of the infantry assault on Castle Hill and the artillery of three corps, totalling over 600 guns, would saturate the objectives over a period of four hours.

The capture of Monte Cassino by the Allies and the defence of it by the enemy had by now become a central issue, not only of the Italian Campaign but of the European theatre of war. Hitler had issued a special order directing that, apart from military forces, Monte Cassino would be held to the death. Towards the end of 15th February, Panzer Grenadier Division was relieved by the 1st Parachute Division in the Cassino sector. It was claimed by the German High Command and agreed by Allied Intelligence that the 1st Parachute Division was one of the finest fighting formations in the German Army. The division was commanded by General Heidrich who had the reputation of being a master tactician in the art of infantry warfare. Seven battalions would defend Monastery Hill and the town of Cassino with a further three battalions in reserve on Monte Castellone. They would be supported by 200 guns plus a heavy concentration of mortars.

In the second week of March the weather improved and on 14th March the long-awaited signal flashed through the 4th Indian Division: 'Bradman will be batting tomorrow.'

There was a pronounced mood of suppressed excitement on gun positions as 15th March dawned bright and clear. At 08.30 hours there came the steady drone of the first waves of bombers of the Strategic Air Force. Coming out of the south west, we watched, fascinated, as the bombs came down on the monastery, Castle Hill and the town. From 08.30 until 12.00 hours over 500 heavy and medium bombers dropped 1100 tons of bombs on the target area. It was unfortunate that in spite of clear target indicators some bombs went astray. Divisional 'B' Echelon, located in the upper Rapido Valley, was plastered. Fifty men and 100 mules became casualties. As the final wave of bombers wheeled away and out over the Mediterranean Sea the gunners crouched behind their guns as the seconds ticked away closing to Zero Hour – 12 noon.

Then it came – the intense post bombing silence was shattered and split open as 600 guns thundered in unison.

The barrel comes back on the buffer-recuperator, No. 2 snaps the breach block open and through a thin haze of residual smoke No. 4 sends the next round into the barrel, the shell running true off his left wrist, the charge replaced and the breech block slams shut. No. 3 has relaid. Over all this activity the detachment NCO or No. 1 watches with intensity, ready to call out the classic artillery order 'STOP!' It is the order that would freeze every man into complete immobility and is only given if threatened danger is perceived. It is the only order that can be given by any gunner regardless of rank and must be obeyed by all regardless of rank. No. 3 reports 'READY!' and No. 1 says quietly 'Fire!' No. 3's right hand sweeps down and back on the firing lever, then the peculiar sharp crack of the 25-pounder and, as the barrel comes back again, the process is repeated.

The massive bombing had reduced Castle Hill to a heap of rubble and as had happened in the first attack, the tanks were effectively neutralized. The Kiwi infantrymen moved forward behind the barrage. From out of the ruins came the stubborn German parachutists, moving through our shellfire. It took four hours of intense fighting, much of it hand to hand, before the New Zealanders could claim a victory on Castle Hill. The Kiwis quickly consolidated, reformed and made a downhill charge into the town. From foxholes, basement ruins and shelters, came the defenders bleary-eyed and caked with dust to challenge the attackers and dispute their advance. It was desperate fighting by desperate men on both sides, led and exhorted by officers and NCOs.

As the dusk settled the rain came. It fell in torrents. It soaked everything and everyone and it achieved the success which had so far eluded both sides by beating them both into submission.

The 5th Indian Brigade advanced through the downpour to relieve the Kiwis on Castle Hill. At 23.30 hours, led by 1/4 Essex, the brigade occupied Castle Hill. In the early hours of the following day, units advanced or climbed to Point 165, 300 yards above the castle. They secured the lower hairpin bend at this point. The division was now on the battlefield; 1/6 Rajputana Rifles followed the Essex and went across the hillside. Their objective was the second hairpin bend at Point 236. Capture of this point would open the way to Hangman's Hill. With only 150 yards to go, the enemy suddenly came alive. Detecting the Rajputs they opened up with a hail of small arms fire supported by artillery fire. The Rajputs were forced to withdraw to the castle.

At about 01.00 hours 1/9 Gurkhas moved into the outskirts of the town. Their role was to support 1/6 Rajputana Rifles, then attack and secure Hangman's Hill. As they moved into the town, one company was ambushed by an enemy spandau team, losing 15 men in less than a minute. 'C' Company under Captain Drinkall moved around the town and started up the hillside towards Hangman's Hill.

The sixteenth of March dawned on a bitter battle. As the Kiwis pushed forward literally brick by brick against fierce resistance by the paratroopers, General Heidrich watched the progress of the battle from his OP high up on Monastery Hill. Concentrating all his strength to hold the vital area around Castle Hill, he was able to move additional reinforcements into threatened areas. Artillery and mortar fire was rained down on the Essex and the Raj. Rifles on Castle Hill.

At the gun positions, the barrage had ended at 14.00 hours. The 11th Field Regiment commenced to put down a smokescreen at 16.30 hours to cover the New Zealanders on Castle Hill. This smokescreen was maintained by all three batteries in rotation for three days. Opinions on its effectiveness were diverse. Some of our infantry officers claimed it was more of a help than a hindrance to the enemy.

On the first day of the attack ammunition expenditure averaged 800 rounds per gun. On the same day Captain D. Blomfield-Smith RA of 83/85 Battery was seriously wounded and evacuated.

During the afternoon of 16th March OP officers reported figures could be detected in the vicinity of the gibbet on Hangman's Hill. A short while later radio signals were picked up. Apparently Captain Drinkall and his Gurkhas had worked their way across the hillside and had seized the summit. They were now almost in the shadow of the monastery walls. This was exciting news. It became imperative to reinforce this gallant force. At 19.00 hours divisional artillery commenced firing on the hillside. After two hours of concentrated fire 1/6 Rajputs made another effort to seize Point 236 and the upper hairpin bend. Although they were successful casualties and shortage of ammunition prevented them from exploiting their initial gains. While this fighting was in progress, the other two companies of 1/9 Gurkhas moved out of Castle Hill under cover of darkness and began to work their way across and up the hillside. Although they came under fire,

147

they worked their way through the enemy defences, using the *kukri* when necessary. They reached the summit shortly before dawn. Now 1/9 Gurkhas had four companies on Hangman's Hill. Shortly after dawn, the enemy mounted a fierce counterattack from the monastery. This assault was beaten back with heavy casualties to the attackers.

About the same time the enemy counterattacked 1/6 Rajputana Rifles on the upper hairpin bend. The Rajputs were just too thin on the ground and Captain Scaife decided to withdraw to Castle Hill rather than face annihilation.

Concurrently with these actions the Kiwis mounted a strong attack on the Continental Hotel in Cassino. The enemy garrison in the hotel had constructed heavy fortifications, bringing the New Zealand Division advance to a full stop.

The supply of water, food and ammunition to 1/9 Gurkhas established on Hangman's Hill now became of paramount importance. Calls came to divisional artillery from Divisional HQ, requesting volunteers for portering duties to carry supplies to the hardpressed Gurkhas. There was a powerful response from the 11th Field Regiment. Sergeant Parfitt and eight gunners were selected and ordered to report to Battalion HQ. The gunners, along with volunteers from our sister regiments, shouldered heavy loads and were ordered to follow a detachment of 4/6 Rajputana Rifles. The infantry had been ordered to fight their way through the enemy if necessary to reach the summit of Hangman's Hill. The party got through with the loss of eight men. Unable to return before dawn, the party remained on Hangman's Hill the following day. The artillery party returned on the night of 19th March, carrying with them a badly wounded Gurkha officer. One of our party, Gunner Skinner, was wounded and had to be left behind for rescue by a stretcher party. He did not return and was believed to have fallen into enemy hands.

One of the features of the fighting on Monte Cassino was the outstanding work of medical personnel and stretcher parties in particular. Due to the complete domination of the slopes by enemy observers, movement was not possible in daylight. Action went in after the fall of darkness and ceased at sunrise. Soon after daylight the stretcher parties went out under a Red Cross flag to pick up dead and wounded. It was not unusual for German stretcher parties to pick up our wounded and vice versa.

It became impossible to maintain sufficient supplies to the force on Hangman's Hill by portering. Allied aircraft, assisted by coloured smoke from the artillery, did a creditable job even if some drops fell on the slopes of Monte Cassino.

The Kiwis continued their slow and costly fighting to clear the town of the enemy. The German paratroopers were tough, resourceful and stubborn. The Maori infantrymen finally rushed and secured Cassino railway station.

It was decided to reinforce 1/9 Gurkhas on Hangman's Hill in order to mount a decisive attack and storm the monastery itself; 1/6 Rajputana Rifles were combined with 4/6 Rajputana Rifles and ordered to relieve 1/4 Essex on Castle Hill and the lower hairpin bend. The 1/4 Essex would then move up the slopes and reinforce the Gurkhas. It was planned that at dawn on 19th March both battalions would charge across the 250 yards separating Hangman's Hill from the monastery. A diversionary attack would be mounted against the rear of the monastery at the same time coming at the enemy from Cavendish Road. These plans called for split-second timing by inadequate forces worn thin and tired by four days of almost non-stop fighting. In addition, they would be under attack on their start lines.

Knowingly or unknowingly, the German commander decided to pre-empt this attack. As dawn came up on the morning of 19th March heavy artillery fire commenced to come down on Hangman's Hill, the lower hairpin bend and Castle Hill. This was accompanied by mortar fire. In addition, spandau teams raked the slopes with fire, designed to catch anything that moved. As the artillery and mortar fire ended and the machine guns ceased their chattering the enemy attacked down the hill from a start line near the upper hairpin bend. It was a determined counterattack by the 1st Parachute Regiment in battalion strength. The Essex and Rajputana Rifles, with only two platoons between them, were overrun at the lower hairpin bend. There were only two survivors. The enemy swept on against Castle Hill. At this time the garrison was composed of remnants of 1/4 Essex, 4/6 and 1/6 Rajputana Rifles with a small group of sappers and miners.

They were under the command of Major Frank Kettley of the Essex. There was an OP party from the 1st Field Regiment RA. In total the defending force numbered a maximum of 160 men. As the Essex and the Rajputs stood up to rake the attackers with Bren gun

149

and small arms fire, enemy snipers on the hillside picked them off with deadly accurate support fire. The first attack was stopped and thrown back. Major Kettley was mortally wounded. Major D.A. Beckett took command and, although twice wounded, continued to direct and rally his men. The paratroopers, urged on by their officers, were now climbing the castle walls in full view of the defenders. Again the attack crumbled under the furious resistance of the Indian and British infantrymen, straining every nerve to break the determination of the attackers. It was an eyeball to eyeball gladitorial battle as from time to time an individual German paratrooper would gain the parapet only to be bodily thrown off to the ground below. The situation was getting serious when suddenly the OP gunnery officer succeeded in bringing down defensive fire. The initial rounds exploded too far up the hillside but as the range was dropped the 25-pounder shells were almost falling on the castle walls. The enemy paused, then broke and backed away, going to ground on the hill. However the garrison was now reduced to three officers and 60 men. Many of these men were wounded but were fighting on behind a Bren gun or mortar. Expenditure of ammunition was enormous. Barrels of the Essex mortars, which had fired over 1500 bombs, had turned red-hot and bent out of shape. This action had now continued for nearly four hours.

About 09.00 hours a German stretcher bearer under a white flag came forward to ask for a truce to pick up wounded. A 30-minute armistice was agreed to. The castle garrison evacuated its casualties during this period and dug out a number of survivors who had been partially buried under collapsed walls. At midday a company of 2/7 Gurkhas under Major D. Drayton reinforced the Castle garrison.

Back at the gun positions, we had now ranged on the enemy positions and under control of our OP officers we were able to bring down accurate defensive fire and break up further attacks during the afternoon of 19th March.

The dawn assault on the monastery from Hangman's Hill, rudely pre-empted by General Heidrich, was rescheduled for 14.00 hours. By noon Corps Command decided to cancel the planned attack. It would have been folly to have mounted a major attack while the enemy was slowly strangling our lines of communications.

For reasons unknown, the diversionary assault by the 7th Indian Brigade on the rear of the monastery was allowed to go forward. Using 19 Shermans from the 20th New Zealand Armoured Regiment and 21 light tanks from US 760th Tank Battalion, the assault proceeded as planned. The tanks encircled Points 479 and 593, destroying enemy outposts placed on the rear ridges. There is little doubt that if it had been possible to mount the attack from Hangman's Hill as planned this armoured assault could easily have tipped the scales in our favour and allowed the 2nd New Zealand Corps to seize Monastery Hill. In consequence, the defenders were able to turn their undivided attention to this attack. The Shermans were unable to negotiate the steep rocky hills and were withdrawn. The American light tanks, supported by Indian infantry, continued the attack. They now came under fire from German artillery. Throughout the day the brigade battled on, holding grimly to each yard of their advance. By 18.00 hours, with tank strength reduced by 50 per cent, Corps Command ordered a withdrawal. There was little purpose in continuing to sacrifice brave men for no reason. Victories at Cassino came quickly or not at all. Prolonged fighting always favoured the defenders.

Under cover of darkness, 7th Brigade withdrew from its forward positions.

By 19th March the third Battle of Cassino was in its fifth day. It was now evident and fully appreciated by both defenders and attackers that the key to success or failure of the battle was the entrance to the battlefield from the Rapido Valley. The pivotal position was Castle Hill. General Freyberg knew it and General Heidrich knew it. The gallant Essex, with remnants of a company of 2/7 Gurkhas, had long since passed the point of complete exhaustion. The 6th Royal West Kent Regiment, commanded by Lieutenant Colonel P. Bryan D.S.O., M.C., was borrowed from the 78th British Division. On the evening of 19th March the relief was effected. One officer and 200 men marched out. They were filthy, haggard, bloodstained and exhausted, but they were able to hold their heads high. They had given more than had been asked of them and achieved more than had been demanded of them.

Shortly after dusk on 20th March a company of the Royal West Kents moved out through the castle gateway and began to deploy against the lower hairpin bend. They had hardly got under way when

151

they were literally blown skywards by a series of land mines. After withdrawing and reorganizing they made a second effort. The second time they ran into one of Jerry's favourite forms of defence – a field of anti-personnel mines. The enemy was now alert and commenced to sweep the area with machine-gun fire. The West Kents were forced to abandon the attack.

Simultaneously, 2/7 Gurkhas advanced downhill from the other side of the ravine. After a two-hour battle, during which they tried to infiltrate through enemy positions, they were forced to withdraw. They sustained 20 casualties.

The paratroopers followed these successes with continuous attacks throughout the night to recapture the ravine and so cut off the supply line to the castle garrison. These counterattacks were beaten back by 4/16 Punjabis, holding positions high up on the hillside.

Early on the morning of 21st March the enemy mounted another determined attack downhill in battalion strength. We responded to a call from the West Kents and brought down defensive fire. Divisional artillery, followed by corps artillery and backed up by mortar and MG fire, finally smashed the attack at the walls of the castle.

General Heidrich made a final attempt to recapture Castle Hill on 22nd March. Again, the stubborn paratroopers, supported by engineers and gunners, came down the hillside from the hairpin bends. Corps artillery broke up this attack on the hillside. The enemy sustained heavy casualties. They retired, leaving 30 prisoners behind.

By now the 1st Parachute Division and the New Zealand Corps had battered each other into insensibility. Neither side was strong enough to sustain an attack long enough to secure decisive success. On 23rd March 1944 the second New Zealand Corps offensive was finally abandoned. In spite of many successes, Monte Cassino was still held by the enemy.

It was agreed by all divisional commanders that there was little tactical advantage in retaining control of Hangman's Hill. In the absence of radio communication with the garrison it was decided to send forward three runners by different routes, each carrying withdrawal orders. From a number of volunteers for this dangerous assignment, three junior officers were selected. Two of the three got through to Hangman's Hill.

Soon after 20.00 hours the withdrawal commenced. The evacuation of Hangman's Hill is best recounted by the senior officer, Lieutenant Colonel Nangle in his own words (from *Fourth Indian Division*):

'Once over the ridge a weird scene came into view. It was a clear fine night with visibility quite good. The Castle could be seen standing up on its knob in the distance. The Brown House (Continental Hotel) stood bold and desolate between us and the Castle. Above the Brown House there was a line of bursting shells stretching right across the face of the hill, their flashes making a queer glow in the clouds of smoke and rock dust they threw up. Just before us a similar curtain of shells was drawn across the hill above the town itself. Between these walls of fire lay the way to the Castle. We continued to move slowly across the face of the hill. The artillery fire quite covered any noise we made as we stumbled over the loose stones. A slight deviation allowed us to give the Brown House a wide berth as we were uncertain whether it was held or not. No sound came from the ruins and we continued, hardly believing our good luck, to the Castle. We filed up the narrow path and were challenged by the West Kents.'

The journey back took three hours. For 10 days these men had been isolated on a mountain top, enduring freezing temperatures by night and battered daily by the elements under direct observation and fire of the enemy less than 300 yards away.

The following came back from Hangman's Hill:

Royal Artillery: two officers and four gunners.

1/9 Gurkhas: eight officers and 177 men.

1/4 Essex: two officers and 30 men.

4/6 Rajputana Rifles: 40 men.

A number of wounded were left behind. The next day stretcher parties went up the hill under a Red Cross flag and brought those men back.

The relief of the 4th Indian Division began on 25th March. The 11th Brigade of the 78th British Division relieved both the 5th and 7th Indian Brigades. The 8th Argyll and Sutherland Highlanders took over Castle Hill while the 5th Northamptonshire Regiment relieved the 1st Royal Sussex, 1/2 Gurkhas and 4/6 Punjabis. The 2nd Lancashire Fusiliers assumed responsibility for Point 175 and the hillsides above the Rapido.

It was with feelings of relief tinged with sadness that our Indian infantry withdrew from their various positions around and on Monte Cassino – it was a relief to get away from the exposure, murder and suffering of that awful mountain but a sadness to have failed and lost so many gallant comrades.

Total divisional casualties over the six weeks of the two assaults totalled over 4000 officers and other ranks. The division lost many of its finest officers and most experienced NCOs. Most of these men had served with the division from El Alamein and before across the North African deserts, through Tunisia to the final victory at Tunis and from Ortona to Cassino. Jointly and severally, they left a little bit of India at Monte Cassino.

The final relief of the 4th Indian Division by the 78th British Division was carried out under cover of a violent snowstorm that assumed blizzard proportions. It seemed at that time that even the elements conspired to draw a veil over the horror and the agony of that awful mountain. It was a fitting finale to the tragedy of Monte Cassino.

On the morning of 24th March the 11th Field Regiment received its withdrawal orders. Our gun positions were to be taken over by the 132nd Field Regiment of the 78th Division. The same day German artillery wished us a happy farewell. They put down a heavy concentration on both the gun positions and Regimental HQ. We were well dug in and sustained only one casualty, Lance Bombardier Gray, wounded by shell splinters.

I spent most of that afternoon working at 83/85 Battery Command Post, computing and cross checking a harassing fire task table. The guns commenced firing on it at 19.00 hours and continued at intervals throughout the night.

At 09.00 hours on 25th March 83/85 Battery came out of action at Cassino, followed shortly by 187 Battery, while 78/84 Battery remained in action until 22.45 hours. As the guns moved out OPs target records and fire task tables were handed over to incoming personnel of the 132nd Field Regiment RA.

The regiment moved into a concentration area in the vicinity of Presenzano. Over the next few days inspection and maintenance of guns, transport, equipment and stores became top priority. The replacement of filthy, stinking uniforms was particularly welcome.

One-day trips for officers and other ranks to Mount Vesuvius were organized. The famous volcano was conveniently in eruption at that time. Visits to the ruins of Pompeii were also arranged.

The parting shot to our Cassino experience was provided by Major W.J. Clements RA. It was, typically, in humorous vein. Friendly and conversational, Major Clements was always ready to talk and offer encouragement to other ranks, whether NCOs, senior gunners or the last joined draft just out from the UK. Stopping at the survey party position one morning, he draped his long gangling frame over the hood of a 15-cwt truck. He pushed his service cap to the back of his head and commented dryly, 'Life looks good for some people.'

'We just try to do our job and stay out of trouble, sir,' Tug Wilson replied as he started to fill his pipe.

'I just thought I'd stop to give you lads your morning laugh,' Clements continued, drawing a well-thumbed letter from the pocket of his battledress jacket. Withdrawing a page which he gave us to read, he went on. 'That's a page from a letter from my mother, which I received the day after I got back after nearly a week at an OP only a few hundred yards from the walls of the monastery: "The news from Italy is encouraging. If you should go there from the Middle East please try to visit the beautiful Benedictine monastery on Monte Cassino, not far from Naples".'

We all looked at each other for a few seconds, then burst out laughing.

Five days later Major Clements handed over command of 83/85 Battery to Captain L.L. Boyd M.C.R.A. He left the regiment on 5th April en route to 159 Transit Camp at Naples and on to the United Kingdom.

On 25th March Major General A.W.W. Holworthy, D.S.O., M.C., took over command of the 4th Indian Division. At about the same time Brigadier Claude Eastman D.S.O. assumed command of divisional artillery.

For his gallantry and dedication to duty Sergeant Parfitt was recommended for and later awarded the Military Medal.

12 BREAK-OUT ON THE ADRIATIC

As we moved into the early days of April the miserable northerly winds that had plagued us with cold rain, sleet and wet snow, moved suddenly around to the south. It seemed like a minor miracle. One day we were freezing in icy dampness and the next balmy air from North Africa coming off the Mediterranean bathed the whole area in pleasant warmth. Our morale, which had dropped to zero following the two abortive assaults on Cassino, began to rise in direct proportion to the temperature. The resilience of youth, with its ability to recover from reverses and disappointments, is immeasurable.

Jackets were thrown off, sleeves rolled up and blankets draped over sundry shrubs to dry out. The RSM strode through our area on the first morning. He looked immaculate, as befits British RSMs wherever they are.

In response to our cheery, 'Good morning, sir,' he barked, 'Your area looks like a bloody gypsy camp.'

We noted he did not make an issue of the situation.

We became hosts to dozens of Italian children who, although pleading poverty and hunger, looked remarkably fit and well nourished. Mammas maintained a close watch on their bambini from a discreet distance.

Our short rest period was soon terminated. We were returning to the Lower Adriatic. Fourth Indian Division would relieve our sister division in Northern Iraq; the 8th Indian Infantry Division was scheduled to move west and into the Cassino mincing machine.

The regiment rolled out of Morroni at 07.00 hours on 6th April, heading back for Lanciano. Stopping near Termoli for the night, we arrived at our concentration area in the Sangro valley soon after midday the following day.

The regiment took over the support responsibilities and gun positions of the 3rd Field Regiment RA. The relief was effected smoothly and flawlessly. On a bright moonlit night, the guns of the 3rd Field Regiment came out of action at 20.00 hours. We commenced moving in at 21.30 hours. The guns were dropped into the same gunpits and transport was parked in the locations vacated by this regiment. The purpose of such unusual care was to deceive enemy intelligence into thinking there were no changes on this sector.

Both 78/84 and 187 Batteries reported 'Ready to fire' by 23.00 hours, while 83/85 Battery had been temporarily detached from the regiment and was now under command of the 111th Field Regiment RA. We occupied positions about 10 miles north west of Casoli with 83/85 Battery west of Castel Frentano.

In contrast to our initial gun positions near Lanciano in January and our Cassino sector positions in the shadow of Monte Trocchio in February and March, we now appeared to be located in a minor paradise on earth. Olive groves paraded up the gentle slopes. Lush green grass liberally decorated with a profusion of wild flowers presented a riot of colour in the valleys. Fruit orchards were showing early growth. Even the wild birds condescended to lower themselves into our manmade pit of iniquity. Swooping low over the gun positions, they would sometimes perch on a gun muzzle. Over this outwardly peaceful scene the early Italian spring, supported by the Mediterranean sunshine, spread feelings of pleasure and well-being over all ranks. But the harsh realities of war soon cast their inevitable shadows over this picturesque panorama.

Captain F.R. Miles of 78/84 Battery and his OP party had their enthusiasm cut back sharply. Upon being assigned to OP duty they discovered their observation position was located in 'no man's land' nearly two miles in front of the divisional forward defence lines! This OP was occupied only through the daylight hours, the party withdrawing soon after dusk. Captain Miles was convinced that this position was taken over by an enemy patrol at night. He claimed he found evidence, some of it unpleasant, that supported his opinion.

Because of the priority being given to the build-up of ammunition on the Cassino sector in preparation for the next assault, we were limited to 15 rounds per gun per day. We fired our first rounds in these positions on 9th April: 10 rounds of gunfire during the night.

On 8th April a 15-cwt 'Q' truck delivering rations and stores to 83/85 Battery was destroyed by a mine on a track running behind the gun positions. Battery Quarter Master Sergeant Ferguson and Driver Savage were slightly wounded. Battery Sergeant Major Franklin was seriously wounded. They were all evacuated. It became necessary to amputate BSM Franklin's left arm and he did not return to the regiment. BSM Franklin was a pre-war soldier. Quiet and efficient he exuded cheerful optimism and positive confidence. His departure was a severe loss to 83/85 Battery. We were both confirmed pipe smokers and exchanging brands had become a tradition.

About this time our divisional artillery genius Brigadier H.K. Dimoline, who had been with us since El Alamein, was posted to the Home Establishment. He was replaced by Brigadier C. Eastman.

The infantry action in this sector, during the month of April, is best described by an Indian Army observer. Quoting from *Fourth Indian Division*, he wrote:

'The bleak looking farmhouses, which dot the countryside, are the scene of many quick murderous encounters. Both Indian and German detachments live in much the same fashion. Downstairs, in tool-sheds and cattle stalls, the infantry platoons are quartered. The cellar serves as a bolt hole in emergency. The upper storey, reached by outside staircases, which give excellent observation, house the machine-gunners, signallers and specialists. Everyone moves discreetly during the day to avoid unwelcome attention from enemy guns. When darkness falls, the danger mounts. These farmhouses nearly all have blind walls behind which a raiding party may approach unseen. Throughout the night, therefore, sentries are stationed on all sides in slit trenches. Alarm wires are strung and likely approaches are mined or booby-trapped. The technique of surprise, like the precautions against it, demand courage and resourcefulness of a high order, as well as skill in battle tactics which are a mixture of gangster and Red Indian practices.'

The regiment was supporting the 11th Indian Infantry Brigade at this time and this arrangement continued throughout the balance of the Italian Campaign and on into Greece. The 11th Brigade was composed of 2 Camerons, 2/7 Gurkhas and 3/12 Royal Frontier Force Regiment.

158

On 22nd April after a heavy artillery bombardment supplemented by mortar fire, the enemy mounted an attack in company strength against 2/7 Gurkhas. The attack was repulsed with fighting at close quarters. Three days later they again attempted to 'rush' the Gurkhas and were thrown back with heavy losses. These actions and many more were all part of the holding pattern by both sides on the Adriatic Front through the month of April.

Meanwhile, at the other end of the Gustav Line on the Cassino sector, the Allied build-up for the next assault continued. Monte Cassino had to be either taken or turned.

Quite apart from the military aspect of the campaign and the tactical considerations arising therefrom, the capture of the Eternal City was exercising its own unique spell over senior Allied military commanders. Even Winston Churchill was pushing Field Marshal Sir Harold Alexander to accelerate the offensive, claiming that 'whoever holds Rome holds the Deeds to Italy'. Another consideration was the abortive Anzio beachhead which had now become a liability. Winston Churchill, employing his genius to turn a phrase, likened it to 'a stranded whale'. Finally the commander of the Fifth Army, American General Mark Clark, had made no secret of his personal ambition to go down in history as the twentieth century conqueror of Rome.

After the failure of the first three assaults on Monte Cassino, Alexander and Clark had now come to the same conclusion, expressed so clearly by General Tuker in his letter to General Freyberg in early February. 'It was one of the great tragedies of the Italian campaign that 25,000 Allied soldiers had to be sacrificed before the stark reality of Monte Cassino became apparent to the two senior commanders.'

The line up for the fourth and final assault on Monte Cassino, with the ultimate objective of opening the road to Rome, capturing the Eternal City, and forcing the enemy to fall back from the Gustav Line, was indeed formidable.

There was the 1st Canadian Corps, with two divisions and one armoured brigade: XIII British Corps mustering two British divisions with the 8th Indian Division; the Polish Second Corps with two infantry divisions and one armoured brigade; the French Expeditionary Corps, totalling four divisions; the US 85th and 88th Infantry Divisions and finally the 6th South African Armoured Division in reserve. It was indeed a massive force totalling 14 divisions. The contrast with

General Freyberg's two divisions for the second and third attacks wasn't just remarkable, it was laughable.

On 11th May at 23.00 hours, after six weeks' preparation, the attack went in. It was a vast coordinated offensive on a 25-mile front stretching from the sea to Monte Cassino. The assault was preceded by intense artillery fire from over 1500 guns. Initial progress was slow. Although three bridge leads were forced over the Rapido and the Garigliano, the enemy was successful in containing each crossing. For 48 hours the battle seesawed back and forth with desperate fighting by both sides. Then the 8th Indian Division broke open their bridgehead over the Garigliano. The key advance, however, was made by a Moroccan division of the French Expeditionary Corps. German defences were relatively light in the Arunci Mountains and the Moroccan Goumiers, fighting in their natural habitat, moved rapidly through the hills. Their lightning move threatened the enemy defences opposing the British and Canadian Corps. By 17th May the Commonwealth forces had outflanked the ruins of Cassino town. The Polish Corps battled their way savagely up and across the scarred slopes of Monte Cassino in the face of fierce resistance and terrible casualties. On the night of 17th May, after six days' savage fighting, the German 1st Parachute Division finally were forced to withdraw from Monastery Hill. They had nothing to be ashamed of. On 18th May the Poles occupied the ruins of the monastery and raised their flag. They had lost nearly 4000 men in the assault.

In a cemetery on Snakeshead Ridge rest the remains of many of the Polish dead. A visitor to this well-maintained cemetery may read the following inscription above the graves:

'We Polish soldiers
For our freedom and yours
Have given our souls to God
Our bodies to the soil of Italy
And our hearts to Poland.'

On 4th June General Mark Clark brought his dream to reality when he made his triumphant entry into the Eternal City.

Total Allied casualties from all sources in the drive to Rome are difficult to assess accurately. It is a reasonable estimate, based upon casualty lists at a divisional level, that over the six months of fighting they would exceed 100,000 men. This figure would include the Anzio landings.

It was a high price to pay for an objective that made such a small contribution to the final outcome of the war.

On the Adriatic front local infantry attacks and counterattacks continued throughout the month of May. Patrolling by both sides was continuous and aggressive. Gunners were kept busy providing defensive and harassing fire. The regiment was continuously engaged in breaking up enemy attacks and supporting our counterattacks. The diarist of 83/85 Battery gives an excellent picture of the day's action for 14th May. It also demonstrates the close support and cooperation between field artillery and infantry in the 4th Indian Division. At this time 83/85 Battery was supporting 3/12 Royal Frontier Force Regiment.

The diary for 14th May is given in its entirety:

'83/85 Battery
11 Fld. Regt. R.A.
West of Lanciano
May 14, 1944

05:50	Capt. R. Bentham R.A. acting as Liaison Officer at 3/12 Frontier Force Regt. Battalion H.Q. orders Bty. to lay on 'SUMATRA'. Requests other two btys
06:00	Regiment fires 'SUMATRA' Scale 1
06:07	Bty fired 2 rounds gunfire-Church in Orsogna
06:17	Regt. fired 'SUMATRA' Scale 1
06:20	Regt. fired 'SUMATRA' Scale 2
06:30	'E' Troop 5 rounds G.F. on Q105 (church)
06:35	Regt. shot on 'BURMA' Scale 1
06:37	Regt. shot on 'BURMA' Scale 2
06:45	Battery shot on 'BURMA' Scale 3
06:45	2 Platoons 'C' Company reported over-run. Capt. P.G. Francis R.A. with them missing. His body was found later trapped in platoon building which had collapsed
06:55	Battery fires 5 rounds gunfire on Q105
06:58	Capt. Bentham reports attack about company strength now developing on 17 Platoon area (241027)
07:00	Battery fires Q105 North 100 yds. 1 r.f.t.

07:05	Battery repeats Q105 N 100 yds. Capt. Bentham reports falling exactly right. Enemy now occupying platoon areas captured from 'C' Company
07:10	Capt. Bentham orders Bty to lay on 235031
07:20	Bty fired 2 r.g.f. on above map reference
07:25	Bty fired 1 r.g.f. on above map reference.
07:35	Battery repeats
07:42	Capt. Bentham gives correction NW 100 yds.
07:48	Bty. fires on corrected map reference
07:57	Repeated. Record as Target M201
	Operation 'TONBRIDGE' coming into force Capt. Bentham arranges Divisional Artillery fireplan for operation
08:00	Bty. continues to fire 1 r.g.f. every 3 min. until 09:25
	Capt. Bentham reports attack on 'D' Company area from 'C' Company area and enemy forming up in area of Church. Enemy engaged with other batteries in 1 Field and 31 Field Regiments at call and are laid respectively on 'SUMATRA' and 'BORNEO' subsequently engaging them on orders of Capt. Bentham
08:35	Capt. Bentham reports fire on M201 effective-attack on 'D' Company held-situation around Church quiet. 'H' hour for operation 09:30
08:55	'E' Troop ordered to open wireless (radio) to Capt. Bentham and remain on listening watch as a precautionary measure
08:56	B.S.M. arrives with first loads of ammunition
09:00	Capt. Bentham engages enemy in 14 Platoon area with 31 Fld. Regt.
09:02	Reports 31 Fld. fire effective
09:05	Battery fire on M201 reduced to 1 r.g.f. every 7 minutes
09:28	Bty. ready on FIREPLAN. Bty. part in plan is 15 minutes
09:29	Postpone H hour Tanks are not ready
09:32	FIRE! Infantry cannot be stopped. Shot
09:36	Capt. Bentham reports smoke bursting too high
09:37	'D' Troop No. 1 Gun ordered to lengthen fuse. 2
09:39	Capt. Bentham orders 'All targets add 200 yds.'
09:47	Battery completed FIREPLAN
09:48	Bty. ordered to engage Q107 (enemy OP) same rates
09:51	Battery shot on Q107

09:53	Capt. Bentham reports all fire coming down O.K.
09:54	Air O.P. reports movement 235034 and requests fire
09:56	Regt. on 'BORNEO' moved to engage above
10:02	Continue firing until ordered to stop
10:05	Counter-attack past 'C' Coy. H.Q. at 14 Platoon moving on objective
10:07	Unconfirmed back on objective Air O.P. can still see enemy 235034
10:14	Capt. Bentham requests move Regt. on 'BURMA' SW 200 yds.
10:16	Capt. Bentham reports not on objective and asks for 1 troop to fire on each platoon position Bty. continues to engage M201
10:21	Reduce rate to VERY SLOW
10:27	'D' Troop on M201 _____
	'E' Troop on Q101 _____ engage rate normal
	1 Troop 187 Bty. on 13 Pl. area _____ 5 minutes
10:38	'E' Troop on Q101 West 100 yds. – rate normal
10:42	'E' Troop reports guns getting hot Capt. Bentham reports (enemy) attack on 'C' Coy. failed
10:44	'D' Troop engage 'BURMA' for 2 minutes – rate very slow
10:48	'D' Troop engage Q101 to very slow
10:49	'E' Troop reduce rate Q101 to very slow
10:56	STOP! Present situation 12 & 24 Platoons O.K. Enemy holds 13 & 15 Platoon areas. One battery laid on 13 Platoon – M203. One battery laid on 15 Platoon – M201. One battery laid on 'BORNEO' south 300 yds. M202
11:04	Battery laid on M201 – Stand easy. During next hour switches and ranges to new 'M' Targets checked between Command Post and troops
11:40	Enemy concentrating near Church
	Capt. Bentham fired Battery of 31 Fld. Regt. on Q105 W.100 Yds. 3 r.g.f.
11:54	Capt. Bentham fired 'A' Troop on Q101 West 100 yds. 5 minutes very slow
12:00	Capt. F.R. Jephson R.A. arrived Btn. H.Q. to free Capt. Benson to man O.P. if necessary

12:15	O.P. radio netted to tanks on 'flick' frequency reports they are heavily mortared
12:18	Bty. fired 3 r.g.f. on M201 for above
12:22	Report from tanks. New attack developing from S.W.O.P. asks for 3 r.g.f. from two batteries on 'BURMA'
12:37	Infantry want O.P. established on PENELOPE O.P.
13:45	Capt. Bentham occupies. Capt. Jephson new Liaison Officer at Btn. H.Q.
13:46	'E' Troop engage Q107 1 r.g.f. followed by 3 r.g.f. Air O.P. ranges 'D' Troop No. 1 Gun on U520 for FIREPLAN
13:52	Target U520 recorded
13:53	Capt. Jephson engaged area 237035 with 'E' Troop at Btn. request
13:57	'E' Troop engaged Q109
15:00	Bty. engaged on FIREPLAN U520 for 10 minutes. Infantry report rounds falling short but after careful checking these rounds found to be enemy defensive fire. Capt. Jephson reports Btn. H.Q. received two direct hits from tank or S.P. gun near ORSOGNA. Btn. H.Q. moved to dug-out in garden. Capt. Jephson at Maintenance Point laying line to new Btn. H.Q.
15:13	Movement near Church
15:15	Engaged Q105 W 200 yds. in response to above
15:23	Infantry request west half of 'BURMA' Scale 2. Fired
15:28	Repeated west half 'BURMA'
15:38	Engaged 238219 where tank shooting up Btn. H.Q. Engaged at intervals with infantry observing until 16:07 hours
16:15	Battery engaged FIREPLAN U520
16:38	Report from friends that rounds falling short again. Most careful check on 'board' – sight tests and registration made. Same conclusion as before
17:00	Gun at 238019 opened up Btn. H.Q. again
17:02	Battery engaged 238019
20:05	Battery laid on D.F. 'WASHINGTON'
20:15	H hour for attack by Camerons Other two regiments on FIREPLAN U520. 11 Fld. Regt. at call of FOO provided by 78/84 Battery – Capt. Bentham in PENELOPE – Capt. Jephson at 3/12 Frontier Ford Regt. Btn. H.Q. Rt. Col. Huntley at Cameron Btn. H.Q. PENELOPE engaged by

50 m.m. anti-tank gun – 6 direct hits – Capt. Bentham forced to evacuate as building in imminent danger of falling down. Line cut but established in garden and 'thru' by '38' set to Btn. H.Q.

20:47 Capt. Jephson reports 105 mm scoring near misses on Btn. H.Q. and mortaring on 'B' Company Requests medium fire with regiment to engage all active H.R.s in FILETTO area

20:48 Counter attack reported thru 'B' Company area going well

20:50 Counter mortar tasks and 'SUMATRA' engaged

21:05 Attack successful – carriers have dumped consolidation stores on position and returned

21:10 Infantry on objective being shelled and mortared from direction of ORSOGNA. Sig. Maidstone wounded by mortar bomb at Btn. H.Q.

21:15 Battery laid on DF 'WASHINGTON' for night. Casualties to-day – 1 officer killed. 1 O.R. wounded. 1 OR reinforcement'

Temperatures continued to rise throughout the month and the change from battledress to khaki drill in early May was more than welcome. At about the same time uniform headdress changed from 'Cap. F.S.' to 'Cap. G.S.' (beret). An attempt by the RSM to demonstrate the correct method of wearing the beret sparked laughter and levity: he made the mistake of selecting the regimental joker for his demo. The 'model' caricatured a male 'gay' to perfection.

In spite of the vagaries of war Jack Parker and I maintained our friendship. Often in the evenings we would get together over a mug of tea and a pipe of tobacco to discuss the day's events. We were both confirmed pipe smokers. On a warm evening around mid-May I arrived at the regimental aid post to find Jack engaged in earnest conversation with two charming and very beautiful Italian girls. During our early months in Italy it was noticeable that adults maintained a discreet distance from our positions. However children, like children everywhere, lacking any inhibitions, were trusting and friendly. By the spring of 1944 the Italian civilian population had learned that Allied soldiers were neither morons nor murderers, robbers nor rapists. Consequently, from time to time our gun positions were visited by young female adults in addition to children pursuing their everlasting hunt for chocolate and candy.

Jack introduced me to the two young ladies who were sisters: the older girl was Magdalene and the younger girl was Maria. They were of medium height with the dark attractive skin colour characteristic of southern Italy. Their eyes were a deep brown with full generous mouth and lips that sent tingles rippling down a man's spine. Their shapeless dresses failed to conceal mature and generous figures. They looked to be eighteen to twenty one years old but their dark hair tumbling loosely to their waists gave them a girlish touch.

Their command of English was far from perfect but good enough to maintain a simple conversation. Our egos were sharply deflated when we discovered that their interest in us was material rather than personal.

Gripping me in a hypnotic gaze with her deep, brown eyes, Maria said, 'Coffee, tea, sugar, salt?' She held out her hands in an expressive, imploring gesture.

'Of course,' I replied, completely bewitched by those warm limpid eyes.

I turned to Jack and he laughed. 'I reckon we had better produce.'

'Jack, we have no damned option and what is more, there will be no payment.'

Jack Parker was a classic scrounger and his position as medical orderly in the regiment conferred on him privileges denied to the rank and file. We dispensed tea, sugar, salt and canned milk to our young friends and were rewarded with a shy and discreet kiss on the cheek. They obtained our names and over the next few weeks came to see us on a number of occasions, rarely leaving empty-handed. We noted they always stayed together and any effort to separate them was politely neutralized with the ever present flashing smile, revealing even white teeth. We assumed that Mamma had laid down a few safety first precautions for her daughters' protection!

One evening in late May the girls approached us as we sat smoking outside the RAP. They appeared to be more serious than usual and after making their habitual old world courtesy, Maria said, 'Mamma and Papa want … you come … supper. Mamma say you good men … very happy you give tea, sugar.'

We looked at each other. 'We can't refuse, Jack. It would be an insult.'

He agreed.

'Maria, tell your Mamma and Papa we will be happy to have supper with your family,' I replied earnestly.

A date and time was arranged and after a short conversation they took their leave.

Maria and Magdalene's home was a small farmhouse about one mile to the rear of Regimental Headquarters. It appeared to have escaped major damage, although bullet holes were in evidence in the white plaster walls and the roof showed extensive repairs.

We were introduced to Mamma and Papa. The former was a small woman dressed in black with dark and slightly greying hair and sharp piercing eyes. The father, who had served in the Italian Army and had been wounded in the early fighting in Libya, walked with a distinct limp. He also favoured his left arm.

They greeted us warmly, expressing thanks for our gifts of foodstuffs. The stone floored kitchen was scrupulously clean and simply furnished.

There were few preliminaries and we sat down at a well-scrubbed wooden table with a hearty appetite. Wine was served. Maria explained that her father had buried their precious supply of wine in the bush ahead of the retreating German forces. Neither Mamma or Papa spoke any English so Maria and Magdalene acted as interpreters. The single course meal was an Italian stew built around what appeared to be rabbit, generously augmented with vegetables and flavoured with a delicious Italian sauce. It was Italian-style cooking at its best.

Upon leaving and after thanking our hosts through Maria, we were both emotionally embraced by Mamma who repeated the only two English words she appeared to know. 'Thank you thank you thank you.'

A few days later Maria and Magdalene paid us another visit. In the course of conversation Jack commented, 'That was very good rabbit stew.'

The girls broke into hilarious laughter. Finally, controlling herself, Maria adopted a mock serious mien and replied, 'No rabbit. Cat.'

Strangely, we were neither shocked or upset. We were, however, deeply moved that this poor Italian family, their farm and their lives ravaged and overrun by the passage of war, had killed their only remaining animal, the family cat, in order to provide a meal for their guests.

Near the end of May I was detailed for OP duty with Lieutenant W. Hopman RA. 'Hoppy' was a quiet serious officer. His behaviour with other ranks was always meticulously correct. At times he appeared to have a problem giving orders, preferring to precede the order with 'Would you be good enough to … ' or 'I would appreciate … '

A jeep took us to within a mile of the OP, which was located on the reverse or enemy side of a ridge. Originally it had been covered by a dense growth of trees and bush. Constant shelling had laid it nearly bare with the ugly stumps of shattered trees pointing to the heavens, as if in supplication. Here and there the fresh new green of spring growth battled gallantly to overcome the tide of war. We finally reached the OP, which occupied the remains of a two-storey stone building. The roof had long since gone. We climbed the crumbling stairway to a small piece of the second floor. Having relieved the out-going officer and his OP ack we took over the signaller who had replaced his colleague several hours earlier. Judging by the few broken pieces of furniture the room we were in had formerly been a bedroom. I noted a small statue of Jesus Christ set into a recess in one wall. Examining it closely, I could see it was completely unmarked. There seemed to be a sad smile on His face.

Placing myself behind what were left of the only windows, I oriented my map and studied the front through binoculars. As Hoppy placed himself on the other side of the window opening, he commented: 'There's a cellar under this building. Jerry has the OP registered. If he opens up we go for the cellar.'

I was about to reply that I would prefer to stay in the open but I changed my mind and replied, 'Yes, sir!'

There was no point in aggravating a decent officer.

The front appeared to be fairly quiet. Infantrymen of the Royal Frontier Force Regiment were established in slit trenches and weapon pits 200 to 400 yards in front and below us. We were looking for signs of an enemy withdrawal. It was now over a week since Monte Cassino had been captured. The Fifth Army were expected to reach Rome in the next few days but the enemy was still holding firm in the Adriatic sector. Recce patrols reported no movement and fighting patrols drew violent reaction. The day passed quietly.

The next day Hoppy gave me the first 'shift' watching the front. About 07.00 hours, as I gulped my first mug of tea, I detected enemy movement. It appeared to be a working party. They were loading materials into a truck which appeared to be around three-ton capacity.

I called Hoppy. Another truck now appeared behind the first.

'They may be getting ready to pull out,' said Hoppy.

We continued to watch intently.

'Can I have a shoot, sir?' I asked hopefully.

Hoppy didn't reply but went on as if talking to himself. 'They are about 500 yards east of an M target.'

He suddenly turned around. 'Right, Oates, see what you can do but don't use all the HE in Italy.' He paused and then added, 'D Troop only.'

Our signaller suddenly became alert. Stubbing out his cigarette he grabbed his message pad.

I rapidly calculated bearing and range, knowing that Hoppy was doing the same and would override my fire orders if they were seriously adrift. It wasn't difficult. We had a registered target within 600 yards.

I commenced my fire orders: 'D Troop-G.F. Target'.

I paused, allowing time for the gun position officer to give orders to the troop to take post. Checking the signaller's pad I continued, 'Right Ranging.'

'HE Charge Three.'

'More eight degrees.'

'Eight thousand eight hundred yards.'

'Fire!'

I then glued my glasses to my eyes and watched the target with some trepidation. After all, this wasn't a practice range; this was a real live target with our own infantry in front of me. The first ranging round was critical. What if it was way off target? What if I couldn't see the fall of shot? Surely Hoppy would have stopped me. It seemed an eternity to that first round; actually it was only seconds.

Suddenly, there it was! As the smoke rose in the still morning air I knew I had to be fast. I calculated it was almost on line and plus 200 to 300 yards.

'Drop 600 yards.'

The second ranging round confirmed the first, just a little too much to the left.

'More one degree.'

'Add 300 yards.'

I paused then almost shouted at my signaller, 'Three rounds gunfire!'

Hoppy remained silent.

The enemy was now reacting but 'D' Troop gunners were too fast. The Germans were caught in the open: as the first rounds exploded three men at least were taken out. The second round appeared to explode harmlessly. I watched for the third and final round. Almost the last shell hit one of the vehicles. The explosion was followed by a massive sheet of flame as the lorry blew up. I gazed in awe. Hoppy said, 'Good work, don't forget to finish your fire orders.'

I came back to earth and called out to my signaller, 'Shoot successful: enemy working party dispersed: vehicle destroyed.'

'Stand easy.'

A modest cheer drifted back on the morning breeze from the infantry positions.

I filled my pipe and picked up my mug of tea. It was still hot. The fact that I had been directly responsible for the deaths of maybe six men between commencing and finishing the same mug of tea did not even register.

We had barely settled down before the familiar whine of 88 shells galvanized us into action.

Hoppy yelled, 'Down to the cellar.'

An enemy observer had decided that if we wanted to disturb the peace of a beautiful May morning he could do the same. As we crouched in the cellar with the enemy gunfire exploding around us Hoppy started to laugh.

I looked at him and said, 'I don't think the situation is funny at all, sir.'

He stopped laughing and replied, 'You're right but I just thought about one of my professors at university. He had a favourite saying: For every action there is a reaction.'

Returning to our observation level, we found an enemy shell had almost removed one of the three remaining walls. I checked the statue of Jesus; it was still unharmed but I was sure His expression was just a little more sorrowful.

That afternoon and the next day we responded to infantry calls for support. Hoppy handled the fire orders. Three days later we vacated

170

our OP and returned to the regimental positions. The enemy had commenced the withdrawal.

The supreme German commander in Italy, Field Marshal Albert Kesselring, had declared Rome an open city. As the German forces retreated north to their next defence line, their long-awaited withdrawal on the Adriatic Front began. In anticipation of a substantial retreat through the mountains of Central Italy, it was decided by Eighth Army HQ to temporarily withdraw 4th and 10th Indian Divisions. We were looking at the four Rs of active service: rest, re-equip, reinforce and retrain.

On the Orsogna-Maiella sector, the 4th Indian Division was relieved by two Italian formations: Utili Gruppo and CIL Gruppo. Their advance parties arrived on the divisional front with flags flying and a band playing them in. The music came to a sudden stop when Jerry put down a few well-aimed rounds of artillery fire.

The 10th Indian Division was first withdrawn and we relieved them on the coastal sector. The 11th Field Regiment RHQ moved to San Tommaso. By 10th June the enemy retreat from the Gustav Line became universal. Supporting the 11th Indian Infantry Brigade, the guns of the 11th Field Regiment moved forward behind the advancing infantry. An initial move was made into positions at Ortona and on 13th June we moved forward again to Francavilla. After sharp fighting with enemy units employing delaying and harassing tactics, our infantry forced the position. The next day the guns advanced again, taking up positions south west of Pescara. Two signallers, setting up communications for an OP in a house in Pescara, were instantly killed when they entered a booby-trapped room.

On 15th June with RHQ at Francavilla, the 4th Indian Division was pulled out of the line. The regiment moved to a concentration area in the vicinity of Sepino.

It was expected that in the mountain fighting in Central Italy that lay ahead the division would operate on a brigade plan. As a result of this decision each field artillery regiment would go into training with the brigade they expected to support. The 11th Field Regiment would continue to support the 11th Indian Infantry Brigade.

At the end of June Lieutenant Colonel J.F.B. Huntley RA relinquished command of the 11th Field Regiment. He was succeeded by Lieutenant Colonel R.H.A. Foster C.B.E. RA.

13 CENTRAL ITALY AND THE BATTLE OF THE GOTHIC LINE

After the capture of Monastery Hill and the Allied occupation of Rome, the enemy retreat became universal across the Italian Front. Their withdrawal from the Adriatic sector was slower and more controlled. Field Marshal Albert Kesselring appeared to have two broad intentions: the first was to slow the Allies' advance in order to obtain maximum time to complete the fortifications of the Gothic Line; the second was to make the Allies pay dearly for every mile of advance.

Field Marshal Alexander's objectives were the exact reverse. He had divided the advance into three sectors. In between the western sector, which had now moved north of Rome and the Adriatic front, he created the Central Italy sector. Alexander decided to use Indian troops exclusively.

The 10th and 4th Indian Infantry Divisions were assigned to the mountain fighting of Central Italy. The 8th Indian Division had been retained in the Fifth Army under command of General Mark Clark.

As the Eighth Army moved further north, the mountain ridges went higher and the valleys deeper. Many rivers were tributaries of the Arno and the mighty Tiber linked historically with ancient Rome. The valleys were fertile, boasting some of the finest farmland in Italy. Attractive villages decorated the high ground, almost appearing to have been created to ornament the lush landscape. The lower slopes were clothed with orchards, vineyards and cereal crops. The lay of the land favoured the defenders. As most of the roads ran east and west the mobility of the assault forces was limited and difficult and almost impossible for effective tank warfare.

The principles of warfare in this rugged terrain are well described in *The Tiger Triumphs*:

'In a war of automatic weapons, an advance through a wooded country-side with few tracks and little visibility, constituted a hazardous enter-prise. The first necessity was to locate the enemy, the second to by-pass his fixed positions. The final task was to mop up. The routine of infiltration varied with conditions, but the usual method was to send reconnaissance patrols of not more than four men to explore the ground ahead. Within close supporting distance a fighting patrol of about one platoon lay in wait. Within equally easy reach of the fighting patrol, a force of one or two companies with machine gunners, mortar teams and artillery observation officers remained on call. The screen of recon-naissance patrols would infiltrate between the enemy posts, or in some instances would bump into them. From these contacts, a pinpointed picture of the German dispositions would emerge from which objectives could be allocated. These objectives were key sectors which, when seized, would force the enemy to withdraw from his other positions.

This type of warfare suited Indian troops. It retained something of the character of the endless little squabbles on the Indian Northwest Frontier. The deep patrols brought out military qualities inherent in the blood of men whose ancestors have been soldiers for a thousand years. Keen sight, silent movement, quick decision and abounding courage were the counters to win in this sort of game, and these abilities Indian troops have always possessed in full.'

The 4th Indian Division relieved the 10th Indian Division on 8th July.

With 1/2 Gurkhas in the van closely followed by 2 Royal Sikhs, 7th Brigade moved into the mountains. They were supported by the 31st Field Regiment RA. In addition, tanks of Warwickshire Yeomanry were on call.

The division was operating on a wide front of over 20 miles. This fact, coupled with the mountainous nature of the battleground, made it necessary to decentralize to brigade level. To a major degree, the three brigades would be fighting independently with liaison at divi-sional level. The 11th Field Regiment would continue to support the 11th Brigade. The 5th Medium Regiment RA were available to supply heavier artillery fire if required.

On 5th July the regiment pulled out of the Sepino area, staging for the night about 10 miles east of Rome. The journey to the new battle area was continued next day via Rome and Narni. This was the first view that our gunners had of the Eternal City. We arrived at Assisi at 17.30 hours. Two days later the guns were in action.

The days of static warfare and artillery duels so familiar to the gunners on a fixed front were now over. The infantry advanced, attacked, bypassed, mopped up and advanced. Calls for neutralizing fire on strongpoints, harassing fire on the retreating enemy and defensive fire to break up counterattacks, came in fast and furious. Fighting had again become a war of movement, reminiscent of the North African and Tunisian Campaigns. Forward observation parties, moving up front with the infantry, often found themselves on the receiving end of desperate counterattacks. OP casualties became serious. The division was now fighting in mountainous country about 140 miles north of Rome and 45 miles east of Florence. Regimental HQ was established in Arezzo. Batteries and troops moved forward from one gun position to another, supporting 2/7 Gurkhas, 2 Camerons and 3/12 Royal Frontier Force Regiment.

From Arezzo the brigade forced the enemy back to Campriano, which we bypassed and the Germans evacuated. Then up, over and down another mountain ridge, supported by our guns and tanks of the Warwickshire Yeomanry. The brigade reached and captured Castelacciao, crossing Route 71 and the River Arno. While the 2 Camerons mopped up the 2/7 Gurkhas pushed forward to Bibbiano. Accurate artillery fire, followed by the awesome sight of a company of Gurkha hillmen charging up a slope, shouting their war cries and brandishing their wicked *kukris*, often demoralized the defenders, forcing them to retreat in terror and confusion. However, it is only fair to state that the quality of the German infantry encountered in central Italy fell far short of the stubborn paratroopers who had defended Cassino and Monastery Hill.

To our left, 7th Brigade crossed the Arno near Route 73, seized Castiglion and pushed on to Talla. On our right, 5th Brigade, having taken over 7th Brigade's original axis of advance, reached Piandi Maggio, bypassed Gello and drove the enemy back to Falciano.

On 24th July His Majesty King George VI paid a brief visit to the 4th Indian Division. From an observation point in Arezzo he was able

174

to observe a concentration shoot put down by the 1st Field Regiment, the 5th Medium Regiment and the 32nd Heavy Regiment. The shoot was in support of 11th Brigade at Campriano. It is possible that this concentration was to some degree at least prearranged. If so the German officer commanding at Campriano must have wondered why his position was selected to be the target of such a massive bombardment!

The 83/85 Battery diarist provides an excellent summary for the month of July 1944, which is reproduced in its entirety:

'From July 12–16 the battery in area Morra supported the 1/9 Gurkha rifles in operations in the area M. Civitella–Mon Terchi until relieved by 1 Field Regt. R.A. when it reverted to support of 3/12 FFR on the arrival of 11 Ind. Inf. Bde. from Sepino. From July 19 – end of month the battery from positions in Arezzo area and Antria supported 3/12 FFR in the occupation of Antria, M Torcellino (July 20), the attack on the Campriano feature (July 24), its occupation (July 27) and the move of Btn. westwards during the last days of the month and gradual improvement of positions, preparatory to a new advance. During these operations the battery suffered the following casualties to its O.P. parties. Wounded in action, Major Aitken, Capt. Bentham, Lieut. Hopman, Capt. Boyd's old wound re-opened and turned septic – he was posted to Home Establishment July 23. O.P.As – Sgt. Juniper killed in action. L./Bdr. Garnett wounded Signallers – Sig. Mullen – Sig. Allen wounded. Carrying party – Gnr. Carvell killed in action. Morter O.P. – 1 N.C.O. killed in action.

One driver injured in battle accident. Owing to the above officer casualties reliefs were almost impossible, but the Battery continued to supply B.C. at Btn. H.Q., one O.P. manned and an FOO in addition for advances. Signallers also were on duty without relief for long periods. Capt. Lindsay from 57 LT. A.A. Regt. and Lieut. Allenbrook (149 A/Tank) candidates. Air O.P. were attached for field experience and although with little previous knowledge were of considerable help as spare officers with B.C.'s party to organize the party, maintenance of communications and replacement of casualties. The B.C.'s party moved on a mule basis (4–6 mules) and acted as Signal Centre, O.P.s having to be manpacked on all advances.

During the attack on Campriano, a simple grouping was made of all known enemy mortars and gun positions and a programme made to be engaged on receipt of a codeword. This eliminated accurate map reading at night in the forward areas: e.g. call for fire simply send 'Being shelled from N.W. request PIGLET' This was a big step over what had before been a stumbling block. Several calls for both CB and CM were answered and fire was most effective.'

On 20th July an item on the regimental noticeboard announced that the late Captain P.G. Francis RA, killed in action on 14th May at Orsogna, had been posthumously awarded the Military Cross. Driver Preedy, also of 83/85 Battery, was awarded the Military Medal.

In early August the regiment moved forward to the Chiassa area in order to maintain effective support to the fast-moving infantry of 11th Brigade.

At 09.30 hours on 2nd August an enemy shell exploded on a jeep. Signaller Hill and Driver Paget of the Royal Corps of Signals were killed instantly and Lance Bombardier Elliott was seriously wounded and evacuated. Lieutenant P.R. Farr, also of the Corps of Signals, was presumed killed in action. It was necessary to write the records in this fashion because, sadly, the remains of Lieutenant Farr could not be positively identified. Five days later Sergeant Neish and Lance Bombardier Bell of 78/84 Battery were wounded and evacuated. Gunner Lock was killed in action whilst laying line to an OP and the battery commander, Major L. Evans, M.B.E., RA was wounded and evacuated.

These August casualties, among the last in the fighting in Central Italy, assumed tragic overtones when on 10th August Eighth Army Command suddenly terminated the campaign.

On the western sector the New Zealand, Canadian and South African divisions, with the 8th Indian Division and American troops, had broken through the enemy defences and had reached Florence. There was little point in continuing the fighting over the mountains and risking further casualties when the enemy defences could be turned and taken from the rear.

The Central Italy campaign had been short, sharp and successful, lasting a total of only 32 days. The 4th Indian Division had advanced over 50 miles, measured by marching distance. This advance was over terrain of more assistance to the defenders than to the attackers. Divisional casualties totalled 1043 men of all ranks.

On 13th August a non-denominational memorial service was held in memory of those men who had lost their lives in this brief campaign. It was a sombre and moving service with sad overtones, depending upon and arising from one's former personal associations with those men now lost forever to their comrades and families.

Coming out of action in the Chaissa area, the regiment moved to a concentration area three miles west of Lake Trasimeno. The first leave party left for Rome. Officers and other ranks were allowed a few days' rest and relaxation, taking advantage of the glorious summer weather. Both guns and transport had taken a terrible beating and soon, as always, it was all hands on maintenance.

Around the middle of the month divisional artillery was honoured by a visit from Sir Oliver Leese, Commander-in-Chief, Eighth Army. With the assistance of a public address system, set up by our indefatigable signallers, Sir Oliver addressed all three field regiments plus the anti-aircraft and anti-tank gunners. He gave a brief overview of the war to date, including both the Second Front in France and the Russian Campaign. Without revealing any future plans, he also supplied a short outline of the fighting that lay ahead.

The regimental rumour mill was now operating at full capacity and the smart money was being placed on a drive through the mountains on the Adriatic side of Italy to the Gothic Line.

From time to time groups of personnel or individuals would leave the regiment en route to the Home Establishment. Many of those men, in addition to active service in the Middle East, North Africa and Italy, had served for three years or more in India. It is a sad fact that many of those men who had survived four campaigns lost their lives in France, Holland and Germany. On 24th August Bombardier Shaw of 78/84 Battery left for Naples on his way home to England.

By late August the division had concentrated at Sigillo on Route 3. On 23rd August the guns were in action in the area of Villa Coldecanali, supporting the commencement of the divisional drive to the Gothic Line.

The Adriatic Front retained the original topographical feature with which we were familiar: a coastal 'plain' varying from just a few miles up to 30 miles. Even along the foreshore the terrain was not flat but rather a succession of rolling ridges with gentle valleys and always the rivers coming down from the Appenines to find the sea. To the left of this coastal plain, as we moved north and west towards the Gothic Line, lay the foothills of the Appenines, rising to heights of 1000 feet.

These foothills then merged into the high mountain ranges of the Italian backbone.

The plan for the advance to, and hopefully through, the Gothic Line developed by 5 Corps, called for the 4th Indian Division with the 46th British Division on its right to advance on a broad front through these foothills, employing a combination of surprise, speed and shock.

According to Intelligence, the fortifications of the Gothic Line were far from completion. In addition, the quality of the work fell far below the generally accepted high levels of German efficiency. This was partially due to the activities of Italian partisans and partially to sabotage by Italian contractors. It seemed that Italian masons had forgotten how to lay brick and concrete block!

The nature of the terrain, coupled to extensive enemy demolitions, made it difficult to operate three brigades simultaneously. At 06.00 hours, on 25th August, the 7th and 5th Brigades moved forward. The 7th Brigade followed Route 3 while the 5th Brigade, equipped with jeeps and mules, followed a parallel course, going across country. The divisional strength had been supplemented by the addition of the 6th Royal Tank Regiment, the 58th Medium Regiment, the 85th Mountain Regiment and a battery from the 165th Field Regiment with jeep-drawn guns. Divisional personnel also welcomed some of their friends from the Cassino battlefield, an American Field Service Ambulance detachment.

In spite of demolitions, Herculean work by the sappers and miners kept the infantry moving. There was light opposition by German mountain troops which was effectively handled with the help of Shermans of the 6th Royal Tank Regiment. On 27th August the 1st Royal Sussex, after passing through the 2nd Royal Sikhs, entered the town of Urbino. They received an enthusiastic welcome from nearly 20,000 inhabitants. This town, like so many in Italy, sits atop a hill. The 46th British Division was moving forward and in contact with the 5th Brigade.

Five miles beyond Urbino lay the outer defences of the Gothic Line. They followed the Foglia River, which twisted and turned on its meandering path to the Adriatic. Beyond the river the ground rose to a high crest. Behind, on top and in front of this crest, were placed the enemy defences. The natural advantages of this high ground was developed and further buttressed with a variety of defence devices –

machine-gun pits, trench systems, wire obstacles and anti-tank ditches. Forward of the Gothic Line proper the defences took the form of a series of individual posts with interlocking fire lines so arranged to cover the maximum area with the minimum number of men. Counterattack detachments stayed safely in the rear, ready to react to any breakthrough.

In order to test the readiness of the enemy defences it was decided to try a surprise night attack. In the early hours of 30th August two companies of 3/10 Baluchis crossed the river and climbed silently to a high spur near the village of Monte della Croce. They were surprised to reach the hamlet without any enemy reaction. It was devoid of defenders. However, when the Baluchis attempted to probe further, the enemy came to life. The Baluchis had caught Jerry with his pants down. Tanks were now moved over the river and 4/11 Sikhs moved forward to the right of the Baluchis with 1/9 Gurkhas coming up behind.

The Eighth Army were now closing up on the Gothic Line along the entire front.

One mile to the north west of Monte della Croce lay Monte Calvo. Following the surprise seizure of the village, it was expected that Monte Calvo would be well defended.

On the night of August 29th, a tremendous artillery concentration was put down on the enemy defences from Monte Calvo to the Adriatic. From the gun positions the shell bursts could be seen dancing along the uneven ridge. As the thunder of the crash shoot died away, three corps (2 Polish, 1 Canadian and 5 British) went forward. The 46th Division advanced one mile against desperate defenders and 4/11 Sikhs with 1/9 Gurkhas surrounded Monte Calvo. Following another artillery bombardment of this heavily-defended feature, supplemented by fighter bombers, the Sikhs and the Baluchis mounted a frontal attack. By nightfall, the 5th Brigade had firmly secured the village. The 46th Division seized Monte Gridola after furious fighting and 1/9 Gurkhas exploited behind the Gothic Line towards the town of Taveleto.

Although the map showed that the division had now broken through the Gothic Line, the success was more apparent than real. The enemy had constructed numerous defensive fortifications in great depth behind the Gothic Line. These took the form of a series of temporary defence lines, taking advantage of the numerous rivers and running back to and beyond Rimini. Between the rivers those defence lines followed the contours of the mountain ranges.

After the breakthrough the only limitation placed on the division was availability of road space. Taveleto was taken and all three brigades surged forward towards the next defence line. The enemy had constructed this line along a ridge overlooking the Conca River. On the extreme right of the divisional front the key German bastion of Gemmano stood firm and resolute. It had been attacked unsuccessfully by the 46th and 56th Divisions at least 10 times.

Fighting to retain our share of road space, we moved the guns forward, maintaining support of the 11th Brigade. Due to the fluid nature of the fighting, friend and foe often became dangerously inter-woven. OP personnel were ordered to wear white armbands. This precaution provided some protection from enthusiastic and trigger-happy Indian infantrymen.

Pian di Castelo and Onferno were captured on 7th September and although 4/11 Sikhs secured Cafrarese on the night of 11th–12th September, they were forced to retire in the face of violent enemy counterattacks, supported by tanks. The 4/11 Sikhs had replaced 1/4 Essex. The latter had been temporarily pulled out of action due to heavy casualties and sheer exhaustion. The division had now bumped the main German defence line behind the Conca River.

A major attack along the entire Eighth Army front was launched on the night of 12th–13th September. It met with local successes but failed to break through the powerful enemy defences. On the left flank of the 46th Division 3/10 Baluchis were brought to a full stop by almost impossible going and deadly enemy fire. The 4/11 Sikhs were barely able to move off their start lines and although the 2 Royal Sikhs captured Schiano north of Onferno, they were forced to go to ground in the face of accurate mortar and artillery fire. The 46th Division, although making some progress in the Monte San Colomba area, were unable to capture their main objective of Gemmano.

Gemmano remained the key that would open the German defences on the River Conca.

The 13th Corps Command decided to throw the 4th Indian Division against the bastion. The 2 Camerons were placed under command of the 46th Division and the 1st Brigade took over the left sector of the

46th Division front. The 7th Brigade was intended to cover the gap thus created. The 5th Brigade remained in divisional reserve.

The assault was scheduled for the night of 14th–15th September. The main objective was Point 449 and when this point had been captured the axis of advance would turn west into and along the Conca River valley.

Artillery preparations for this assault were both comprehensive and intensive. Bofo guns would be employed to provide deceptive shoots in the form of tracer shells, well clear of the main axis advance and 7.2 howitzers and medium guns would support divisional field artillery. A total of 260 guns would support this attack. The 11th Field Regiment moved into new gun positions on 14th September. Some confusion arose when 83/85 Battery and 187 Battery tried to occupy the same gun positions. Fast thinking and firm action by Lieutenant Rigby restored order and by early morning both batteries were able to report, 'Ready to fire!'

The 83/85 Battery sustained the loss of one trailer overturned and one tractor with a broken axle during this move.

The 11th Field Regiment fire plan called for support of the 'point' battalion, 2 Camerons. Having taken Point 449, the Highlanders would be relieved by 3/12 Frontier Force Regiment. They would then push on to Zollara which would be the recipient of a concentration shoot of about 2000 shells. In addition to the 11th Field Regiment, the 3rd Field Regiment, the 6th Medium and the 1st Heavy Regiments would support the Camerons. In addition to these concentrations and crash shoots, all field guns would join in a barrage moving ahead of the initial advance. Limited time, coupled to difficult weather conditions, aggravated the complexity of the calculations involved in the artillery preparations of this assault. Finally came the monster task of moving sufficient ammunition over limited and shelltorn access roads and then down tracks cut deep by mud and rain to the gun positions. The 11th Field Regiment alone needed over 15,000 rounds of high-explosive, nearly 200 tons.

This attack, carefully planned and executed and carried through with determination, was successful. By 04.00 hours the Camerons were in Zollara and by 10.00 hours the crest of Gemmano ridge was firmly secured. Although tanks had been brought forward for support, they were not required at this stage of the battle. Enemy casualties exceeded 1000 men. Regimental casualties were light – Captain Butler of 78/84 Battery was wounded and evacuated on the night of 14th September. With Gemmano ridge firmly in our hands, rapid gains were made along the river valley. The 5th Brigade was now moved up from reserve. Crossing the Conca River, they commenced to close in on Montescudo, two miles beyond the river by 17th September.

The division was now approaching San Marino State. This tiny independent republic, reputed the oldest in the world, lies entirely within the boundaries of Italy. Like Switzerland, San Marino State had maintained its neutrality throughout the war. The German command in Italy had respected this neutrality. However, in early September, Field Marshal Kesselring, after appraising the high ground and observation advantages of San Marino, decided to terminate this neutrality. San Marino was occupied by German troops.

The eastern side of the mountain on which San Marino was located dominated the country towards the Adriatic to the south of Rimini. Although the normal pre-war population of San Marino was less than 15,000 persons, Italian refugees had swarmed into the republic, hoping the tide of battle would pass them by. In late September it was estimated that the population of San Marino was close to 100,000.

Montescudo proved to be a bottleneck. Although cleared of the enemy, who had fallen back to the Marano River, it presented natural built-in resistance to the advance of the 4th Indian Division. The only road capable of supporting heavy traffic passed through Montescudo. The weather was now deteriorating, turning cold and wet. The 3/10 Baluchis were the point battalion and forced a bridgehead across the Marano near Faetano. However, when 1/9 Gurkhas attempted to broaden this bridgehead they encountered fierce enemy resistance, who were holding a dominating ridge formation overlooking the river.

In this initial engagement over the Marano, both the Baluchis and the Gurkhas were without artillery support. Divisional gunners were fighting their way through almost impossible traffic conditions. When we finally arrived in the gun area we were faced with a muddy morass. The rain continued to fall. Somehow the thought of those poor bloody infantrymen, trying to hold their positions against enemy machine-gun and mortar fire, pounded by German artillery and at the mercy of the elements, drove the gunners to superhuman efforts. Hauling, winching and manhandling, they brought their guns into position and

182

hen into action. Finally the gun position officers were able to report
o their OP officers, 'Ready to fire!'

Then, as the first rounds of gunfire exploded on the enemy posi-
ions, many an infantryman could echo that famous quote from the
'irst World War: 'The guns, thank God, the guns!'

It was at this time and during the action of the Marano River that
here took place one of those shining and sustained acts of almost
nspired heroism that sets the Gurkha above almost any other
nfantryman in the world.

The following account is taken from *Fourth Indian Division*:

'Rifleman Sherbahadur Thapa and his section commander stormed an
enemy strongpoint, killing the machine-gunner and putting the remainder of the garrison to flight. A group of Germans struck back, and the
section commander was wounded. Single-handed Sherbahadur Thapa
charged his assailants, swept them before him and gained the top of the
ridge, where he brought his Bren gun into play against groups of the
enemy on the reverse slopes. For two hours, he bore a charmed life
under a hail of fire destroying numerous detachments which sought to
regain the crest. When his platoon had spent its last round and was
virtually surrounded, the intrepid rifleman covered their withdrawal. He
then dashed forward under heavy fire and brought in two wounded men
lying on the forward slopes. While returning a second time in full view
of the enemy, he fell riddled and joined the sublime company of those
who have not lived to know of the accolade of a Victoria Cross.'

The enemy was now digging in and making the division fight for
very yard of gain. There were strong indications that we were facing
nother setpiece battle. Brigadier Lovett moved the 7th Brigade
urther north, relieving 2/7 Gurkhas. Because of the impossibility of
apturing San Marino from the south, it was decided to bypass the
own, then launch an assault from the north.

On 19th September 2 Camerons wrestled Valdragona from the
nemy, supported by tanks and all divisional artillery. Under cover of
moke the Highlanders closed in on San Marino. Then, supported by
anks following the main road, they worked their way into town. Then,
s the rain came down in torrents, they 'rushed' the last strongpoints
s the tanks shot up stubborn points of resistance. The success of this
ttack and the relatively poor resistance of the enemy was due, in part

at least, to the fast encircling movement to the north of the town The Camerons sustained a total of only 36 casualties in this action.

The neutral Republic of San Marino was liberated. A major facto in the story of this tiny republic was the decision by Corps Comman not to use either aerial bombardment or artillery fire against the town No doubt the horror of the bombing of the Cassino Monastery wa still fresh in the minds of senior Allied commanders.

On 21st September the 11th Brigade moved up to point brigade a the division continued its drive into the west. Royal Frontier Force reg ment captured Monte Cerreto between San Marino and the valley c the Maracchio River and 2/7 Gurkhas drove onto the high ground wes of Scorticata. Although they met with initial success the enemy coun terattacked in strength and the Gurkhas sustained over 100 casualties

In order to maintain effective artillery support to these lightnin infantry thrusts, the gunners were kept constantly on the move. In on 72-hour period 83/85 Battery alone occupied seven different gu positions. Some of these moves brought the guns into territory onl recently vacated by the enemy. German artillery officers becam expert in recording for future use as counter-battery targets, strategi points and their own former gun positions. Regimental casualties ros sharply at this stage of the Gothic Line fighting.

Near Faetano on 20th September 78/84 Battery OP was heavil shelled and the house in which it was located, literally collapse around the OP party. Miraculously, there were no major injuries. Gu positions of 83/85 and 187 Batteries were plastered by enemy gun on 25th September. One gunner was killed in action, two gunner seriously wounded and evacuated and eight gunners slightl wounded. One of the seriously wounded men, Gunner Catling of 18 Battery, died of wounds the following day.

Towards midnight on a black and inky night in late Septembe Battery Sergeant Major MacLaughlan of 83/85 Battery was watchin his driver negotiate a sharp bend on a narrow road winding around hill in the La Grotto area. He had gone back earlier in the day to pic up stores but the battery had made one of its lightning moves whil he was away. He was now trying to find his way to the new gu position. In addition to his driver, the BSM had a loading party of fou gunners. Coming around the bend without lights, the road suddenl disappeared. The three-ton vehicle plunged down a precipice but for tunately lodged on a narrow outcrop. The BSM and his party crawle out, bruised, cut and shaken but not seriously injured. They were picked up by another vehicle and after treatment at an ADS, returned to duty.

One day later, however, while in action at Aquaviva, the enemy brought down a heavy concentration on the 83/85 gun positions. There were four casualties: one gunner killed in action and three men wounded and evacuated.

Due to continuing and accurate enemy artillery fire the battery moved to alternate positions at 19.30 hours on 26th September. They had recorded zero lines and had just opened fire when they were on the receiving end of German counter-battery fire. BSM Slawson was wounded and Gunner Farnsworth was killed in action.

Royal Frontier Force Regiment had now crossed the Marecchia River with two companies and had thrown the enemy off the crests of Montebello. For 24 hours they clung to their hard-won positions in the face of desperate and successive enemy counterattacks. All divisional artillery was called on for support. The situation required a two-hour concentration before the enemy called it quits. The following night the RFFR moved up the other two companies and the position was secured.

Concurrently with this action the 2 Camerons crossed the river to support the hard pressed Gurkhas. After bloody and violent hand to hand fighting with bayonet, knife and *kukri*, the enemy was thrown off the high ground. The divisional bridgehead over the Marecchia was now firm and secure. The 11th Brigade was ordered to dig in and hold their positions.

The 11th Brigade casualties to date in the Battle of the Gothic Line had now reached awesome proportions. For 25 days, since breaking through the Gothic Line, the brigade had been in constant contact with the retreating German forces. Average company strength stood at about 30 other ranks and the loss of junior officers was particularly high.

Brigadier Lovett's 7th Brigade was now ordered to cover the widening gap between the 46th Division and the 11th Brigade, 2 Camerons came under command of 7th Brigade and all divisional artillery was switched to its support.

After crossing the Rubicon the Royal Sussex and the Gurkhas, supported by the 6th Royal Tank Regiment, advanced north east towards the Borghi ridge. After vicious fighting with no quarter asked or given, both sides fell back exhausted.

After recce patrols discovered a more favourable crossing with no defences in place, the redoubtable 2 Camerons went across the Rubicon. The Highlanders penetrated four miles into enemy territory in a daring thrust, reaching San Giovanni. The enemy now mounted a series of fierce counterattacks, all of which were broken up and neutralized by crash shoots from divisional artillery. The 2/7 Gurkhas came up in support of the Camerons and occupied San Giovanni.

The near exhausted infantry had long since passed the limit of human endurance. Brigadier Lovett called for one final effort and in the early morning hours of 1st October, behind a barrage put down by over 300 guns, the men of Sussex and the Highlanders, the Gurkhas and the Sikhs, advanced behind the bayonet and the *kukri* through the mud and the rain against the stubborn German defence. The Camerons reached their objective at Eight Trees by 03.30 hours. The 2 Royal Sikhs reached Borghi at 07.30 hours and the Royal Sussex captured Reggiano. Although 2 Royal Sikhs battled their way into their final objective, San Martino, strong enemy counterattacks forced them to withdraw.

The weather continued to deteriorate and by the end of September it had reached a crescendo of fury. Torrential rain filled and overflowed creeks and rivers. The ground softened to the consistency of marshland. Vehicles dug in to their axles and even tracked vehicles were reduced to immobility. Gunners winched and manhandled guns from one position to another. For the poor bloody infantryman, soaked to the skin by day and freezing by night, life had become a battle for survival in a sea of mud. The weather succeeded where the enemy failed; the 4th Indian Division ground to a halt.

It was now 32 days since the Gothic Line battle had begun. During this period the three brigades had advanced over 60 miles – an average of two miles per day. Nearly 30 miles of this advance had been in constant contact with the enemy: an enemy who fought desperately and gallantly, extracting maximum casualties for every mile he retreated. Divisional casualties were getting close to 2000 men of all ranks.

The agony was ending. At the end of September, news came that the 10th Indian Division was moving up to the front to relieve the 4th Indian Division. The news came slowly, first by the usual rumour then by fact filtering down to the lower echelons. The 5th Brigade ending the battle in reserve, were the first to be relieved and started their

186

journey back to Perugia. On 3rd October 11th Brigade was relieved by 20th Indian Brigade, Two days later, Brigadier Lovett pulled his shattered and exhausted battalions out of the firing line.

In order to effect the smooth artillery transition so necessary for infantry support, the 11th Field Regiment was retained in the line an additional week. On the night of 9th–10th October we fired our final fireplan. The following morning we brought the guns out of action and concentrated in the regimental area. At 20.45 hours the same day the regiment commenced its line of march to the rest area; RHQ in the lead followed by 83/85 Battery, 187 Battery, 78/84 Battery and a troop of light anti-aircraft. Light aid vehicles brought up the rear. We arrived in a staging area near Fabriano before first light the following morning. Pushing on, we pulled into a concentration area at Passignano soon after midnight on 17th October.

Regimental Orders decreed that there would be an eight-day rest period. A leave party of three officers and 60 other ranks left for a seven-day leave to Rome.

It was generally assumed by all ranks that after a reasonable period to allow time for vehicle and equipment servicing or/and replacement and the arrival of reinforcements, the division would move back into the line. However, in the last week of October, it was confirmed that the regiment would be moving back to Taranto. Hot on the heels of this information came the news that the 4th Indian Division had been ordered to Greece. This latter revelation was not only welcome, it was greeted with a modest degree of enthusiasm.

The average soldier's knowledge of Greece at that time ranged from scant to zero, standing at the level of Grade 8 Social Studies today. We knew it was a mountainous country with many similarities to Italy. Initially, Greece had been occupied by Italian forces earlier in the war. The feisty Greeks were a little too much for Italian troops with little enthusiasm for soldiering in such an inhospitable and unfriendly country. Hitler was finally forced to come to Mussolini's assistance and from then on German troops remained firmly in control. Such was the sum total of knowledge concerning Greece by divisional rank and file in October of 1944.

On 29th October the 11th Field Regiment moved out of Passignano on line of march to Taranto and back to where we had landed in Italy nearly one year earlier. Under Convoy Serial Number 10/D1/067 we maintained a speed of 15 miles per hour with a density of 12 vehicles to the mile. The route was shown as Route 75 – Route 3 – F8363 – F78–64 – Route 7 Capua – Caserta – Benevento – Foggia – Cerignola – Taranto. We anticipated a four-day journey with staging areas at F8363 – Caserta – Stadia – and Canosa.

14   THE GREEK CAMPAIGN

In the afternoon of 1st November, under overcast skies, the regiment pulled into its prepared concentration area about two miles from Taranto.

There were still a number of other ranks who had been unable to take advantage of the leave opportunities after Cassino, Lanciano and the Gothic Line battles. On 4th November 260 men commenced six days' leave at the 8th Armoured Division leave camp at Bari.

The first hints of the future were conveyed to all ranks by the sudden cessation of gun drill, followed by an immediate switch to small arms training. Musketry practice and Bren-gun instruction became a daily routine. Regimental orders failed to give any information: warrant officers and senior NCOs were equally uninformed. It was, therefore, with a high degree of interest and anticipation that all ranks assembled, on a battery basis, for a lecture by their respective battery commanders on 9th November.

Of all the Nazi-occupied countries in south east Europe in the Second World War Greece maintained a special place in the hearts and minds of the British people. The major factor involved was the special relationship between the royal families of both countries. Of much more importance was the future of post-war European politics. It was well known in informed circles even at that time that Winston Churchill did not share Roosevelt's trust in Joe Stalin. Post-war histories have also revealed that Churchill tried to move British and American troops into Poland to foil the spread of Soviet expansion. His efforts were frustrated by the Americans who had no wish to be involved in what they perceived to be British empire building.

Churchill was quick to realize that at least in Greece, using British and Commonwealth troops, he could halt the inevitable tide of post-war Communist domination of the Balkans.

Following the occupation of Greece by the Axis powers, the King of the Hellenes and his cabinet set up a government in exile in Cairo under the protection of the British Government. Sir Henry Maitland-Wilson, Commander-in-Chief, Middle East, was charged with the responsibility of returning the Greek Government to its homeland. This responsibility included maintaining peace and order until the new administration was capable of exercising government control. In a country torn apart by three years of German-Italian occupation, coupled to the anti-monarchist sentiments of a strong Communist-dominated partisan movement, this would prove to be almost an impossible task. Fostered in part by the Allied Powers and Soviet Russia and encouraged by Joe Stalin's political machine, the Greek Communist Party had achieved formidable powers by late 1944.

The Greek Communist movement was broken up into a number of groups: EAM represented the political left wing coalition, KKE being the dominating Communist block and ELAS its armed forces. Forces and factions loyal to the current right wing Greek Government were known as EDES. Complicating the foregoing was the invasion of Northern Greece by an undisciplined army of Bulgarian Communist partisans.

With time on their hands after the German withdrawal from Bulgaria they crossed the frontier, ostensibly in pursuit of German troops. They plundered, pillaged, raped and terrorized the province of Macedonia, murdering Germans and Greeks alike. They destroyed what little was left by the retreating Germans, reducing the unfortunate Greek civilian population to starvation.

Early in 1944 ELAS had set up a 'political committee' claiming the right to represent and speak for the Greek people. Basically ELAS and EDES were at war – civil war, the worst type of war in any country or between any factions.

Although Sir Henry Maitland-Wilson had convened two meetings between the opposing groups, the first in Cairo and the second in Caserta, trying to reconcile widely diverging views and opinions, he was unable to achieve consensus.

Another complication which produced sharp disagreement was the question of the 'security battalions'. In the later stage of the war, pressed as they were for manpower, the Nazi Command in Greece resorted to the dubious expedient of employing 'security battalions' manned by Greek volunteers to maintain order. Although classed as traitors by many Greeks and particularly so by ELAS partisans, many of these men had joined just to secure food for their families. EDES negotiators argued that those men should be given a fair trial. ELAS claimed they should just be executed. In 1944 Greece was a boiling cauldron, a devil's brew of conflicting emotions, opinions, hatreds and personal vendettas. Only rural Ireland in the nineteenth century could have produced a similar scenario.

Coupled to this volatile situation was the increasing tragedy of the Greek population in general. Quoting from *Fourth Indian Division* and referring to the depredations of the Bulgarian Communists in Northern Greece, Lieutenant Colonel Stevens goes on to say:

'With equal callousness the Germans set about the devastation of the remainder of Greece. Nearly two thousand villages were destroyed, thousands of Greeks shot, imprisoned or deported, schools closed, the press and radio muzzled. With less than ten thousand square miles of arable land in the Kingdom, it was essential to import three million tons of foodstuffs annually. The Germans made no effort to meet this requirement. Famine stalked the land. Infant mortality rose to 90% of all births. But for the efforts of Great Britain and her Allies, who managed to supply cargoes of foodstuffs through neutral channels, at least half the population of Greece would have died of hunger.'

Early in 1944 Middle East Command had assembled and trained a carefully selected group of officers and specialists, including signallers to be parachuted into Greece. Their objective was to give guidance to the partisans. Under their directions, arms and equipment were moved into Greece by air. This group was identified as Force 133.

It soon became apparent that ELAS personnel were going to be difficult to handle. Directions from the government in exile in Cairo met with undisguised hostility. Eventually the Commander-in-Chief, Middle East was able to persuade both parties to agree to bury differences during the liberation period and to accept orders from Allied

High Command. Both parties also agreed that British troops could enter Greece subject to the following objectives:

(1) To eject the enemy.
(2) To maintain law and order.
(3) To repair communications.
(4) To distribute civil relief.
(5) To remain strict political neutrals.

Although agreement had not been reached concerning the form of government, there appeared to be some understanding that democratic elections would take place to decide which party would form the constitutionally elected government of Greece. Later events were to prove that although this may have been the intention of EDES, it certainly did not figure in the plans of ELAS.

Late in September, as the Fifth and Eight Armies drove the Wehrmacht north towards the Gothic Line, as France was liberated and the Russians pressed ever closer to the German Fatherland enemy forces vacated the Aegean islands. The withdrawal from Greece had commenced.

As German forces retreated northwards from Athens they devastated the country behind them in a fashion reminiscent of the Russian scorched earth policy. It was senseless, wanton, vengeful destruction, devoid of any military necessity. In many villages civil leaders were shot without cause. There was a strong garrison of 12,000 German troops on Crete and Middle East Command decided to bypass this important island. It had now lost its former strategic significance.

Around the middle of October, the 2nd Independent Parachute Brigade and 23rd Armoured Brigade had landed near Athens. The British troops were welcomed enthusiastically by the civilian population. Not long afterwards the Greek prime minister and his cabinet arrived from Cairo. Lieutenant General Sir Ronald Scobie had been designated Supreme Allied Commander of British Land Forces Greece.

The divisional plan for the Greek Campaign would continue decentralization to brigade level. The 11th Field Regiment would continue to support the 11th Brigade, which would be based at Patras in Western Greece. This area would include Missolonghi and the Peleponnese. The 7th Brigade had been allocated the wild and woolly area of Macedonia and Thrace in Northern Greece and would headquarter at Salonika.

Originally the 5th Brigade had been scheduled to support an assault on Crete. This plan was changed to reconnoitre the islands of the Dodecanese and Cyclades for the purpose of reinforcing or relieving British commandos operating against German garrisons on their islands. Brigadier Saunders-Jacobs' recce party was at point of embarkation when these orders were countermanded. The 5th Brigade was ordered to southern Greece where trouble had broken out with ELAS partisans in Piraeus.

On 1st November a brigade reconnaissance party under Brigadier H.C. Hunt D.S.O. had proceeded to Patras. On 17th November the regimental advance party, having joined the brigade advance party, sailed from Taranto en route to Patras.

Brigadier Hunt divided his area of responsibility into four sectors: 2/7 Gurkha Rifles were given the northern sector; 3 Royal Frontier Force Regiment were allocated the central sector which would include Missolonghi. The Peleponnese was awarded to 2 Camerons. The 149 Anti-Tank Regiment was ordered into the Ionian islands of Kephallinia and Zante.

By the end of November the main body of the 11th Field Regiment, with guns, transport and equipment, was moving to Greece. The speed of this move was dictated by limited shipping. RHQ was established in Patras.

On 1st December a troop from 83/85 Battery, moving from Missolonghi to Agrinion, was aboard the SS *Empire Dace* when the ship struck a mine in the channel entrance to Missolonghi, blew up and sank. The ship was carrying approximately 125 personnel. It was several days before the final casualty list was known. Total figures were six killed, 51 wounded and 64 missing believed killed. Casualties of 83/85 Battery were three killed, 20 wounded and 25 missing believed killed. The channel where the disaster occurred had been cleared by a naval minesweeper and the *Empire Dace* had completed eight trips prior to the tragedy. It was believed but never proven that ELAS had been responsible for the mining of the channel.

Unloading of guns, equipment and stores was interrupted by a dockers strike at Patras Harbour. It was proven that ELAS agents had threatened dockers' families with reprisals if the dockers continued to unload British military equipment. Unloading was completed by military personnel under the direction of Royal Engineers.

193

Partially to 'show the colours' and partially to impress the civilian population, Lieutenant Colonel Page decided to hold a ceremonial parade and march past. On 5th December the 11th Field Regiment Royal Artillery marched through the streets of Patras behind the Pipe band of the 2 Camerons. The enthusiastic reception by the Greek civilians appeared to be genuine, sincere and spontaneous.

The situation in Patras at this time was described by the regimental diarist as being 'sticky'. This is a classic example of British understatement. The situation in Patras in early December was explosive. There were the supporters of the Greek Provisional Government. This group, although not necessarily committed royalists, believed the democratic process should be allowed to function through the medium of free elections. There were Communist supporters of ELAS. There was a broad mass of the civilian population more concerned with the daily struggle for survival and obtaining the basic necessities of life. Most of these groups welcomed the British troops. Finally scurrying for shelter and seeking escape from the summary vengeance of ELAS were former members of the German Security Battalions. In many instances these unfortunate men were taken into protective custody by British forces.

One of the first duties of brigade commanders was to contact the senior ELAS officer in their sector. They would bring this officer up to date on the overall military situation and request he disband his forces and commence surrendering their arms. Those local ELAS commanders proved to be doublefaced liars, recognizing no moral code. They procrastinated, they lied, they double-dealt, often making commitments they had no intention of honouring. A few examples in 11th Brigade area illustrate what became a pattern of negotiation and action throughout Greece by ELAS commanders.

In Patras the ELAS commanding officer assured Brigadier Hunt he would comply with the instructions of the Provisional Government. The same night the National Guard detachments (government troops) were surrounded and disarmed, then taken out of the city into the mountains. When questioned the following day, he denied all knowledge of the kidnapping. In Pyrgos the ELAS commander, a Major Mandukos, disarmed the National Guard and seized the local radio station. His political commissar broadcast that the Greek Provisional Government had fallen and that the Communist Party would assume power. When Lieutenant Colonel Noble, commanding 2 Camerons, demanded an explanation the Greek officer called a strike!

In all of these meetings with ELAS commanders British officers, negotiating under difficult circumstances, kept their cool. Often under pressure by highly emotional Greek officers who believed that a good negotiator was a good liar, they refused to be stampeded. Many of those meetings were handled with an interpreter. The interpreter would change the British statement and in some cases threw in his own opinion to really confuse the issues.

The situation became daily more tense. Provocation and insult to British troops was a regular occurrence. Only the military discipline and good humour of British and Commonwealth soldiers prevented a major explosion.

On 14th December a small convoy of infantrymen from the Royal Frontier Force Regiment, with a number of gunners from the 11th Field Regiment, were moving from Agrinion to Krioneri. At a lonely pass ELAS troops ambushed the convoy. They seized three British officers, including Captain R. Bentham RA of 83/85 Battery and four other ranks, including BQMS Ferguson and Driver Richmond of the same battery as hostages. Lieutenant K.O. Evans RA, who was sent to negotiate, was given a safe-conduct pass but was also seized as a hostage.

The following day ELAS forces mounted a major attack against the garrison in Krioneri using heavy mortars. Frontier Force sustained 17 casualties and three 11th Field Regiment gunners were killed in action. Losses might have been substantially higher were it not for the well-directed fire of a Royal Navy ship offshore. The garrison was withdrawn that night. Although it was necessary to destroy a number of vehicles, the guns were saved in a hair-raising withdrawal at high speed.

By late December, ELAS enjoyed complete control of the countryside. Patras itself was still controlled by British troops.

The 2/7 Gurkhas were on their way to garrison Corfu when their orders were cancelled and they were directed into Patras. A company of the Camerons were withdrawn from Pyrgos and detachments of the RAF Regiment were moved into Patras from Araxos Airfield. It was estimated that ELAS forces surrounding Patras were now at divisional strength. There were, of course, ELAS soldiers within the city, but because of the presence of British troops they maintained a low profile.

There were two features of the ongoing war of nerves in the city which we eventually discovered were peculiar to Greece. The first of these was the public loudspeaker system covering many of the main streets and park areas. From time to time Commonwealth troops were verbally bombarded with a diatribe of vituperation and insults following the familiar pattern of Nazi propaganda made infamous by Josef Goebbels. These vicious verbal attacks were broadcast in both Greek and English. The second phenomenon was the newsheet which appeared on the streets from unknown sources but obviously originated from ELAS sympathizers. They were usually filled with abuse of the occupying forces, both British and Greek.

The patience of British and Indian soldiers was now wearing thin. They had seen their comrades rolled and robbed, kidnapped and murdered. The proverbial good humour of the British Tommy was fast approaching explosion level. All troops were under strict orders to resist all provocation, ignore insults and literally turn the other cheek.

Although British forces in Athens and Piraeus had already taken full scale offensive action against ELAS troops, 11th Brigade Command continued to hope that the situation in Patras could be settled without bloodshed. It was a vanishing chimera. ELAS commanders entirely misunderstood Brigadier Hunt's statements and actions. They assumed our lack of action was due to timidity and fear of ELAS forces.

Brigadier Hunt had the necessary authority to take offensive action as the following extract from Operation Order No. 2 will attest:

'GP O.O. No. 2 11 IND INF BDE
6 December 1944 Top Secret
INFM.
3(b)   Personal from Gen. Scobie to Gen. Holworthy and Brig. Hunt.
BEGINS. H.M. Govt's Prime Minister has given me full powers to act in dispelling as follows Communist attempt to overthrow constitutional government. This power I delegate to you as far as your area is concerned – if possible arrest forthwith ringleaders of ELAS and politicals – I rely on you to prevent utmost any bloodshed but you have my authority to use force should this be necessary – ends.
INTENTION
4.   11 IND INF BDE GP will:
(a)   carry out the arrest of Communist leaders and liquidate ELAS forces in No. 2 District Greece.

(b)   Give max SP to Greek military and Govt. authorities in enforcing Martial Law.
6.   Action in Sp. of Martial Law
(a)   The capture and liquidation of ELAS/EP troops in Patras and Pergos.'

It became obvious that taking the current attitude of the Communist commanders, in order to comply with the preceding orders, blood would be shed – capture and liquidate were words that could not be misunderstood.

Although Brigadier Hunt continued to exhort and negotiate, plans were quietly being drawn up for offensive action. By the end of December preparations were well advanced. Lieutenant Colonel Page had been given complete responsibility for planning artillery support for the brigade plan of action. Guns were placed in carefully selected positions and zero lines recorded. OPs were established. In order to obtain a clear arc of fire for the guns it was necessary to cut down a number of trees. A security perimeter was established within which civilians were denied access.

One of the unusual features of the gun positions in Patras was the necessity to provide defence. It was well known that ELAS soldiers in civilian clothes were continuing to infiltrate into the city. Our infantry were already overextended and were unable to supply man-power for artillery defence. Major Brooke RA, the new Battery Commander of 78/84 Battery, was given the task of organizing the defence of the gun positions using regimental personnel. All ranks now carried personal weapons.

In addition to the defensive preparations within Patras a number of mobile armoured columns were formed to move out into the country in support of the infantry. Their objective was to capture and disarm, if possible, ELAS troops. The alternative would be liquidation. The overall name of these armoured formations was PATFORCE, and they were all composed of three elements: the first component was tanks usually Shermans manned by Royal Tank Regiment, armoured cars and infantry in Bren carriers. In addition lorried infantry might also be attached. The 11th Field Regiment was to supply and man six armoured cars for PATFORCE under command of Major Bromley-Davenport of the Highland Light Infantry. Our section was under the command of Captain J. Mayes RA of 187 Battery with Lieutenant J. Elles RA of 78/84 Battery 2 i/c.

On 16th December there was a confrontation between an ELAS patrol and Lieutenant Colonel Page at Andante House in Patras. The CO was conferring with officers of 78/84 Battery when the Greek officer commanding the patrol demanded that the house be turned over to him. Lieutenant Colonel Page refused and warned the officer that any attempt on his part to enter the house by force would be met with gunfire. Tension mounted as both groups raised their small arms in readiness. The Greek patrol withdrew abruptly.

Later that same day, a cache of small arms ammunition was discovered in Andante House. This explained the unusual interest of the Greek partisans.

The regiment hosted a Christmas party for local children on Christmas Eve. In addition, a total of over 200 pounds sterling was collected and donated to the Mayor's Fund for Poor Children.

New Year's Day 1945 was ushered in with a ceremonial parade in Patras Stadium at brigade level. The 11th Field Regiment contributed 100 officers and other ranks with four guns and four armoured cars. The salute was taken by Brigadier Hunt D.S.O.

On 4th January the Royal Navy Cruiser HMS *Ajax* anchored in Patras Harbour. Lieutenant Colonel Page and the regimental adjutant went aboard to arrange and co-ordinate the 11th Field Regiment and naval fire plans. The CO had developed those fire-plans in anticipation of the worst possible scenario with regard to ELAS forces surrounding Patras. Artillery officers with regimental signallers were put aboard HMS *Ajax*. Naval guns would come under command of the 11th Field Regiment. The continuous build-up of tension waiting for an invisible enemy to strike was now coming to an end.

Even as Lieutenant Colonel Page was completing the artillery preparations, Brigadier Hunt was informed by 3 Corps in Athens that the final meeting with ELAS representatives had proved abortive. The 11th Brigade must take immediate action to defend Patras and furthermore take such action that would pre-empt any planned assault on the city by ELAS forces. The brigade command was also informed that the 139th British Infantry Brigade with two squadrons of the 50th Royal Tank Regiment and a brigade of the Greek National Guard were on their way to Western Greece.

Martial Law was declared and the notices posted in both English and Greek. They read as follows:

'1. Military Law has been declared today by the Government Representatives of the Districts of Achaia and Elam and the surrounding District of Patras.
2. British Forces have been called to help the Greek Government to keep law and order.
3. The EAM/ELAS Forces have been called upon to lay down their arms and give themselves up. The Military Commander has forbidden anyone to carry arms except the National Guard, The Royal Greek Navy and the Police.
4. In order that there shall be no bloodshed and to keep law and order I advise all the inhabitants of Patras and its environs that until further orders, all troops under my command have orders to search all persons, houses, buildings and cars in the whole area which has to be cleared of ELAS forces and that this will be carried out.
5. I call on every law-abiding citizen to help me as well as the Forces under my command in bringing law, order and peace at the earliest possible moment in Patras and to help in the collection of arms and ammunition etc. belonging to the forces of EAM/ELAS.
January 1945
(signed) John Hunt
Brigadier DSO'

Units of 139 Brigade commenced disembarking on 9th January with tanks of 50th RTR coming ashore first. Brigadier Block, commanding officer of 139th Brigade, took over command of PATFORCE as senior officer. Brigadier Block had some experience negotiating with Greek Communists. He had come to the conclusion that any form of negotiation was misconstrued as a sign of weakness. Although the Bishop of Patras offered to mediate, he was politely shown the door.

Brigadier Block ordered all ELAS formations to evacuate Patras within 48 hours. This ultimatum would expire at 06.00 hours 11th January.

Four days earlier, and coinciding with the Declaration of Martial Law, 11th Brigade Sergeants' Mess was nearly torn apart by a bomb explosion which was apparently timed to go off during a dance. A six-piece band provided by 187th Battery absorbed most of the shock. Total casualties amounted to 17 men. Lance Bombardier Grounds died from injuries.

Injured either seriously or less seriously included BSM Edwards, Sergeant Kemp and Gunners Gaskin and Holt. That Communist operatives were responsible for this outrage was never in doubt.

ELAS commanders, upon receipt of Brigadier Block's ultimatum, put on a major exhibition of indignation, claiming their honour was on the line. They demanded, what else, a conference. In a series of phone calls, they made an effort to lead the commander of 139th Brigade into the now familiar conference trap. They were told that negotiations were now closed and if they failed to vacate Patras as per ultimatum, they would be taken prisoner or liquidated if they chose to resist.

In the early hours of 10th January ELAS troops commenced their retreat from Patras. Their bluff had been finally called.

House to house searches throughout Patras were conducted following the expiry of the ultimatum. Substantial quantities of arms and ammunition were discovered and confiscated. Vehicles were checked and any individual unable to give a satisfactory explanation of his actions was detained.

Brigade patrols now began pushing out of their wired in beach-head into the country. Captain Cullen RA commanded a troop of guns supporting a 139th Brigade column. The recapture of Araxos Airfield was completed without casualties.

On 13th January Brigadier Hunt issued orders to battalion commanders to intercept, detain and disarm all ELAS forces in the brigade area. This area could be described as a mountainous belt along the Gulf of Corinth and about 40 miles in depth. The weather had turned cold in early January with intermittent snow falls. Deep snow covered much of the country.

At first light on 14th January the three battalion columns moved out of Patras into the high ground.

Two Camerons were allotted the south east boundary of the brigade area. They clashed with a number of ELAS patrols which were detained and disarmed without a major incident. On the third day the Camerons reached their objective at Kalavrita.

The Royal Frontier Force Regiment drove east along the Gulf of Corinth. ELAS troops set up heavily defended road blocks along their line of advance. Ambushes at critical points were a feature of their resistance. It became obvious that although the Communist partisans may have withdrawn quietly from the city, they had no intention of yielding in the country without a fight. At Kamarais on the coastal road to the east of Patras, the RFFR were brought to a halt. The 11th Field Regiment guns were deployed and brought into action. On 15th January a company of RFFR joined up with the Camerons at Kalavrita and closed the ring. Patrols, supported by Bren carriers and armoured cars, now moved out into the country.

ELAS troops in this area, who had apparently decided that the war games were now over, surrendered with little resistance. ELAS leaders in the area of Klauss were particularly hostile to the Provisional Government and had threatened to fight to the death. The 2/7 Gurkhas were given the task of bringing this area under control.

The strategy involved in dealing with this explosive area called for Gurkha infantrymen to take the partisans from the rear while a mobile armoured column from 139th Brigade would advance frontally driving the enemy into the Gurkha positions. Force marching through the mountains by night, the Gurkhas arrived in the rear of the partisans by dawn on 14th January.

The report to RHQ 11th Field Regiment by Captain J.S. Mayes RA on 17th January covered the actions by this mobile column. Captain Mayes commanded the armoured cars in this column. This report is quoted in its entirety:

'Report on 'Mobcol' operations
13 January 1945
O.C. Mobcol – Major Bromley-Gardener
Composition: (2 Bn. H.L.I.)
1 Troop Sherman tanks – 50RTR
1 Troop Armoured Cars – 11 Field Regt. R.A.
1 Troop Bren Carriers – 2/7 Gurkha Rifles
1 Det. A.D.S.
Object:
    To capture 'Klauss' and push enemy onto 2/7 Gurkha Rifles
Method:
    08.00 hrs
    'Mobcol' entering village Kourouli in following order:
1st Column
    Tank
    Armoured Car (with Public Address loudspeakers attached)

Tank

3 Carriers

2nd Column

Armoured Car

3 Carriers

ADS

1 Tank

Fired on by Spandau. Column halted and swept area to left of road with M.G. fire.

Broadcast telling ELAS to surrender. Enemy resistance ceased.

08.30 hrs

1st Column pushed on, leaving second column in Kourouli. Encountered a roadblock composed of felled trees. Both blocks disintegrated by 75 mm on leading tank at 10 yds. range.

09.00 hrs

Encountered third road block at 667823. 6–75 mm HE put into it and remains had to be towed away. Loudspeakers produced 20 male civilians unarmed.

09.45 hrs

Advanced into wadi 671820. Came under LMG and MMG fire from direction Saravali. Replied with 75 mm and LMG. 1 tank temporarily v/s with clutch trouble. Owing to plunging fire carriers left behind a wall in wadi, and advance made by 1 tank and 2 armoured cars. Fired on all the way up to Klauss Hill. Encountered infantry battle and supported with LMG and 75 mm second and third tanks called up to head of column to support with 75 mms.

12.00 – 13.00 hrs

2 tanks and 2 armoured cars advanced to Saravali. Fired on by snipers from hill. Broadcasting produced two ELAS officers who were put on the air to tell their men to surrender. Resulted in 20–30 surrenders.

14.00 hrs

Return to Klauss to regroup leaving one tank guarding arms and ammunition in Saravali church. Mobcol remained in Klauss night 13/14 with 2/7 G.R.

Results:

Enemy killed – 27

Wounded – 32

Disarmed POW 80

Own casualties – nil

Arms and Ammunition taken

10 heavy and medium machine guns

90 (approx.) rifles
20 tons (approx.) Ammunition mines explosives 17 January 1945
(signed)
J.S. Mayes Capt. R.A.'

The armoured mobile column achieved its objective of driving the communist partisans onto the waiting Gurkha infantrymen. A number of sharp skirmishes and fire fights developed but by mid-afternoon it was all over. The Gurkhas were fighting in their natural element and the ELAS irregulars were no match for the disciplined and battle hardened hillmen. The ELAS troops finally surrendered having lost 27 men killed and 32 wounded. Eighty-four partisans laid down their arms. Gurkha casualties were two killed and two wounded. The districts of Achaia, Elam and Patras were now neutralized.

The 5th Brigade was originally ordered to land on the Dodecanese and Cyclades groups of islands. The brigade was to reinforce and support British commandos operating against German garrisons making a final stand. However, before Brigadier Saunders-Jacobs commenced a planned reconnaissance, his orders were cancelled and the brigade was directed to land at Athens. Trouble had broken out with the ELAS partisans in southern Greece.

ELAS forces in the south totalled nearly 75,000 men. They were well armed and more disciplined than their compatriots in the north. Long experience fighting German occupying troops had made them masters of street warfare. They were dedicated, determined and resourceful.

On 3rd December ELAS troops, abrogating the treaty with the Provisional Greek Government, had taken to the streets fully armed. They surrounded British Headquarters, located in the Hotel Grande Bretagne. Simultaneously they invested British and Greek Naval Headquarters in Piraeus. Elements of 2/5 Leicesters and 16th Durham Light Infantry were ordered into position to defend these headquarters against impending attack. They were hopelessly outnumbered by ELAS troops and called for reinforcements.

The initial objectives of 5th Brigade were to land at Piraeus, clear the harbour and maintain sea communications with Athens.

Piraeus is an ancient harbour town located about five miles south west of Athens. Although the area surrounding the town is generally flat, the harbour is dominated by a hill named Lofos Castella. The summit of Lofos Castella rises to a height of nearly 100 metres. This feature was held by ELAS troops in strength. It appeared that the tactical plan of the Communist commander was to maintain the harbour under siege while ELAS troops in Athens would engage British forces and destroy them before they could be reinforced. They would then take prisoner or liquidate the Greek Provisional Government and declare a Communist state.

On 9th December the 5th Indian Infantry Brigade began to come ashore, protected by 2/5 Leicesters. Led by 1/4 Essex, they had advanced about three-quarters of one mile by nightfall. Resistance was relatively minor. Early the next morning the remainder of the brigade came ashore.

Brigade HQ had drawn up a five-stage plan to relieve Athens and Piraeus, defeat ELAS and restore the power of the Greek Provisional Government:

1.   Cordon the Kharikou-Trikoupi road and mop up all partisans caught behind barricades.
2.   Advance to the road Yeoryiou 800 yards further north.
3.   Assault and seize the hill Lofos Castella.
4.   Advance to the line of the railway skirting Phaleron Bay.
5.   Clear enemy forces from the northern and opposite side of the harbour.

The first phase of the operation was completed by 13th December. The 1/4 Essex held a barbed wire barrier while 1/9 Gurkhas and 3/10 Baluchis moved out, destroying or capturing ELAS enemy troops. The Royal Greek Marines supplied valuable assistance in this operation.

The advance to Yeoryiou was continued in the morning of 14th December. The 1/9 Gurkhas were now withdrawn to prepare for the assault on Lofos Castella.

Street fighting slowed the advance as ELAS troops fought stubbornly and contested every yard and every house. Many of these houses had been converted into strongpoints and were heavily fortified with mortars and machine guns. Sherman tanks were rushed forward and houses were battered down using 75 mm high explosive. As the defenders broke cover, infantry following behind cut off their escape. Street barricades manned by determined partisans were also blasted clear by tank gunners. During this phase of the fighting the local ELAS HQ was overrun and captured by 3/10 Baluchis.

On 15th December the action against the defences on Lofos Castella opened with a naval bombardment. This was supplemented by a battery of the 1st Field Regiment which had deployed its guns on Psittalia, a small island in Phaleron Bay. Shooting under observed fire, the battery searched the hill for enemy strongpoints and machine-gun emplacements. At 01.40 hours the following morning 1/9 Gurkhas made contact with the enemy near the base of the hill. They were supported by gunners of the 1st Field Regiment turned infantry-men and commanded by Captain R. Harrison RA. With rifle, bayonet and *kukri* they fought their way up the hill. By mid-morning they had gained the summit. Soon afterwards Lofos Castella was reported clear of the enemy. The advantage of observation provided by the hill was a major by-product of this action and the road to Athens was soon opened. Communication between Athens and Piraeus was restored and the Kallipolis Peninsula cleared of the enemy.

Only the inner harbour now remained under ELAS control. The 57th Light Anti-Aircraft Regiment had occupied the power station on St George's Bay. It was heavily attacked by ELAS troops on 20th December. An amphibious operation was mounted by a company of 3/10 Baluchis supported by detachments of 1/9 Gurkhas. They linked up with gunners and established a tenuous bridgehead. On 22nd December the enemy fought back violently. This was probably the most vicious and fiercely contested battle of the Greek campaign. ELAS troops fought with bravery and determination and only the support of rocket firing Beaufighters saved the bridgehead. Further attacks were mounted during the night. These attacks were thrown back after fierce hand to hand fighting.

On 23rd December the advance was resumed in the face of heavy machine-gun fire. The action now resembled the fighting in Orsogna against the Germans – it was house by house and from factories into warehouses.

On the morning of Christmas Eve the brigade mounted an attack on the powder house, a strongpoint blocking access to Avenue Dhionisiou. Utilizing heavy mortar fire, with artillery concentrations supported by rocket-firing Beaufighters, the resistance disintegrated and the objective was occupied.

Christmas Day arrived, cool and overcast, but the spirit of Christmas failed to reduce the intensity of the fighting. During the morning the Essex, supported by Shermans, attacked and occupied the Papastratos Cigarette Factory, taking over 300 prisoners. The factory cellars were crowded with women and children in a pitiable state of terror and misery. They had had neither food nor water for several days.

Events were now building rapidly towards the final action of this short and vicious campaign. ELAS commanders gathered in their forces to make a last desperate stand in the area of the power station on St George's Bay. The 5th Brigade deployed 1/4 Essex and 3/10 Baluchis supported by 2/5 Leicesters who came under brigade command.

They attacked towards the power station with their flank protected by mortar fire directed along the Anatasis Cemetery. ELAS troops resisted valiantly, taking heavy casualties from both naval gunfire and the 25-pounders of the 1st Field Regiment. By early afternoon on New Year's Eve it was all over. The defenders broke and began to retire in disorder towards the north of Leoforos Salaminos pursued by armoured cars.

It was a sad ending for the Communist partisans. They had battled bravely for their cause and although they possessed both the numbers and the determination, they lacked the fire power and the battle experience of the 4th Indian Division.

The power station assault brought the campaign in Athens and southern Greece to an end. Athens was relieved and the port of Piraeus was open. Brigade casualties were relatively light: 18 men killed and 175 wounded. Although the brigade took nearly 1000 prisoners ELAS casualties in killed and wounded were never revealed.

Unknown to the soldiers of the 4th Indian Division, a strange meeting had been convened in Athens on the afternoon of 26th December. It was a meeting which would have historic consequences, leading eventually to a peaceful settlement of the Greek holocaust, although many lives were yet to be lost.

In an unheated conference room in the building housing the Greek Ministry for Foreign Affairs, Archbishop Damaskinos of Athens sat at the centre of a large oval table. In the absence of electric power the light was provided by a number of oil hurricane lamps. On the right of the Archbishop sat the British Prime Minister, Winston Churchill, and on his right was the British Foreign Secretary, Anthony Eden. To his left were Field-Marshall Harold Alexander, Allied Military

206

Commander in the Mediterranean Theatre, and Harold MacMillan, Churchill's personal representative who had convened the meeting under Churchill's direction. Opposite him were M. Papandreou, Greek Premier Designate, and George Kaplandoris, Greek Prime Minister in 1924. There were three ELAS representatives: Dimitrios Partsalides, Secretary of EAM; Georgios Siantos, Secretary General of KKE and General Emmanuel Mandakas of ELAS.

Also present as observers were Colonel Popov, head of the Soviet Military Mission to Greece; Mr MacVeagh, the American Ambassador and a French minister. Major Matthews provided interpreting services.

After opening remarks by the Archbishop who chaired the meeting, Churchill addressed the group, speaking for about 20 minutes. He made it clear that he supported the candidacy of the Archbishop for the office of regent; that he wanted peace and reconciliation and increased effort in the work of relief to all Greeks, regardless of political affiliation, that he not only supported but demanded that the future form of government for Greece be constitutionally elected. Churchill reminded the ELAS representatives of British military power which he was prepared to use in order to achieve Allied plans. He closed his address by urging all Greek representatives to reach agreement between themselves without outside intervention.

Field-Marshall Alexander then addressed the gathering briefly. He is quoted as saying: 'Instead of putting my brigades into Greece, I would like to see Greek brigades coming to help me in Italy against the common enemy.'

After shaking hands all around, Churchill led the British delegation out of the room. They were followed by the observers, leaving the Greek delegates to forge an agreement between themselves under the chairmanship of the Archbishop of Athens.

In his *War Diaries*, Harold MacMillan noted, referring to Greek negotiators that: 'The Greeks are really oriental in their methods. Time wasted, as long as it is wasted in talk, is time enjoyed. Nothing takes place at any ordinary hour and, above all, at the hour arranged.'

ELAS commenced a general withdrawal of their forces from Athens on 5th January. Ten days later, the conference opened by Churchill on 26th December finally produced an agreement between the Provisional Government and ELAS, culminating in a truce. Orders were issued to all brigade commanders that no further action was to be taken against ELAS forces in southern Greece. They were to be allowed to withdraw north of an agreed delineated line or truce boundary, taking their arms, ammunition and equipment with them. Four days later patrols reported that all partisans had complied with the terms of the armistice.

The 5th Brigade now faced the daunting task of feeding and caring for tens of thousands of starving and homeless civilians. Athens, with 1,250,000 inhabitants, was without water, food, heat or light. Piraeus had been devastated and almost destroyed by the German Army long before the Communist partisans embarked on their reckless civil war. Homeless civilians, taking shelter in deserted factories, warehouses and public buildings, were devoid of the basic essentials of existence.

The 5th Brigade opened a Brigade Clearing Centre in Athens. Reserve ration dumps were used to feed starving civilians. As many as 22,000 meals were served daily to over 10,000 civilians in this area alone. First aid posts supplemented by medical treatment centres were set up by the 26th Field Ambulance. Those were often staffed by British, Indian and Greek doctors working side by side. Indian sappers and miners demolished dangerous buildings, constructed water points, erected temporary tents and installed public latrines. These temporary and makeshift arrangements alleviated the extreme level of misery to which the population had been reduced initially by the occupying forces, but intensified and prolonged by the civil war.

The action at Krioneri produced another Military Medal for the regiment. The regimental medical orderly Bombardier Jack Parker was the recipient. Under heavy mortar fire he had repeatedly gone forward to bring wounded gunners to safety.

15   FINALE: NORTHERN GREECE

While the 11th Brigade was occupied in Patras and the Peleponnese and the 5th Brigade was fighting in southern Greece, the 7th Indian Infantry Brigade was engaged in northern Greece. This wild and totally unpredictable area is composed of three provinces. In the west, Epirus shares its borders with Albania and Yugoslavia; in the centre Macedonia faces Yugoslavia and Bulgaria and in the east Thrace faces both Bulgaria and Turkey. With the exception of Turkey, which preserved its neutrality in the Second World War, all of these countries by the end of 1944 were either Communist or occupied by Russian troops. The total area measured about 350 miles from west to east as the crow flies and averaged about 50 miles from its northern border south to the Aegean Sea.

Even before the war and the eventual Nazi occupation, life in northern Greece was uncertain, frugal and threadbare; living on or below the poverty line was the norm in Macedonia and Thrace. Poor communications exacerbated a dangerous lifestyle and family feuds were a way of life. Under the excesses of German military discipline a situation that was already chronic became acute.

The concept of the security battalions which caused so many post-German withdrawal problems throughout Greece was a complete disaster in Macedonia. Former members became immediate targets for ELAS troops bent on revenge and the settlement of old scores, real and imagined. The area of Kozani and Drama was particularly serious and only timely action by units of 1/2 Gurkha Rifles saved the lives of many of those unfortunate men.

The Macedonia Corps of ELAS was commanded by General Bakardzis who, although technically under the command of ELAS HQ in Athens, had decided to operate his own campaign. He considered northern Greece to be his own personal fiefdom, disregarding all directives from Athens unless they meshed with his own plans. Into this devil's brew of anger and animosity, supported by Joe Stalin in Moscow, Brigadier Lovett led his 7th Brigade in December of 1944. Setting up his headquarters in Salonika, he quickly realized that he faced an impossible task. At this point in the Second World War the 7th Brigade could muster less than 3000 front line troops. There were over 4000 armed men in Salonika alone. In the countryside ELAS could call upon three to four times this number. Until reinforcements arrived Brigadier Lovett, supported by Brigadier Eastman, C.R.A. 4th Indian Division, decided to play a game plan calling for patience linked to diplomatic negotiation.

A favourite method of obtaining funds to support their operation were levies placed against the shopkeepers by ELAS. Those who resisted would have their merchandise seized. As at Patras, public loudspeaker systems were used to insult and pour invective on British and Indian troops.

In late December an incident occurred at a Salonika soccer stadium which proved to be more humorous than serious. During a match between a Greek civilian team and the crew of a British minesweeper, a heavily armed detachment of ELAS appeared on the soccer field and marched off all the Greek spectators!

The truce, concluded with ELAS on 14th January 1945, was divided into two stages. This initial stage called for ELAS troops to withdraw north of the provincial boundary between Thessaly and Epirus, running roughly east and west from the Aegean Sea, circling Mount Olympus and ending at the Albanian frontier. It was also agreed that those men who opted to move north would be allowed to take their arms and equipment with them. ELAS soldiers who decided to remain in southern Greece surrendered their arms. The second stage of the truce would extend the authority of the Provisional Government throughout northern Greece. This stage was scheduled to commence some time in February. Once again, the 4th Indian Division was called on to spearhead the enforcement of the authority of the Provisional Government.

In late January the division was relieved of its responsibilities in Patras, Athens and surrounding areas by two British Divisions. The division was ordered to move into a concentration area near Salonika.

Preceding the divisional move but following the truce, the commander of 3 Corps, General Hawkeworth, arrived in Salonika. A meeting between him and General Bakardzis almost ended in violence. General Hawkeworth informed the Greek commander that the terms of the truce would apply to the northern provinces and would be enforced. The partisans were given four days to evacuate Salonika and withdraw to defined areas. ELAS forces immediately commenced their withdrawal from Salonika.

On 18th January two battalions of the Greek National Guard arrived from Athens. They immediately relieved 7th Brigade of their police duties in the city. The brigade was now free to move out into the country. Later on these duties were taken over by newly-enlisted and British-trained Greek police. It may be superfluous to add that would-be recruits for this police force were carefully screened for their political sympathies before enlistment.

Through the month of February, 5th and 11th Brigades sailed north through the Aegean Sea without incident disembarking at Salonika.

On 31st January the first group from the 11th Field Regiment embarked in two LSTs in Patras Harbour. The group was under the command of Captain Mayes with three junior officers and numbered 84 other ranks. They were equipped with six guns, eight trailers and 72 vehicles. The balance of the regiment followed through February.

The division would continue to operate at a brigade level and for this purpose northern Greece was divided into three areas which coincided with its Greek political and geographical divisions: 5th Brigade was allotted Epirus in the west; 11th Brigade made responsible for Macedonia while 7th Brigade moved east into Thrace, which included the islands of Thasos and Samothrace.

A plan was drawn up by Divisional Command and Greek National Guard commanders. It was hoped that with care and ongoing consultation the risk of open warfare with ELAS could be maintained to a minimum. Initially each province was divided into a number of manageable areas. Expressed in its simplest form, this plan would operate as follows: British and Commonwealth troops would move into a single designated area; one week later National Guard units would follow; in week three British troops would commence collecting arms and at the same time Greek authorities would commence call-up for service in the National Guard; in weeks five and six, equipment and clothing would be issued to conscripts and training would begin. Each area had to be safely under the control of the Provisional Government before troops would move into another area, where the process would be repeated.

The 4th Indian Division was ordered to cross the truce lines on 2nd March and on that date 7th and 11th Brigades moved out of Salonika, leaving a strong garrison in the city. The 11th Field Regiment continued to support the 11th Brigade. OP parties moved with battalion headquarters; it was deemed advisable to be prepared for a hostile reception. Generally speaking, 4th Indian Division troops were well received. This friendly reception did not necessarily apply to government troops or Greek civil administrators. The departments of Khalkidke, Thessalonica and Kilkis were occupied and disarmed without serious problems.

The 7th Brigade worked their way into Thrace following the operational plan previously laid down. They occupied and disarmed a number of departments. By late March 1/2 Gurkhas had reached Alexandroupolis, moving close to the Turkish frontier. Some fighting started between ELAS supporters and Greek troops and it was necessary to call in Central India Horse with their armoured cars. Close to the Turkish border about 300 German soldiers were seized by ELAS troops. Only the timely intervention of units of 1/2 Gurkhas saved these unfortunate men from summary execution.

The 1/4 Essex moved steadily through the countryside, surrounding Edhassa, and continued on to Florina close to the Yugoslav border. The 1/9 Gurkhas handled the dangerous area of Kozani in the centre of the Province of Epirus while 3/10 Baluchis searched Naosa encountering a form of sullen but passive resistance. The 3rd Royal Frontier Force Regiment remained in the vicinity of Salonika ready to provide support to the National Guard if necessary. The 2 Camerons made their presence felt in the area of Seres while 2/7 Gurkhas patrolled the difficult and potentially dangerous town of Kilkis close to the Bulgarian border. Drama and Kavalla were allotted to the Royal Sussex while 1/2 Gurkhas disarmed the partisans in and around Xanthe. Komotini in eastern Thrace was pacified by 2 Royal Sikhs.

This left the islands of Thasos and Samothrace. The latter island was only about 80 miles west of the Straits of the Dardenelles and Gallipoli in Turkey, the scene of terrible losses by British forces in the First World War. The 7th Brigade provided garrisons for these two islands.

In many of these operations gunners of the three divisional field regiments with men of the anti-aircraft regiment and anti-tank gunners were employed in an infantry role, providing direct support to the regular infantry formations.

Macedonia was the scene of some bloody fighting when Communist troops of the Macedonian Autonomists Movement, sponsored by Tito in Yugoslavia, refused to be disarmed and attacked British and Indian troops. They were commanded by a ruthless guerrilla leader named Gotsis who feared neither God nor man. His forces were finally routed by 1/4 Essex and Central India Horse, supported by Sherman tanks of the Royal Tank Regiment. Although the power of this lawless group of criminals was broken Gotsis escaped the sweep and was believed to have found refuge across the border in Bulgaria.

Although living conditions were bad throughout Greece in the final year of the war in Europe, the civilian population in northern Greece were scraping the bottom of the barrel. Even under pre-war peacetime conditions the inhabitants of Macedonia and Thrace had eked out a precarious existence, living close to the poverty line. In 1945 the condition of those unfortunate people resembled the height of the great famine in southern Ireland between 1840 and 1850.

The retreating German soldiers had wantonly destroyed what they couldn't remove. The Greek partisans were too busy settling their everlasting private feuds to concern themselves with the welfare of civilians. Communications were non-existent and both national and local governments had been swept away. Starvation, malnutrition, sickness and death of ancient Biblical proportions lay like a black static cloud across the face of the earth.

Following the restoration of law and order the immediate priority was the supply of food, clothing and medical services to the civilian population. The following report by a British officer in respect of just one village was typical of many others.

'Village of ...
1.   Communications – none

2. Education – school burned by Bulgars
3. Religion – Priest killed by Bulgars.
4. Employment – none
5. Food reserves – none
6. Clothing – rags
Comment: Supplies of everything urgently needed.'

In the mountainous broken terrain of northern Greece, cut and intersected by many rivers, bridges of all types were a vital necessity. To a major extent these had been destroyed by partisans trying to restrict and immobilize enemy troops. Whatever survived was destroyed by the retreating German forces.

Divisional field engineers moved rapidly to repair or replace the most important of these bridges. On the main highway to Athens a bridge over 800 feet long was one of the first to be returned to service. Another, over the Axius River, had a total length of 1800 feet (above 600 metres) with 14 spans. The broken spans were replaced with Bailey bridge sections. On the Verroia-Kozani road permanent masonry bridges were built. An important and vital bridge over the Aliakman River was repaired. The civilian administration deemed this bridge important enough to warrant an official opening. The Bishop of Macedonia was called upon to officiate and the bridge was renamed Red Eagle Bridge in honour of the 4th Indian Division. Where and when possible, local civilian labour was employed on many of these bridge and road repair projects.

The following table dramatically demonstrates the work of Indian Divisional Sappers and Miners (field engineers) in northern Greece through the late winter and spring of 1945.

CLASS OF STRUCTURE	NUMBER	LENGTH (IN METRES)
1. Permanent structures in masonry or concrete	15	125
2. Temporary lumber bridges	5	310
3. Temporary Bailey bridges	13	315
4. Semi-permanent Bailey bridges	5	330
5. Semi-permanent Flambo bridges	6	275
TOTALS	44	1355

The repair and maintenance of the main highway running south to Athens was another major project handled by divisional engineers. This road rendered some spectacular views when it made its way through a pass on the slopes of Mount Olympus. It was very often snowbound from December through March. After repair the division maintained road maintenance crews with equipment to keep the road open.

Working concurrently with the sappers and miners, British and Indian signal detachments commenced work on the telephone system. This had been almost completely destroyed by German occupation troops. The initial priority was to reestablish communications between Salonika and Athens. Feeder lines were then erected into the country districts and finally the frontier posts which had been reestablished were connected to the main telephone system.

It was, however, in the field of medical services that the division made its greatest contribution to the population of northern Greece. In many areas houses and even whole villages had been destroyed by explosives or burnt to the ground. The former inhabitants, without any form of shelter from the harsh winter temperatures and weakened by hunger, died in hundreds. Thousands more were surviving on a day to day basis, reduced to the level of an animal existence.

The 17th Field Ambulance was established in Kavalla, the 26th Field Ambulance in Verroia and the 32nd Field Ambulance remained in Salonika. Medical detachments were sent into the country districts.

Epidemic diseases which were a direct result of malnutrition were slowly brought under control. A major crisis almost swamped the 26th Field Ambulance which had set up a medical post in Volos. They found themselves with thousands of sick, wounded and dying prisoners of war on their hands. A full scale general hospital was eventually developed in this area supplying a complete range of medical services. Additional tents and equipment were rushed to the scene from Athens and again, as in southern Greece, military and Greek civilian doctors worked side by side. Through the late winter, spring and summer of 1945 this hospital treated over 400 civilian outpatients daily.

In the early summer of 1945 a delegation from UNRRA arrived in Macedonia to develop and continue the services commenced by the 4th Indian Division. This delegation was under the command of a Colonel von Spach, a former United States Army officer. Colonel von

215

Spach proved to be an inspiring leader. He sent the following report (found in *Fourth Indian Division*) to his superiors upon the completion of his duties in Greece:

'Before leaving Greece, I wish to report to you on the outstanding co-operation I have received in operating our programme in Western Macedonia from Fourth Indian Division of the British Army commanded by Major General Charles Boucher.

To gain my objective I was constantly calling on various units of this Indian Division for assistance which they most willingly gave. We used their transportation – all kinds, from jeeps to three-ton trucks, to haul supplies to every part of Western Macedonia. We used their gas, oil and repair services to keep our own transportation in operation. We used their staging areas to park our large convoys which remained over-night guarded by their soldiers. Officers and men helped us in fair distribution of our supplies to villages far up in the mountains. We used their quarters to house and feed truck drivers. The Officers Messes were always open to UNRRA personnel. We used their ambulances to haul people to and from hospital. Their doctors were a big factor in our public health programme.

We used their barracks to store our supplies, at times even drawing upon them for rations to keep our soup kitchens going. They built our public baths and disinfectant centres and soup kitchens and provided us with materials to rebuild hospitals and schools.

Without the help and co-operation of the above, it would have been impossible for us to get even a small part of our programme over in Western Macedonia. I assure you that I am most grateful for what they have done.'

However, for the men of the 4th Indian Division, the compliments that were most remembered came from Greek civilians. They were expressed simply, without emotion, and consequently carried sincere honesty – a smile or courtesy. Maybe a bottle of ouzo. After the passage of time, as the population came to realize that British and Indian troops were neither murderers nor rapists and lost their initial fear, individuals would approach officers and NCOs with warning of possible danger.

In the town of Verroia there is a street named Sherwood. It was renamed by the Mayor of Verroia in 1945 in memory of Lieutenant Colonel L.V. Sherwood D.S.O., Commanding Officer of 3/10 Baluch

Regiment, who was killed in an unfortunate accident.

Early morning May sunshine was flooding the mountains and valleys of northern Macedonia as an armoured car with the battle colours of the 11th Field Regiment Royal Artillery drew slowly to a halt on a rocky outcrop near the Bulgarian border. As the crew climbed out and began brewing tea a company of Gurkhas dismounted from their vehicles on the road below. An officer searched the country ahead with his binoculars.

The burnt-out ruins of a Greek frontier post about 300 yards ahead marked the Greek side at the international boundary. Nearly a mile to the west the Struma River snaked its way through a winding valley. Here and there an area of shallows would disturb its placid surface and reflect the sun's rays in sparkling silver. On the Greek side of the border the river became the Strimon, pursuing its way south to the Aegean Sea.

The 2/7 Gurkha patrol had been making a sweep and the previous day had caught up with a group of Communist partisans. Contact had been lost during the hours of darkness.

It was evident that, outnumbered and outgunned, their quarry had fled across the border into Communist Bulgaria. Self-exile, usually into Bulgaria, was the final move of diehard ELAS troops who refused to surrender and turn in their weapons and ammunition. Gotsis, the fierce ELAS leader, had made this decision two months earlier. How many ELAS soldiers elected to take this extreme path out of their dilemma has never been established. Their final fate is revealed in the second chapter of *The Gulag Archipelago*, the international bestseller written by the famous Russian author Aleksandr I. Solzhenitsyn:

'In 1948, one more nationalist wave went into exile – that of the Greeks who inhabited the areas around the sea of Azov, the Kuban and Sukhumi. They had done nothing to offend the Father (Josef Stalin) during the war, but now he avenged himself on them for his failure in Greece, or so it seemed. This wave too, was evidently the fruit of his personal insanity. The majority of the Greeks ended up in Central Asian exile; those who voiced their discontent were thrown into political prisons.

Around 1950, to avenge the same lost war, or perhaps just to balance those already in exile, the Greek rebels from Markos' army who had been turned over to us by Bulgaria, were themselves shipped off to the Archipelago.'

After a final check of the border area the patrol commander gave orders to terminate the operation. Soon afterwards the patrol started its journey back to its temporary base at Sorrai.

Although the gunners in the armoured car did not know it, they had, at the Bulgarian border on that May morning, reached the furthest point travelled by the 11th Field Regiment since it left Meerut in India three years and nine months earlier. To Bombay and then by sea to Basra, then north through Baghdad to Mosul and Kirkuk and the Persian frontier. Next the forced march west through Syria and Palestine to Egypt and the Western Desert. Then Alamein with its panzer tank battles and the chase of the Afrika Korps across Northern Africa culminating in the Tunisian Campaign. Then Italy with its horror of Cassino, and finally Greece.

In a total of five campaigns spread across three continents, the 11th Field Regiment had sustained 516 casualties in killed, wounded and missing.

As spring advanced into the summer of 1945 UNRRA continued to assume greater responsibility for the problems of northern Greece. The military issues were now settled, not necessarily to everyone's satisfaction, and the war in Europe had ended in May. With the end of hostilities in the Far East later in the year the work of the 4th Indian Division was completed. The inevitable break-up of the division commenced in early July when the 1st Royal Sussex and 2nd Camerons embarked at Salonika. In early August, the 57th Light Anti-Aircraft Regiment and 1/4 Essex left Greece for the Home Establishment.

It was January of 1946 before the divisional field artillery, including the 11th Field Regiment, sailed west to England and the Indian infantry sailed east home to India.

It was a sad parting. The bonds of trust, respect and dependence, forged in steel and tempered in blood from Keren in East Africa through the battles of El Alamein, across North Africa to Tunis and finally welded on the bloody slopes of Monte Cassino, now had to be broken. The friendship that developed between white man and coloured over five years of conflict disintegrated the racial animosity of centuries and placed every man in the 4th Indian Division, whether English or Rajput, Scottish or Madrasi, Irish or Gurkha, Welsh or Sikh, on the same level and equal before God and the judgement of history.

In five years of almost continuous action the 4th Indian Division had suffered over 25,000 casualties or almost 200 per cent of its normal strength and captured more than 150,000 prisoners. The divisional sign, the Red Eagle, had been carried across every battlefield in the Middle East and the Mediterranean.

EPILOGUE

The years have passed and the diminishing number of the survivors of the 4th Indian Division, including the 11th Field Regiment, Royal Artillery, are now in their declining years.

Although it may well be true that the story of the 11th Field Regiment could be equalled by several other field regiments the wartime record of the 4th Indian Infantry Division must stand at the very top of all Allied infantry divisions in the Second World War.

The foreword to the history of the division written in 1948 by the late Field Marshall Lord Wavell (from *Fourth Indian Division*) may be quoted here:

'For the fame of this Division will surely go down as one of the greatest fighting formations in military history: to be spoken of with such as the Tenth Legion, the Light Division of the Peninsular War, Napoleon's Old Guard.

Those who fought under the sign of the Red Eagle will always be justly proud of it; and those commanders who, like myself have known the worth in the field of that magnificent Division, will be the first to acknowledge their debt of gratitude, and to salute one of the greatest bands of fighting men who have ever served together in this troubled world of wars and warriors.'

To the many gunners of the 11th Field Regiment who were killed in action or died from wounds and left their own little plots of England, Scotland, Wales, or Ireland on a foreign field from Egypt across North Africa to Italy and finally Greece we who have survived remember you and salute you.

It is said that even today, if one stands at the Tel El Eisa feature near the Egyptian coast road and looks south across the west end of the Ruweisat Ridge on 2nd or 3rd July at midday, one can see British gunners firing, as the *khamseen* winds carry the metallic sounds of breechblocks slamming shut, followed by the sharp crack of 25-pounder gun howitzers.

REMEMBRANCE DAY

Remember now the dead, but think
As well of them that came
Back from the terrifying brink,
The men of nameless fame,
Unlike the dead, they do at last grow old,
Those comrades of a half forgotten fold.

Do not go down dismayed, old men,
Do not go down dismayed,
For you possessed the strength of ten
Against the hordes arrayed
To seize your island fortress and enslave
A Nation that no longer ruled the wave.

Though bearded boys, who never knew,
May now presume to mock,
It was yourselves, the ageing few,
Who then withstood the shock
And held it high and cast it back again
As once your fathers cast back France and Spain.

Therefore do not go down, old men,
Dismayed, for in your day
You dared the devil in his den
And slew him where he lay;
And nothing that these feckless times may do
Shall smirch the honour which belongs to you.

J.H .B. Peel

Reproduced by permission from *This England* magazine

List of Honours and Awards gained by 11th Field Regiment RA

Distinguished Service Order
Lt-Col. A.E.H.   HOWELL
Lt-Col. F.C.G.   PAGE

Military Cross
Major J.F.B.   HUNTLEY
Major F.R.   JEPHSON
Captain L.L.   BOYD
Captain P.G.   FRANCIS   (Killed In Action)
Captain J.B.   TYLER

Distinguished Conduct Medal
B.S.M.   KEELAN

Military Medal
Sjt   WILKINSON
S/Sjt   FOWNDE
Gnr   SELLARS
Sjt   PARFITT
Gnr   PREEDY
L/Bdr   LANG
Sjt   HICKMAN
L/Cpl   SALES   (Royal Corps of Signals)
Bdr   PARKER

Mentioned in Despatches
L/Sjt   WARD
Sjt   TURBERFIELD
Bdr   CLEMENTS
RQMS   STOKES
Lieut   MOTT   (Royal Corps of Signals)
Major   DOUGLAS   (Twice)
Sjt (AC)   TYDEMAN
Capt   BOYD
L/Sjt   YOUNG
Sjt (FCG)   KING

Capt	CLEMENTS	
Gnr	WALLACE	
Gnr	EDWARDS	
Bdr	GELDING	
Capt	WILLIAMSON	
Major	DUNCAN	
Bdr	JUNIPER	(Killed In Action)
RSM	CLARK	
BSM	CROFT	(Twice)
Capt. J.S.	MAYES	
Sigmn	REED, C	(Royal Corps of Signals)
ASM	BOWEN	
Major	DICKSON	
L/Bdr	BARBER	

BIBLIOGRAPHY

Barnett, Corelli, *The Desert Generals*, Pan Books, 1961

Barnett, Corelli, *The Battle of El Alamein*, The MacMillan Company, New York, 1964

Blomfield-Smith, Denis (compiler), *Fourth Indian Reflections*, privately published, Cambridge, 1987

Caidin, Martin, *The Tigers are Burning*, Hawthorn Books Inc., New York, 1974

Carver, Michael, *El Alamein*, B T Batsford Ltd., 1962

Heckmann, Wolf, *Rommel's War in Africa*, Doubleday and Company, New York, 1981

India Defence Dept., *The Tiger Triumphs*, Director of Public Relations, New Delhi, 1946

Irving, David, *The Trail of the Fox*, Dutton, New York, 1977

Liddell-Hart, B H, *History of the Second World War*, G P Putnam Sons, New York, 1970

Lucas, James, *War in the Desert*, Beaufort Books, New York-Toronto, 1982

Montgomery, Field-Marshall, *El Alamein to the River Sangro*, Barrie & Jenkins Ltd., 1973

Moorehead, Alan, *The March to Tunis*, Harper and Row Inc., New York, 1943

Solzhenitsyn, Aleksandr I, *The Gulag Archipelago*, Harper & Row, New York, 1973

Stevens, Lt. Col. G R, OBE, *Fourth Indian Division*, McLaren & Son Ltd., Toronto, 1948

Stevens, Lt. Col. G R, OBE and Hingston, Lt. Col. W G, *The Tiger Kills*, Director of Public Relations, Bombay, 1944

INDEX

Adams, Jock, 13–14, 16
Adriatic Front, 118, 121, 161, 171,
    177–78
Afrika Korps
    and Battle of Alam el Halfa, 51–53
    at Battle of Ruweisat Ridge, 26–29,
        31–34, 36–39, 41–43
    at Mareth Line, 81–83, 88, 89
Agrinion, 193, 195
Alam Baoshaza, 33
Alam el Halfa, Battle of, 50–53
Alamein, El. *See* El Alamein
Alexander, Field Marshal Harold, 48,
    56, 62, 101, 107
    directs Italian campaign, 118,
        159, 172
    at meeting with ELAS, 206–207
Alexandria, 74–76
Altun Kopru, 17–19
American Field Service
    Ambulance, 178
ammunition, 142, 157–58
Andante House, Patras, 198
Anti-Tank Battery, 265th, 31
Anti-Tank Regiment, 149th, 41, 193
Anzio landings, 128, 159, 161
Aquaviva, 185
Arezzo, 174–75
Argyll and Sutherland Highlanders,
    8th, 153

Armoured Brigade, 22nd, 50
Armoured Brigade, 23rd, 50, 192
Armoured Brigade, 4th, 47
Armoured Brigade, 8th, 50
Armoured Division, 1st, 90
Armoured Division, 7th, 47, 90, 98,
    101, 103, 104, 106
armoured observation vehicles
    (AOVs), 50
Armstrong, Major Geoff, 33
Arnim, General Jürgen von, 97, 104
artillery. *See also* guns
    command post, 61–62
    creeping barrage, 60, 100
    field survey, 10–11
    field training, 79–80, 114
    gun control, 61–62
    systems of fire, 100
Arunci mountains, 123, 126, 160
Assisi, 174
Athens, 208
Auchinleck, General Claude, 21,
    48–49, 56, 62
Australian Brigade, 20th, 41
Australian Division, 9th, 41, 42, 47, 57,
    58, 77, 98

Backlund, Signaller, 144
Baia E Latina, 125, 133
Bailey, Gunner, 133

Bakardzis, General, 210, 211
Baluch Regiment, 3/10
   in central Italy, 179, 180, 182
   at El Alamein, 41
   in northern Greece, 212
   in southern Greece, 204, 205, 206
   in victory parade, 79
barbed wire, 62
Barber, Signaller, 144
Bari, 189
Barty, Driver, 29
Basra, 15–16
batteries
   78/84
     in central Italy, 184, 187
     in Italy, 157
     at Matmata Hills, 86
     at Monte Cassino, 132, 133, 135,
       144, 154
     in Orsogna area, 119
     at Ruweisat Ridge, 33, 36
     in southern Greece, 197
   83/85
     on the Adriatic Front, 161
     after Ruweisat Ridge, 33
     "B' Echelon, 23, 27, 30
     in central Italy, 157, 158, 175–76,
       181, 184, 187
     crossing Matmata Mountains,
       85–86, 87
     'D' Troop, 31, 32
     'E' Troop, 28–32, 29, 30, 31, 32
     in India, 4
     in Italian Campaign, 119
     at Monte Cassino, 133, 154, 155
     on ship when mined, 193
   187th
     in central Italy, 181, 184, 187
     'F' Troop, No.3 Gun, 135
     in Greece, 199
     in Italy, 119, 157
     at Monte Cassino, 132, 133, 143,
       154
Battle Group, 83
battlefield, cleaning up, 70–73

Beaufighters, 205
Beckett, Major D.A., 150
Beda Fomm, 80
Bell, Lance Bombardier, 176
Bentham, Captain R., 133, 195
Bernhard-Gustav Line. *See* Gustav
   Line
Bibbiano, 174
bivouac, one-man, 117–18
Block, Brigadier, 199
Blomfield-Smith, Captain D., 147
Bombay Sappers and Miners, 86
Bond, Captain A., 138
booby traps, 62, 138. *See also* mines
Boon, Brigadier, 133
Borghi, 186
Boucher, Major General Charles, 216
Boyd, Captain Laurence L., 33, 34–35,
   155
Breakell, Captain, 27, 29
Brigade, 1st, 101, 180–81
Brigade, 31st, 101
Brigade, 5th
   in central Italy, 174, 178, 181, 182,
     186–87
   at El Alamein, 63
   in Libya, 80, 81
   at Matmata Hills, 90
   in southern Greece, 203, 206, 208,
     211
   in Tunisia, 95, 101
Brigade, 7th, 80
Brigade, 11th
   in central Italy, 173, 175, 180, 184,
     185, 187
   at Monte Cassino, 153
   in northern Greece, 192, 211, 212
   sergeants' mess bombed, 199–200
   in southern Greece, 192, 196–97
   in Tunisia, 101
Brigade, 139th, 198, 199, 201
British Division, 1st, 102, 103
British Division, 51st, 93–94
British Division, 5th, 127
British Division, 44th, 50, 52, 57, 98

British Division, 46th, 127, 178, 179, 180, 185
British Division, 50th, 57, 83, 89, 90, 93–94, 98
British Division, 56th, 127
British Division, 78th, 124, 128, 151, 153–54
British Other Ranks, 31, 33
Bromley-Davenport, Major, 197
Brooke, Major, 197
brothels, 75
Brown, Topper, 11, 12, 13–14, 18
Brown House. *See* Continental Hotel, Cassino
Bryan, Lieutenant Colonel P., 151
Burroughs, Sergeant, 38–39
Butler, Captain, 182

Cafrarese, 180
Cairo (village), 136
Cameron Highlanders, 2nd
    in central Italy, 174, 180, 181, 183–84, 185–86
    in Italy, 158
    leaves Greece, 218
    in northern Greece, 212
    in southern Greece, 193, 194, 195, 200
Campriano, 175
Canadian Brigade, 11th, 120, 122
Canadian Corps, 1st, 159
Canadian Division, 176
Cap Bon Peninsula, 104
Cassino, Battle of. *See* Monte Cassino
Cassino (town), 126, 144, 145, 148, 149, 153
Castelacciao, 174
Castle Hill, 144–47, 151, 152. *See also* Monte Cassino
Catling, Gunner, 184
Cavendish Road, 144, 149
Central India Horse Regiment, 212, 213
Chiassa area, 176

Churchill, Winston, 17, 159, 189–90, 206–207
CIL Gruppo, 171
Clark, General Mark, 118, 126, 159, 160
Clements, Major W.J., 33, 118–19, 155
Coates, Corporal, 135
Colley, Gunner Matt, 13–14, 43–44, 74
Conca river, 180, 181
Continental Hotel, Cassino, 148, 153
Corps, 10th, 127, 128
Corps, 13th, 65, 180
Cowley Camp, 20–21
creeping barrage, 60, 100
Crete, 192
Cullen, Captain, 144, 200
Curry, Lieutenant P., 33

Damaskinos, Archbishop, 206–207
Deir el Shein, 30, 31
Desert Air Force, 51, 52, 53, 89
Desert Battle Group (ROBCOL), 31–34, 36
Desert Rats, 47, 103. *See also* Armoured Division, 7th
Dickson, Captain R.B., 91
Dimoline, Brigadier H.K., 99, 130, 158
dive bombers, 33, 42–43, 52, 144
Djebel Garci, 98
Douglas, Major, 84, 85
Drama (town), 212
Drayton, Major D., 150
Drinkall, Captain, 147
Durham Light Infantry, 28, 29
Dyce, Colonel G.W., 12–13
Dyebel Zemlet el Beida, 93

EAM, 190
East Yorkshire Regiment, 22
Eastman, Brigadier Claude, 31, 155, 158, 210
Eccleston, Bombardier, 33
Eden, Anthony, 206–207
EDES, 190, 191, 192
Edhassa, 212

228

Edwards, BSM, 200
Eight Trees, 186
Ein el Asker, 104
Eisenhower, General Dwight, 118
El Alamein, 21, 110
   cleanup of battlefield, 70–73
   final battle of, 56–64
   2nd Battle of, 50–53
   1st Battle of, 26–40
El Daba, 21, 24
El Djem, 97
El Media, 94
El Midou, 92
ELAS, 190–92, 193, 194–201,
   204–207, 210
Elles, Lieutenant J., 198
Elliott, Lance Bombardier, 176
Enfidaville, 97
Epirus, 212
Er Regina, 78–79
Essex Regiment, 63–64, 151, 206
Essex Regiment, 1/4
   'C' Company, 31
   in central Italy, 180
   at El Alamein, 41
   in Greece, 204, 206
   leaves Greece, 218
   at Monte Cassino, 146, 149–50, 153
   in northern Italy, 212, 213
   at Ruweisat Ridge, 62
   in Tunisia, 98, 100, 103
Evans, Lieutenant K.O., 195
Evans, Major L., 176
Evans-Lawrence, Captain J., 22, 27, 28,
   30, 43

Falciano, 174
Farnsworth, Gunner, 185
Farr, Lieutenant P.R., 176
Fatnassa feature, 93, 107
Fedjadi salt marsh, 93
Ferguson, BQMS, 158, 195
Field Ambulance, 32nd, 215
Field Ambulance, 17th, 215
Field Ambulance, 26th, 215

Field Company, 12th
   'B' and 'C' companies, 136
Field Regiment, 32nd, 43–44, 84
Field Regiment, 132nd, 154
Field Regiment, 3rd, 157, 181
Field Regiment, 1st, 43–44, 84, 175,
   205, 206
Field Regiment, 31st, 173
Field Regiment, 11th, 49, 53–55
   ambushed, 195
   assigned to 4/16 Punjab Battalion, 57
   casualties of, 95, 218
   under command of Lt.Col. Howell, 56
   under command of 4th Indian
   Division, 57
   commanded by Major Waterfield, 43
   at Cowley Camp, 20–21
   crosses Wadi Zigzaou, 84
   to go to Italy, 114–15
   in India, 3–6, 9–12
   in Italy, 119, 157, 173, 181, 187
   in Matmata Hills, 86
   at Monte Cassino, 135, 147, 148, 154
   moves to San Tommaso, 171
   in northern Greece, 211
   in PATFORCE, 197
   in Patras, 192, 194
   returns to Egypt, 109
   at Ruweisat Ridge, 31–34, 36–40, 41
   on way to Alamein, 24–25
Field Regiment, 165th, 178
fighting patrols, 48
Florence, 176
Florina, 212
Flying Fortresses, 134
Foglia River, 178
Foster, Lieutenant Colonel R.H.A., 171
Francis, Captain P.G., 141–43, 176
Franklin, Sergeant Major, 158
Free French forces, 57, 98, 104, 127
French Expeditionary Corps, 127, 159,
   160
Freyberg, General Bernard, 23, 58, 101,
   128, 129, 134, 144, 151, 159
   compliments 4th Indian Division, 106

funerals, military, 9. *See also* memorial
service

Garci-Takrouna battle, 99, 101, 124
Garfield, Les, 12, 13–14, 16
Garigliano River, 127
Garry, Brigadier R.V., 18
Gaskin, Gunner, 200
Gemmano, 180–82
George VI, King
inspects 4th Indian Division, 108,
174–75
German army. *See also* Afrika Korps
retreat from Greece, 191–92, 213
retreat from Italy, 171, 172
Goodey, Gunner, 133
Gothic Line, 177–79, 185, 186
Gotsis (ELAS commander), 213, 217
Gough, Lieutenant A.G., 118, 124–25
Gray, Lance Bombardier, 154
Greece
bridges in northern, 214
children, 198
communism in, 190, 206
highway repairs in northern, 215
living conditions in, 191, 213–15
medical services in northern, 215
National Guard, 194, 198, 211–12
occupation by Axis powers, 189–91
partisans, 206. *See also* ELAS
people of northern, 213–14
Provisional Government, 194, 207,
212
retreat of Germans from, 191–92, 213
4th Indian Division ordered to, 187–88
Green Howards, 22
Grounds, Lance Bombardier, 199
Guards Brigade, 201st, 98, 101
guns
calibration of, 57–58
18-pounders, 9–10
25-pounders, 9–10
six-pounders, 81
Gurkha Rifles, 1/2
'B' Echelon, 134

at Bou Huaker, 103
in central Italy, 173
at Garci–Takrouna, 100
in Greece, 209
in Italian campaign, 119
in Matmata Hills, 90
at Monte Cassino, 136, 138–39, 153
in northern Greece, 212
surrender of General von Arnim to,
104
at Wadi Akarit, 94
Gurkha Rifles, 1/9
'C' Company, 138, 139, 147
in central Italy, 179, 182
in Greece, 204, 205
at Monte Cassino, 136, 138, 147–48,
149, 153
in northern Greece, 212
in Tunisia, 98, 100, 103
at Wadi Akarit, 94
Gurkha Rifles, 2/7
in central Italy, 174, 183, 184, 185,
186
at Monte Cassino, 150, 151, 152,
158, 159
in northern Greece, 212, 217
in southern Greece, 193, 195, 201, 203
Gurkha Rifles, 2/9, 91
Gurkha soldiers
in central Italy, 174
in house to house fighting, 120
on infantry patrol, 48
on night patrol, 78
at Ruweisat Ridge, 62
at Wadi Akarit, 94, 95–96
Gurung, Subedar Major Narbahadur,
95, 108
Gustav Line, 118, 119, 123, 126, 127,
159, 171

Hadera, 19–20
Hall, Sergeant, 19, 30
Hallouf Pass, 90–91
Hangman's Hill, 144, 146–47, 152–53.
See also Monte Cassino

Harrison, Captain R., 205
Harvey, BSM, 23, 28, 29
Harvey, Major-General C.O., 18
Hatfield, Sergeant S., 19, 27, 29–30
Hawkeworth, General, 211
Heavy Regiment, 32nd, 175
Heavy Regiment, 1st, 181
Heidrich, General, 145, 147, 150, 151, 152
Hermann Goering Division, 101
Hewetson, Gunner, 133
Highland Division, 51st
   at El Alamein, 57, 61, 63, 64
   at Mareth Line, 81
   in Tunisia, 98
   at Wadi Akarit, 93–94
HMS *Ajax,* 198
Holgate, Basil, 13–14
Holt, Gunner, 200
Holworthy, Major General A.W.W., 155
Hopman, Lieutenant W., 167–70
horses, 4–5
house to house fighting, 120
Howell, Lieutenant Colonel A.H.E., 56, 111
Hunt, Brigadier H.C., 193, 194, 196–97, 198, 200
Huntley, Major J.F.B., 56
Huntley, Lieutenant Colonel J.F.B., 171
Hussars, 11th, 104

Independent Parachute Brigade, 2nd, 192
Indian Division, 5th, 43–44
   attacked by Ramcke's parachutists, 49
   relieved by 4th Indian Division, 57
   11th Field Regiment under command of, 41
Indian Infantry Brigade, 161st, 41, 57
Indian Infantry Brigade, 5th
   on Castle Hill, 146
   at Lanciano, 119
   in Matmata Hills, 85
   at Monte Cassino, 153

in Ruweisat sector, 41, 79
In southern Greece, 204
in Tunisia, 104
at Wadi Akarit, 94
in Wadi Zigzaou, 89
Indian Infantry Brigade, 7th
   in central Italy, 173, 174, 178, 181, 183, 185
   at El Alamein, 57
   in the Greek campaign, 192
   at Matmata Hills, 90
   in Matmata Hills, 85
   at Monte Cassino, 134, 135, 136, 138, 151, 153
   in northern Greece, 209, 212
   at Orsogna, 119
   in Tripoli, 81
   in Tunisia, 101–102, 103
   at Wadi Akarit, 94
Indian Infantry Brigade, 9th, 41
Indian Infantry Brigade, 11th, 158–59
Indian Infantry Brigade, 18th, 18, 27, 30, 32
Indian Infantry Brigade, 20th, 187
Indian Infantry Division, 4th
   break-up of, 218
   in central Italy, 171, 172, 173, 176, 178, 180, 186
   at El Alamein, 57, 58, 62
   at Er Regina, 80
   and Mareth Line, 82, 83
   at Matmata Hills, 90
   at Monte Cassino, 122–23, 128, 134, 135–36, 144, 153–54
   in northern Greece, 212
   ordered to Greece, 187–88
   praised, 106–107
   returns to Egypt, 109
   Sappers and Miners, 142
   in southern Greece, 206
   in Tunisia, 98, 101, 102
   visited by George VI, 174–75
   at Wadi Akarit, 93
   at Wadi Zigzaou, 84
Indian Infantry Division, 5th, 41, 47, 57

231

Indian Infantry Division, 8th, 14, 15–19, 156, 159–160, 172, 176
Indian Infantry Division, 10th, 171, 172, 173, 186
Indian Other Ranks (IORs), 29
Iraq, 16–17
Italian soldiers, 65, 71–73
Italy. *See also* Adriatic Front; Gustav Line; Monte Cassino
    central, 171–87
    children, 118, 156
    weather in, 116–19, 122, 125

Jephson, Captain F.R., 91
Jews, European, in Palestine, 69–70
Johnston, Bombardier, 33
Juin, General, 127

Kairouan, 97
Kamotini, 212
Kaplandoris, George, 207
Kavalla, 212, 215
Keable, Sergeant, 133
Keddy, Gunner, 135
Keelan, Sergeant John, 35, 39
Kemp, Sergeant, 200
Kesselring, Field Marshal Albert, 171, 172, 182
Kettley, Major Frank, 149–50
khamseen, 23–24, 36–37, 44, 50
Khanpur Camp, 11–12
Kidney Ridge, 63, 64
Kilkis, 212
King Tuk's Fort, 6
KKE, 190
Kozani, 212
Kram, General, 104
Krioneri, 195
kukri, 48, 78
Lancashire Fusiliers, 2nd, 153
Lancer Camp, 19
Lanciano, 119
leaguers, 77–78
LEAS, 197
Leavesley, Sergeant, 133

Leclerc, General, 57
Leese, Sir Oliver, 177
Leicestershire Regiment, 2/5, 204, 206
Light Anti-Aircraft Regiment, 57th, 136, 205, 218
Light Infantry Division, 90th
    at El Alamein, 49, 51, 52
    at Garci mountain, 99
    at Mareth Line, 89
    at Ruweisat Ridge, 27, 29
    surrender of, 104–105
    at Wadi Akarit, 95
Limba, Rifleman Sargahana, 104
Liri valley, 128
Lock, Gunner, 176
Lofos Castella, 203–205
Loftus-Tottenham, Lieutenant, 139
London Division, 56th, 100, 180
Long Range Desert Group (LRDG), 83, 85
Lovett, Brigadier, 88, 91, 136, 183, 186, 187, 210

Macedonia, 190, 213
Macedonian Autonomists Movement, 213
Mackensen, General von, 128
MacLaughlan, BSM, 184–85
Macmillan, Harold, 207
MacVeagh, Mr., 207
Madras Sappers and Miners, 86, 89–90, 91
Magdalene (Italian girl), 166–67
Maiella, 171
Maitland-Wilson, Sir Henry, 190
Mandakas, Emmanuel, 207
Mandukos, Major, 194–95
Maori Battalion, 28th, 140
Maori soldiers, 149
Marano River, 182–83
Marauders (bombers), 134
Marecchia River, 185
Mareth Line, 82–83, 89
Maria (Italian girl), 166–67
Markham-Lee, Major, 137, 138

marriage, an Alexandrian view of, 112–14
martial law, in Patras, 199
Matmata Hills, 82, 85, 86–88
Matthews, Major, 207
Mayes, Captain J.S., 198, 201–203, 211
McCarthy, Lieutenant Colonel A.O., 18, 19, 22, 32, 43, 56
McGregor, Lieutenant A.M., 33
Medinine, 81
Medium Regiment, 51st, 99
Medium Regiment, 5th, 173, 175
Medium Regiment, 6th, 181
Medium Regiment, 58th, 178
Medium Regiment, 64th, 99
Medium Regiment, 69th, 99
Medjez el Bab, 102–103
Meerut, 3–4, 12
Meida Kopje, 94
memorial service, in central Italy, 176–77
Mersa Matruh, 21, 23, 24
Miles, Captain F.R., 44, 119, 157
military funerals, 9
mine fields, 47
mines
    anti-personnel, 47, 62, 138, 152
Misurata, 108
Mitchell bombers, 134
Monastery Hill, 130–31, 132, 151, 160. *See also* Monte Cassino
Monte Belvedere, 127
Monte Cairo, 131–32
Monte Calvo, 179
Monte Cassino, 123–24
    final battle of, 151–53
    first assault on, 126–40
    monastery, 129–34, 141–42
    2nd assault on, 144–48
Monte Castellone, 127, 131
Monte Cerreto, 184
Monte della Croce, 179
Monte Gridola, 179
Monte Trocchio, 128, 131–32, 134
Montebello, 185

Montescudo, 182
Montgomery, Field Marshal Bernard Law, 48, 56, 101, 118
    battle plans of, 83
    compliments 4th Indian Division, 106–107
    and favouritism, 58
    holds victory parade, 79
    re Mareth Line, 90
    use of Indian troops, 62
Moroccan Goumiers, 160
Morroni, 156
Motor Brigade, 7th, 47
Mountain Regiment, 85th, 178

Nangle, Lieutenant Colonel, 153
Naosa, 212
Neal, Sergeant Norman, 38, 84–88
Neish, Sergeant, 176
New Zealand Armoured Brigade, 4th, 128
New Zealand Armoured Regiment, 20th, 151
New Zealand brigade, 41
New Zealand Brigade, 5th, 119
New Zealand Brigade, 6th, 144, 147, 148
New Zealand Corps, 128, 131, 134, 140, 146, 149, 152
New Zealand Corps, 2nd, 151
New Zealand Division, 176
New Zealand Division, 2nd
    congratulates 4th Indian Division, 106
    at El Alamein, 47, 49, 57, 58, 63, 64
    at Mareth Line, 81, 83, 85, 92
    at Mersa Matruh, 23, 31, 78
    at Monte Cassino, 124, 139
    and surrender of 90th Light Infantry Division, 105
    in Tunisia, 98, 99
Noble, Lieutenant Colonel, 195
Northamptonshire Regiment, 5th, 153
Northumberland Fusiliers, 31, 32

233

Oates, Edward A., 102
  arrives in Italy, 116
  chats with Polish officer, 121
  checks out trig point, 46
  cleans up battlefield, 70–73
  on convoy to Tobruk, 76–78
  dines with rich Alexandrian, 111–14
  drinks kümmel, 66–67
  drinks tea with Gurkhas, 108–109
  in Er Regina, 78–79
  experience with corpse, 7–8
  finds Italian shelter, 46–47
  on horseback, 4–5
  in India, 1–14
  on leave in Alexandria, 64
  on leave in Palestine, 65–70
  at Misurata, 108
  in Monte Trocchio area, 131–32
  and one-man bivouac, 117–18
  on OP duties at Monte Cassino,
     141–43
  on OP duty with Lt. Hopman, 167–70
  promoted to war substantive
     bombardier, 65
  reaction to Stukas, 43
  receives first stripe, 13
  returns to Egypt, 109
  and Sergeant Wilson, 115
  visits dentist, 65–66
  visits Italian family, 165–67
  visits Tunis, 107
  on way to Tripoli, 80–81
  weekend in Alexandria, 74–76
observation post officers, 49–50
O'Connor, General, 57, 80, 84
O'Day, Lieutenant, 23, 28
O'Halloran, Major D.N.E., 95
Onferno, 180
OP ack, 49–50
Operation Lightfoot, 59
Operation Supercharge, 63
Ormsby, Major, 139
Orsogna, 118, 120, 171
Ortona, 118, 120

Page, Lieutenant Colonel, 194, 197,
  198
Paget, Driver, 176
Panzer Division, 21st, 27, 49, 51
Panzer Division, 10th, 104
Panzer Division, 15th, 30, 49, 51, 89
panzer divisions, 82
Panzer Grenadier Division, 145
Papandreou, M., 207
Papastratos Cigarette Factory, 206
Parachute Division, 1st, 145, 152, 160
Parachute Regiment, 1st, 149
Parfitt, Sergeant, 148, 155
Parker, Bombardier Jack, 208
  in Alexandria, 64, 74–76
  dines with rich Alexandrian, 111–14
  drinks tea with Gurkhas, 108–109
  on leave in Palestine with E.A.
     Oates, 65–70
  in Tripoli with E.A. Oates, 81
  visits Italian family, 165–67
  visits Tunis, 107
Partsalides, Dimitrios, 207
Passignano, 187
PATFORCE, 197–99
Patras, 193–200
patrols, 47–48
Pemberton, Max, 36–40
Penny, Sergeant, 28
Phaleron Bay, 205
Pian di Castelo, 180
Piandi Maggio, 174
Pietrogalla, 116
Piraeus, 203–206, 208
Polish Corps, 2nd, 159, 160
Polish forces, 120, 124
Popov, Colonel, 207
Preedy, Driver, 176
Presenzano, 154
Psittalia, 205
Punjab Battalion, 4/16
  at El Alamein, 57
  at Monte Cassino, 136, 138, 152, 153
  in Tunisia, 100, 103
  at Wadi Akarit, 94

Pyrgos, 194

Qutb Minar, 6–7

Rajputana Machine Gun Battalion, 136
Rajputana Rifles, 94, 104
Rajputana Rifles, 1/6, 146–47, 148,
    149–50
Rajputana Rifles, 4/6
    at Monte Cassino, 136, 148, 149–50,
        153
    at Ruweisat Ridge, 41
    in Tunisia, 98, 100, 103
    in victory parade, 79
Ram, Jemadar Mara, 138
Ramcke, Major General, 49
Ramsey-Brown, Major, 139
Rapido river valley, 126, 127, 131, 145,
    151
Rashid Ali, 16–17
Raw, BSM, 43
Red Eagle (divisional sign), 57
Reeve, Gunner, 46–47, 79
Reggiano, 186
Richmond, Driver, 195
Rigby, Lieutenant, 181
Ritchie, General Sir Neil, 21, 56
Roach-Rooke, Captain N., 91
ROBCOL, 31–34, 36
Roberts, Gunner, 79
Rome, 160–61
Rommel, Field Marshal Erwin, 63, 78,
    81, 83–84, 97, 100
Roosevelt, Franklin D., 189
Roumana, 93
Royal Artillery, 153
Royal Corps of Signals, 176
Royal Engineers, 193
Royal Frontier Force Regiment, 168,
    184, 185, 195, 200–201
Royal Frontier Force Regiment, 3/12,
    158, 161, 174, 181
Royal Frontier Force Regiment, 3rd,
    193, 212
Royal Greek Marines, 204

Royal Horse Artillery
    'A' Battery, 33
Royal Northumberland Fusiliers, 41
Royal Sikhs, 2nd, 173, 178, 180, 186,
    212
Royal Sussex Regiment, 136–37, 185,
    186, 212
Royal Sussex Regiment, 1st
    in central Italy, 178
    in Italy, 119
    leaves Greece, 218
    at Monte Cassino, 153
    surrender of 10th Panzer Division to,
        104
    in Tunisia, 103
    at Wadi Akarit, 94
Royal Tank Regiment, 197, 213
Royal Tank Regiment, 6th, 178, 185
Royal Tank Regiment, 50th, 198, 199
Royal Warwickshire infantrymen, 37
Royal Warwickshire Regiment, 5
Royal Warwickshire Yeomanry, 173,
    174
Royal West Regiment, 6th, 151–52
rum ration, 122
Ruweisat Ridge, Battle of, 26–40, 110

Salonika, 192, 211, 212, 215
Samothrace, 213
San Elia, 131
San Giovanni, 186
San Marino, 182–84
San Martino, 186
San Michele, 131
Sangro valley, 157
Sardhana, 12
Saunders-Jacobs, Brigadier, 193, 203
Savage, Driver, 158
Sbeitla, 102
Scaife, Captain, 148
Schiano, 180
Scobie, Lieutenant General Sir Ronald,
    192
Scott, Lieutenant Colonel, 137
security battalions, 191, 209

Seres, 212
Shaiba Camp, 15–16
Shaw, Bombardier, 177
Sherwood, Lieutenant Colonel L.V.,
    216–17
Showers, Lieutenant Colonel, 104,
    138–39
Siantos, Georgios, 207
Sicily Landings, 109
Sidi Haneish, 21–22, 24, 27
Signaller Hill, 176
Sikh Regiment, 4/11, 179, 180
Sikh Sappers and Miners, 89–90
Singh, Subedar Narinder, 108
Skinner, Gunner, 148
Slawson, BSM, 185
Slight, Lieutenant W.E., 33, 38
Snakeshead Ridge, 127, 160
Solzhenitsyn, Aleksandr I., 217
Sorrai, 218
Sousse, 97
South African Armoured Division, 6th,
    159
South African Division, 176
South African Division, 1st, 24–25,
    30–31, 47, 57, 63, 98
Spach, Colonel von, 215–16
SS *Empire Dace,* 193
Stevens, Lieutenant Colonel G.R.,
    30–31, 95–96
Strategic Air Force, 145
stretcher parties, 148
Struma River, 217
Stukas, 33, 42–43, 52, 144
Sturdee, Lieutenant L.P., 33
sun-compass, 20–21
Superga Division, 104
surveys, field, 10–11
Tabage, 100
Takrouna, 98
Talla, 174
tanks
    Grant, 50
    Mark III, 48
    Mark IV, 48

at Monte Cassino, 151
    salvage of, 79
    Sherman, 57–58, 151
Tapahe, Sherbahadur, 139
Taveleto, 180
Tel Aviv, 66–70
Tel El Eisa, 37, 42
Termoli, 156
Thapa, Naik Birbahadier, 139
Thapa, Rifleman Sherbahadur, 183
Thapa, Subedar Lalbahadur, 95–96,
    108
Thasos, 213
Tobruk, 109–10
Toujane, 82
Trasimeno, Lake, 177
Tripoli, 81
Tughlakabad, 6–7
Tuker, General, 80, 88
    in El Alamein, 62
    at Garci-Takrouna, 101
    at Mareth Line, 82
    at Matmata Hills, 90
    at Medjez el Bab, 102, 103
    report on Monte Cassino monastery,
        129–31, 134, 159
    surrender of Afrika Korps, 104
    at Wadi Akarit, 94–95, 96
Tunisian Campaign, 89–105
Turberfield, Sergeant, 11
Tynesiders, 89

UNRRA, in northern Greece, 215–16,
    218
Urbino, 178
US II Corps, 98
US 34th Division, 127, 128, 135–36
US 36th Division, 127, 128
US 85th Infantry Division, 159
US 88th Infantry Division, 159
US 760th Tank Battalion, 151
Utili Gruppo, 171

Valdragona, 183
Verroia, 215, 216–17

Volos, 215
Volturno River, 127

Wadi Akarit, 93–96
Wadi Zigzaou, 82–84, 89–90
Walker, Gunner T., 95
Walker, Lieutenant J.P., 133
Waller, Brigadier Rob, 31
Waterfield, Major P.R.M., 17, 43, 56
Watkins, Lance Bombardier, 12, 13–14, 34
Watts, Brigadier, 44
Watts, Sergeant, 109, 115
Wavell, Field Marshal Archibald, 17, 62, 220

Wellbeloved, Lance Bombardier, 144
Western Desert, conditions in, 44–46
Wilkinson, Sergeant George E., 35
Wilson, Sergeant Tug, 115, 116–17, 123, 131–32, 155
Winter Line. *See* Gustav Line
Wolff, Dr. Hede, 65–66
Woodward, Gunner, 29
wounded, 70–73

Xanthe, 212
XIII British Corps, 159

Zagreb Mountains, 17–19
Zollara, 181